The Book of Lyle

*A Spiritual Adventure
From Our Beginning
To Beyond Death*

Daniel B. Lyle, Ph.D.

LylePublishing
Sulphur, Oklahoma

The Book of Lyle
A Spiritual Adventure from Our Beginning to Beyond Death
Copyright © 2006, 2013, 2014 by Daniel Basil Lyle

All rights reserved. No part of this book may be reproduced or transmitted in any form or by any means without written permission from the author, except in the case of brief quotations embodied in critical reviews and certain other noncommercial or educational uses permitted by copyright law. For permission requests, or any other questions, e-mail the author at DanLyle@LylePublishing.com.

ISBN 978-0-9794101-2-3

Published by LylePublishing
505 W. 12th Street, Sulphur, OK 73086
(www.LylePublishing.com)

Printed by CreateSpace, An Amazon.com company. Available from Amazon.com and other retail outlets. Also available as an ebook on Kindle and other devices.

First ebook edition 2006
Paperback edition 2013
Expanded ebook edition 2014
Expanded paperback edition 2014

PREFACE

What do you want? I invite you to join me on a dangerous spiritual adventure. Although anyone is welcome to come along for the ride, "unsatisfied seekers" will enjoy it the most: those both blessed and cursed with a nagging itch to understand life. For all those who are irritated and confused by ritualistic religion, seeing it as too-often boring and unproductive---there is a better way. For all those who have deep spiritual yearnings, yet find cults or unsubstantiated beliefs poor vehicles---there is a better way. For all those who suspect they are greatly talented, yet find religion and society unsupportive and dismissive---there is a better way. Come with me to our beginning and continue beyond death---and we, together, will discover that better way! Yes, it is dangerous. Everything has to be re-evaluated. We must go back to our beginning and start all over with religion/spirituality, while being careful to not forget the lessons mankind has learned in the last several thousand years. We must explore all aspects of human behavior. We must question ourselves and our deepest assumptions. We must pursue our true motivations. We must do all this by allowing God to put us on trial. There, we must have the courage to listen to our enemies and allow them to dictate our fate. By this process we will excavate our own minds---not for vague generalities but hard specifics. We will confront our greatest fears. We will admit our greatest weaknesses. We will discover and be reconciled with the true nature of evil. The way ahead is difficult and at times uncertain. But hang in there with me and we will make it through the acid fog of confusion into a new and wonderful place. Prepare to have your mind boggled and your heart uplifted. I believe in you. Together we will triumph over all the naysayers, the doubters, and the haters. God believes in us. After all, He made us as we are: perplexed, struggling, fragile seekers. It's tempting to settle for what is safe, easy, and simple---or even to just give up and quit! All of us, after all, have our breaking points. There are terrible forces arrayed against us. But be comforted that the reward goes not to those that win some great success... rather, the best prize of all goes to those that dare to try! What do you want?

Dan Lyle, 3-20-2014

TABLE OF CONTENTS

Preface 3

Lyle 1:1-5 --- At the Beginning 6

Lyle 1:6-11 --- Humanity 7

Lyle 2:1-12 --- Rejection of God 8

Lyle 2:13-21 ---From Confusion Faith 10

Lyle 3:1-21 --- Wisdom from Above 11

Lyle 4:1-20 --- The Birth of Lyle 13

Lyle 4:21-34 ---Raised in Church 15

Lyle 5:1-36 --- Creativity versus Control 17

Lyle 6:1-24 --- Destroying Joy of Learning 21

Lyle 6:25-45 ---Tunnel Vision Exploded 24

Lyle 7:1-12 --- Abstractions versus Details 26

Lyle 7:12-53 ---Startling Revelations 28

Lyle 8:1-87 --- Parable of the Wanderer 32

Lyle 9:1-56 --- Parable of the Last Survivor 45

Lyle 10:1-39 ---Parable of the Sick Child 50

Lyle 11:1-45 --- Wise Sayings 54

Lyle 12:1-49 ---School & Learning 58

Lyle 13:1-21 --- Work, Business, & Commerce 63

Lyle 13:22-48 -Money & Success 65

Lyle 14:1-27 ---Food & Drugs 68

Lyle 14:28-49 -Sex, Love, & Marriage 71

Lyle 15:1-24 ---Family, Community, & Church 74

Lyle 16:1-17 --- Formal Religion 77

Lyle 16:18-44 - Spirituality	79
Lyle 17:1-39 --- Charity & Compassion	82
Lyle 17:40-74 - The Human Condition	86
Lyle 18:1-23 -- Science & Medicine	90
Lyle 18:24-40 - Animals & Nature	93
Lyle 18:41-61 - Competition & War	95
Lyle 19:1-14 --- Devotions & Obsessions	98
Lyle 19:15-30 - Inspiration & Creativity	100
Lyle 20:1-18 -- Balance & Health	102
Lyle 20:19-39 - Pain, Injustice, & Suffering	104
Lyle 21:1-26 --- Society, Art, & Beauty	107
Lyle 22:1-19 -- Politics & Power	110
Lyle 23:1-22 -- Quality Relationships	113
Lyle 24:1-27 -- Sickness, Illness, & Injury	116
Lyle 25:1-22 -- Fun, Humor, & Joy	119
Lyle 25:23-35 - Endings & Death	122
Lyle 26:1-18 -- Connections & Humility	124
Lyle 26:19-37 - Sin, Evil, & Punishment	127
Lyle 27:1–34 -- Creative-Theology ®	130
Lyle 28:1-20 -- Music, Dance, & Singing	134
Lyle 29:1-95 -- Songs & Prayers	137
Lyle 30:1-420 - Debates & Discussion	147
Lyle 31:1-458 - The Meaning of Life	221
Lyle 32:1-40 -- Beyond Death	292
About the Author	297

Lyle 1:1-5

AT THE BEGINNING

[1] *In our beginning, God created our Universe---seeding into its texture the potential of evolving life;*

[2] Spreading His Spirit through all, endowing every law of physics---substantiating every particle and energy;

[3] Expressing a grand, glorious Creativity so gigantic and colossal in its scope to gather everything into a pinpoint---then explode to the ends of Space and Time;

[4] Across billions on billions of years a vast array of Galaxies, Stars, Planets, and Worlds---*all concentrated and set into your mind*:

[5] Endowed with SELF-AWARENESS, FREEDOM, AND A CHOICE TO REJECT ITS OWN FIBER... *that only those with a true desire might find their way back home.*

Lyle 1:6-11

HUMANITY

⁶ *And God saw that his creatures could think. Arrived at a state of curiosity, they reached out and He touched them again, giving them souls*:

⁷ Beyond a mere piece of His Spirit, they were sanctified... made distinct, brilliant, and eternally individual;

⁸ *Blessed with God-like sensitivities to perceive far beyond what could be seen*: not as mere illusions but in hope that the accumulated weight of evidence was more than the sum of its separate parts;

⁹ Reflected in their ability to touch each other, man turned to woman, females turned to males---passing on now not just shared genetics, but the stuff of souls:

¹⁰ From physical pleasure to merge halved cells crying-out from ecstasy and pain of birth... joined at the genes, minds, and visions;

¹¹ A fresh Creation of potential joy, humor, and worthiness... set-into a magnificent world, a GARDEN OF ABUNDANT LIFE---*endowed with the greatest Gift of all in transcending love: the potential to exercise themselves a God-given Creativity!*

Lyle 2:1-12

REJECTION OF GOD

¹ *And so humans were given a grand Awareness beyond immediate circumstance---which they promptly rejected in favor of the fleeting taste of the moment*;

² Embodied in the first God-aware man---who promptly turned from God to sex; and in the approval of his mate found his ultimate satisfaction; rejecting enlightenment for immediate sensation... EVEN WILLING TO HURT OTHERS IN ORDER TO DERIVE PERSONAL PLEASURE...

³ An evil arrogance for which God cursed man, driving him and his family from the comfort, beauty and innocence of the Garden---to which mankind his ever after sought, in vain, to return...

⁴ And though it blinded him to his greater potential, he led his growing family into even-greater, easily-justified selfishness: *using his elevated mentality and spirituality to dominate and destroy the world about him* CHOSING TO ACT NOT AS WISE CARTAKER, BUT AS HEELDESS DESPOILER---incurring the wrath of a vengeful Mother Nature;

⁵ Stupidly choosing to fight with the trees, flowers, and animals... forcing them to bend to his will---he happily sank back into his own genetics: hating and killing, content to be just another smart animal rather than celebrating his freshly-allotted portion of Divinity...

⁶ *Even going so far as to leave his own kind stilled and dead in spreading pools of their own blood*: that his bestial, selfish, short-sighted lust might be expressed above all else;

⁷ Which God certainly knew would happen, allowing them to reject whatever they wanted... such that each person might be certified for what they freely chose to be; that their ultimate fate might be richly deserved:

⁸ A final purging of their retained spiritual flaws, beyond their control to be burned away---as tribute to their own fear and stupidity... *while they still stubbornly continued to turn to God only out of fear or "last-resort" desperation, seeking magical solutions to largely self-generated problems*;

⁹ When, caught in their own webs, they at last face the onrushing heavy

tread of the ultimate Consumer---hungry for their tasty, contaminated, festered souls;

[10] *As, lost and alone, they fall into smothering blackness*---only a few choosing at last to reach up and grasp God's ever-outstretched hand;

[11] To be snatched-away from the fangs of the rabid Grim Reaper, their struggles rewarded beyond their ability to comprehend or appreciate... finally truly safe and satisfied in the Arms of their loving Creator.

[12] But for many it is simply too late for them to change: as mired in a futile pursuit of the Garden THEY TRADE A TASTE OF HEAVEN FOR LIVING THEIR EARTHLY LIVES IN HELL...

Lyle 2:13-21

FROM CONFUSION FAITH

¹³ *So God made man complex: of many minds and diverse types... their words diverging into distinct forms and sounds*;

¹⁴ And COMMUNICATION BECAME A RAGING BLOOD SPORT even while all thoughts remained the same; a contradiction perversely dividing humanity from itself;

¹⁵ Such that security was sought in conformity, with so-called "enemies" defined by subtle differences of skin, tribe, or territory;

¹⁶ *God allowing humans to wallow in their fears while holding out to them rays of bright hope*:

¹⁷ That their short little lives might not be crushed in the overwhelming floods of disease, starvation, predation, wars, and injustice---but saved by an Ark within arm's reach, there to clamber into and carry them upward;

¹⁸ Soaring high over all the surrounding destruction and uncertainty; protected from the cold winds of fragile existence; *a reward to those who dare Struggle to rise above it all; on troubled waters to serenely float; a Golden Path out of the tempest*;

¹⁹ Safe, happy, well-fed, and secure with their loved-ones and families---if only they would take a leap of transcending faith: not into the unknown, blindly... but lighted by His love to step forward boldly on the springboard of existential Truth;

²⁰ *Actually believing in commitment to something higher than they*: trusting to not be totally abandoned, but rather taken to a beautiful, desired, and peaceful shore... where their lives would be utterly saved forevermore:

²¹ Given a fresh start, a new beginning, a different Adventure merged into A COMMON LANGUAGE OF THE SOUL---a solid Connection cementing them together with themselves and with their God!

Lyle 3:1-21

WISDOM FROM ABOVE

¹ Seeing their great confusion, then, *God sent forth repeated guidance embedded within the thoughts of Prophets: speaking Godly Wisdom for their particular time, society, and place*---a prick-of-the-collective-conscience, a reminder of realities largely forgotten; a ray of hope to those daring to lift their gaze beyond immediate pleasure, problems, and prejudice...

² KEY CONCEPTS CAREFULLY STAGED AND FRAMED FOR HUMAN COMPREHENSION filled with noble strivings for growth; endowed with uncommon notions of higher love, grace, responsibility, devotion, reverence, unselfishness, transcendence, and faith;

³ Left to great Visionaries to fully translate, filling many letters, then books, with specifics impacting the present state of humanity's varied societies: for workable structure, helpful regulations, and useful boundaries;

⁴ *Which man took and promptly perverted into suffocating bonds, crushing chains, deadening constrictions, mindless traditions, and exclusionary walls*;

⁵ Such that "organized" religion often became merely a bad joke: all of them without exception or excuse less than their potential, standing on feet of clay---often corrupting rather than uplifting:

⁶ Shamelessly practicing the very things they fervently preached against;

⁷ Mutating inspired fresh Godly discussions into repetitive, boring monologues;

⁸ Painful plodding duties made the norm rather than exciting Adventures of productive exploration;

⁹ Merely going through the motions made more important than striving for lofty goals; *trading action for boredom, productivity for predictability, and creativity for control*:

¹⁰ Cherished Prophets one by one viciously and gleefully murdered by their own followers;

[11] Organizations loudly celebrating their Founder's words flaunting or ignoring underpinning God-given constructive objectives;

[12] Thinking they'd achieved glory and acceptance in God's eyes by rigorously adhering to time-honored tradition, while ignoring God's constant inner urgings in their day-to-day lives:

[13] *Turning written words into Icons while forgetting their underlying Meaning;*

[14] Mandating ritual "check-lists" of little impact or note;

[15] Such that hearts that should have melted into vibrant liquid crystals instead congealed into cold, formless lumps;

[16] As those rare, precious Prophets shuddered and wept, fearfully glancing down from God's higher realm at the ordered stagnation of earthly neglect...

[17] Institutions and hierarchies once fluid and dynamic now solidified into drab perpetuators of ceremony;

[18] *God's Teachings twisted and made unrecognizable, the dead Prophets shaking their ghostly heads in disbelief... shocked and dismayed at what was done in their names*:

[19] Their dutiful followers happily marching on in generational lock-step: saying all the right things but dishonoring the Spirit of their Holy Teachings; bringing shame on the few true practitioners standing lonely at long-lost unmarked graves...

[20] ---dropping a flower to signal their visit to WHAT MIGHT HAVE BEEN IF ONLY GOD'S PROPHETS HAD SURVIVED IN MAN AND WOMAN'S MINDS...

[21] Those fine religious folks refusing to walk through the fire lest their elegant clothes be singed... embarrassed at the courage of their immolated Founders.

Lyle 4:1-20

THE BIRTH OF LYLE

¹ *In the middle of the 20th century, Daniel Basil Lyle was born of a holy union between Basil Kenneth Lyle and Mary Lee Gillaspie*: their marriage producing a normal, kicking, crying baby boy;

² In no way particularly unique or different from millions of post-World War II "boomer" kids growing up in middle-class tract homes in the U.S.A., a prosperous developed nation;

³ Just a small-town boy, blessed by God as all others with regular intelligence and talents; claiming no special revelation or inspiration; set-into the ceaseless flow of time as is any youngster...

⁴ But THE WORLD WAS MADE ANEW---*the past became history, and the future filled with fresh possibilities---as yet again a baby experienced a whole new perspective*:

⁵ For the very first time (yet again) amazed at biological life hopping or crawling-about as toads, frogs, birds, lizards, spiders, caterpillars, praying mantis, cat, dog, snake, or human---all manner of freshly-fascinating living creatures!

⁶ In complexity and form dazzling; biochemical underlying mechanisms arguing for powerful logic; yet itself offering an alternative to simplistic origins...

⁷ *Lyle as a young boy taken by his parents each week to hear Preachers loudly proclaiming God-in-a-box, a tightly-constrained "divinity"*: a form *not* credible to underpin millions of stars above; where many of those heavenly dots were themselves galaxies each containing yet billions of more stars...

⁸ ---sources of streaming light almost without number... the vistas made even more incredibly huge by man's invention of satellites and massive telescopes peering back to near the "big bang" origin of the Universe:

⁹ A nearly incomprehensible distance in both space and time begging to be made sense of in terms other than just physics; yet superficially seemingly completely explained by that very same science!

¹⁰ *Such that "God" outside of religious groups was argued as a vanishing temporary crutch*; a "god of the gaps" made continually smaller every

time one of the gaps was filled, thus with the advent of Science quickly shrinking almost to vanishing...

[11] Lessening the need for some super-intelligent super-human to sit on a cloud tossing down lightning and thunderbolts: now recognized as just molecules colliding, friction, and electricity;

[12] Defining the workings of Nature in evolving conflicts selecting efficient usage of sun-energy; a wealth of adaptations allowing fitness to increase;

[13] *Lyle seeing all of this and wondering, puzzled, thinking:* "*What does it all mean?*" *and* "*Where is it all going?*" *and* "*How will it end?*" *and* "*What's with having to learn it over and over again?*" *and* "*What's behind the curtain... and behind the curtain behind that... and the one behind that?*" *and* "*What do I really want, and why?*"

[14] AS YET AGAIN THE SAME BABY CRIED-OUT IN CONFUSION: setback to "zero" renewing the tradition of accumulating knowledge, the fuel of science... in which one might yet hear the voice of God speaking with amusement and compassion... "*SEE ME! I AM AWESOME!*"

[15] ---as yet another young boy again sees spiders, frogs, and snakes: lifting his curious, blinking eyes to the night-time sky and wondering out loud...

[17] "*What?*"

[18] "*How?*"

[19] "*Why?*"

[20] and "*Why not?*"

Lyle 4:21-34

RAISED IN CHURCH

²¹ *Raised going to church, Lyle began crying in the pew seat at the wee age of two weeks old,* his form of singing---as if he were lecturing on the "why" to everything;

²² Quite the regular attender, thoroughly indoctrinated from a baby, sitting patiently on hard pews, listening to lofty lectures:

²³ *Far above his head, this adult chattering somehow soothing but long and immensely boring, filling childhood times as he actively drew and scribbled on a sheet of paper*---his earthly Father's portentous, predictive, proper, "religious-time" relief from boredom paper gift; frowned-at by the other tall adults to use such "sacred" time frivolously transcending droning lectures; only many years later understanding his Dad's wonderful respectful leadership into Godly protest, tribute, and inducement.

²⁴ Singing with enjoyment not childish soprano, but alto then tenor then base; quickly happily wrapped-up in friendships and loving appreciation by his church brethren; induced to ignore ritualistic waste for severely-limited creative license.

²⁵ *A spiritual family kindly affording some opportunity to stretch his talents within accepted modes and formats*: as young song leader of approved songs, Bible class discussion leader of approved Bible doctrine, and even featured speaker on approved Bible topics;

²⁶ *Comforted in a small town's cozy little congregation; nonchalantly excluding nonbelievers and misbelievers as "in-error" heretical "others"*; settling into a comfortable certitude and routine---fundamentals secured and ordered on the wide spiritual landscape by set ceremonies and constraining rituals;

²⁷ Preached lectures woven tight into exclusionary warm blankets: proclaiming strong, defined, set, and absolute boundaries;

²⁸ Not even consciously aware of the traditional security constantly informing religious actions and reactions; coloring and clouding the lenses of one's mind often blithely ignoring Purpose;

²⁹ Lofty Goals sacrificed for blind perpetuation of Procedure; initial justifying reasons forgotten or simply no longer important;

30 *Lyle was shocked to realize that others might do things better*: actually coming closer to scriptural Purpose; MERGING BOTH LETTER AND SPIRIT INTO DYNAMIC ACTIVITY rather than mere static Law;

31 And furthermore recognizing that Holy Words might not just have superficial simple interpretations (or, worse yet, imposed rationalizations as to why they don't say what they clearly say); but rather that deep Meaning might reside behind the noise of their utterance: *unrecognized Mysteries blithely unacknowledged---a Deeper, Higher, Wider, More Complex, and More Substantial layer always present...* not just "black or white", "yes or no", "right or wrong", or "do or don't" but unseen spectrums of brand-new colors!

32 Superficial connections originally radically initiated... but now mutated and congealed: set into stone, built-up as perpetually hardened sequential layers; a multi-generational monument to repetition, momentum, and complacency;

33 *Established Tradition blithely rejecting all questioning as heresy; opting for comfortable, safe conformance; killing excitement and productive exploration bowing down to established orthodoxy rather than transcendent Divinity*:

34 THE GROWTH OF ALL TALENTS ATTEMPTING TO ACCOMPLISH NOBLE GOALS FORGOTTEN... lost in the false illusion-delusion to find "The" Answer critical to getting everything comfortably and undeniably "Right".

Lyle 5:1-36

CREATIVITY VERSUS CONTROL

¹ *Thus the eternal, deadly, and TOTALLY UNNECESSARY CONFLICT of God-inspired Creativity seemingly clashing with fear-soothing Control*:

² Man's animal-inherited genetically-programmed "instinct-for-survival" demanding rigid Walls, craving Set-Boundaries to one's life---an environmental security-Stabilization;

³ Yet the dynamic-tension is often *snapped*: where new horizons stretch the balance between dynamic Growth versus Conservation of vital resources;

⁴ Abrogating solid established bases set but always ever advancing; Rejecting thoughts accelerating yet still protectively considering;

⁵ *One's pathologically FEAR enhanced by tightening and restricting Chaos causing a paralyzing, awful, and strangling blindness making us fall twitching, convulsed, and suffocated...*

⁶ ---as COMPLACENCY steals joy, inspiration, and hope; STAGNATION cripples the Spirit; and RITUALISM-LEGALISM chokes-out Joy... leaving but a stinking, rotting, dying corpse.

⁷ Or Godly impulses are lost to self-destructive splurges... where HATE envelopes, explodes, then implodes the soul; complacency and conformity corrupts the spirit; and Creativity is crushed into petrified stone.

⁸ As vibrant-directed, productive-beautiful God-force is stopped dead in its tracks... self-emulated into holy dead ashes:

⁹ *In the name of a beautiful God spreading horror ruling from fear*, converting by the sword, executing "heretics", bayonetting even little children in the zeal to be "righteous";

¹⁰ Stoning one's women for flashing a nose or baring a toe; beheading men who dare to cut their beards a bit too short;

¹¹ *Justifying anything as the Almighty's stern Laws giving free license to do every manner of evil*;

12 In the name of all that is pure, good, and holy---burning at the stake all types of "witches" or "heathens" or nonbelievers or different-believers or just plain-vanilla "sinners";

13 *More worried about real or imagined splinters in the eyes of others---agonizing over those tiny specks!---while ignoring actual spears skewered deep through one's own eye sockets into savagely-scrambled brains*:

14 Confusing one's reason, skewing true perspective, smearing the line between productivity and destruction, and tangling one's neurons into perverse, unnatural connections;

15 *In one's heedless zeal to tame chaos, instead mush-rooming into an iron grip of discipline*: confounding and confusing devotion, love, and duty---into unrecognizable, distorted, mad-house reflections:

16 Seeking to be God's Hand while degenerating and grossly mutating God's Word... outwardly appearing no different than the sick spasms of the worst demon;

17 *Or, again, conversely seeking enlightenment at any cost... reasonable boundaries shattered and forgotten, allowing all desires to be satiated to the extreme*:

18 As a female heroin addict awakens from ecstatic dreams to find her starved baby lying bloated at her side; a stinking little blue corpse casually sacrificed to getting a fleeting taste of heaven in exchange for living a life in hell...

19 Or making-money become a compulsion to the point of selling one's soul piece-by-piece; trickery and scams killing the ability to feel real pleasure... significance lost in accelerating-downward spirals;

20 Self-reinforcing negative cycles sucking out the joy... dry husks the only existing reminder of former glory;

21 Men skipping gleefully from sexual conquest to casual "hook-ups"; using-abusing-hurting others secondary to personal pleasure; in testosterone-fueled orgies, self-respect drifting away; even fervently-religious men justifying keeping women under their heels...

22 Dark smutty acid clouds settling onto bright canvases: once startling-beautiful masterpieces now burned, torn, and shrouded in dirt and feces;

23 Fresh-faced young children laughing and playing... quickly wrinkled and twisted; shriveled, embittered, and crippled---prematurely aged;

24 *Seeking to help but swamped by heartfelt hurt; creative-strivings slowly strangled by lustful destruction;*

25 Pleasure-worship rewarded with unrelenting pain: a sweet trap, a dark pit---whose occupants seek escape by digging themselves yet deeper down;

26 Significance pursing mighty stars shrunk infinitely tiny: leaving mere grains of sand strewn on an endless, grey beach; pounded forever by ice-cold, eroding, thundering waves;

27 Caught on the edge of disdainful despair: a bleak, black ocean of weariness replete with lost AIMs... where survivors of horrendous sea-wrecks frantically paddle their lifeboats in circles until they die from exhaustion...

28 ...unchangeable-traditions, irrational values, heedless principles, uncaring regulations, illogical rules-laws-habits drowning the lone struggling swimmers; cause-and-effect forgotten:

29 *In their proper place, though---fully acknowledged and appreciated for both their positives and negatives---accepted boundaries providing solid foundations, honorable-helpful structures, and enabling frameworks... from which can sprout magnificent integrated extensions:*

30 *Expanding the limits of human purpose, supporting forward-surges of body-mind-spirit; helping controlled curiosity to carefully and delicately explore the dangerous Unknown:*

31 Viable pathways forged upward-inward-outward... discovering new and stronger connections to the Almighty;

32 Exquisitely-choreographed in a delicate, precise dance; but easily broken, shattered, and stopped... snapped legs dangling at odd angles---the ballet and performers stopped in their tracks!

33 WHEN PURPOSE IS FORGOTTEN, overly-constrictive, mindlessly-restrictive laws senselessly cripple Creativity;

34 *Or random, compulsive, heedless thrusts skewering wise sensibilities lacking healthy tension between Creativity and Control... allow DESTRUCTION and CONSTRUCTION to COLIDE and EXPLODE---rather than to meet in dynamic balance orbiting and energizing each other:*

35 Put into a healthy 2-dimensional perspective swaying gently on a fulcrum's pointed, exact center... humbled, ever-learning, open-minded, carefully-progressing---ever-searching for the Deeper, Wider, Higher, More-Detailed substantiation that fills in the gaps not with more restrictions but with yet-wider possibilities;

36 *Faith not imposed... but rather built-up from within: by detailed self-questioning in a never-ending, exhilarating, dynamically-respectful search for the Divine!*

Lyle 6:1-24

DESTROYING JOY OF LEARNING

¹ *Formal school for Lyle began in fascinating kindergarten... a wonderful time of discovery, skill-building, exploration, and rampant creativity truly learning profound life-blocks*:

² Supporting the fun application of foundational mathematics forging concept-crystallizing, communicable logic units;

³ Enhancing interspersed lazy naps when one got sleepy; yummy cookies and slurped milk when one got hungry keeping energy high;

⁴ With personal guidance helping each student recognize particular talents, abilities, capabilities, interests, and aptitudes... all well supported and even applauded!

⁵ Put to work on marvelous, specific "stretching" projects exercising one's imagination making something from nothing:

⁶ Wet amorphous clay molded into mighty pyramids & castles, people & animals, or starships & cars;

⁷ Without limits intermixing-smearing colors on blank paper: wet fingers directly forging rippling rainbows, shining suns, bizarre animals... merged with bright-glowing flowers exploding bloody-reds, sunshine-yellows, ocean-blues, gleaming-gold, growing-greens, or passionate-purples;

⁸ Swirling reading & writing deceptively-simple stories investigating complex & fantastical relationships... laughing & crying, or sulking & beaming;

⁹ Running-about exercising, playing ball at recess, lifting and moving: a well-spring of creative activity, excitement, and growth flowing freely from education's wonderful, initial "Garden of Eden";

¹⁰ Lyle, moving on, expecting only more and better of the same but, sadly, FINDING OUT THAT KINDERGARTEN WAS THE PINNACLE OF THE PEAK... and "schooling" from there on was only a downhill tumble...

¹¹ *Mind-numbing rote-repetitions pushing out the Joy of learning*;

¹² *The exhilaration of fresh discovery painfully deadened and denied*;

¹³ *Temporary memorization dominating and then killing engrained true learning;*

¹⁴ *Tortured, brutal competition for top grades blistering the psyche;*

¹⁵ *Frequent exams obliterating prideful customer service...* a concept ignored then forgotten;

¹⁶ *Clashing unrelated subjects conflicting*: promoting brain-dumping, fighting for limited short-term memory, slashing fresh neural linkages, and pushing-out details leaving just a vague notion of having studied something...??

¹⁷ Swamping and deflating the ready & eager biologic people-bags filled-to-the-brim with developed abilities & talents... scattered, made-useless, and condemned to irrelevancy, lost;

¹⁸ Mountains of time & effort & energy wasted avoiding true synergism of cooperative talents: all *sacrificed on the altar of brutal "G.P.A" (grade point average) rankings;*

¹⁹ In terrified fear of career-killing, medium grades... impressively-tangible beautiful achievements are discarded and thrown aside: traded instead for stupidly-acquired, real-world-useless, test-taking "skills".

²⁰ Lyle at that time, though, knew nothing of these bad bargains... only that the initial excitement of kindergarten was long-faded: fascination of discovery shrunk to almost nothing, true fun evaporated, and school devolved into a horrible, never-ending, grinding sentence in a bleak prison:

²¹ A constant torture even into the heights of "graduate school" supposedly focused finally on cutting-edge research... yet still the flawed system prevailed again: *substituting courses and tests for true learning; dampening the exhilaration of "O.J.T." (on-the-job-training); blurring keen curiosity by rigid disciplines, walls, barriers, roadblocks, and stovepipes aimed straight into tight academic ruts;*

²² And finally, society demanding money to pay bills crushing even the loftiest of dreams;

²³ *Too soon the "freedom to explore" that should have been the greatest time of one's young life was lost to sad tradition and time-honored arrogance of "teachers":* a collapse of lofty potential, largely unrecognized... applauding their own incompetency by training others to follow in their ruts plodding exactly the same...

[24] ---but somehow having survived all those many difficult and painful years of spirit-smashing agony, Lyle hoped that the true Joy of Learning might yet return: after an accumulated twelve brutal years of certified full-time college credit, finally emerging at the highest level as a Ph.D. "Doctor", LYLE FINALLY BEGAN HIS TRUE EDUCATION....

Lyle 6:25-45

TUNNEL VISION EXPLODED

25 *All that which had come before by way of formal "education" was not totally useless to Lyle---but perversely taught him lessons of interminable bloody battle and exhaustingly-heroic STRUGGLE...*

26 Trying in vain to shape & contain vast oceans counting drops amorphously-surging, flowing, and changing---ephemeral details obscuring powerful general awareness of huge, nebulous forms supporting interlocked, linked realities:

27 *Vast complexities of life swarming across chasms unimaginable*; insinuating-into every crack and fissure, nook and cranny; permeating our globe while ceaselessly moving & changing:

28 Expanding & contracting, reaching ever upward-outward, *combining and recombining, self-consuming interdependent biospheres*;

29 Driven by an indomitable ingrained instinct for survival;

30 Drinking deeply of fusion-spawned, limitless solar-power: infernal perpetually-offering streams of energy, exciting atoms;

31 *Perceiving cosmic lights blazing from a sea of twinkling stars: sparking eager minds*, pricking heaving hearts, and expanding powerful mentalities:

32 *Tweaking a curiosity imbedded in delicate strands of perpetual-change*; eternal scrolls detecting, directing, and celebrating birth, death, and rebirth;

33 Gigantic black holes collapsing... space & time fabric ripped, strained, shredded, punctured, then punched-through---perhaps many pin-prick "Big Bang" EXPLOSIONS cataclysmically birthing:

34 *Yet more universes elevating our concept of "God" far beyond our tiny minds* awakening to discover inside & outside ourselves billions of billions of billions set-into even the tiniest speck of matter;

35 Moving simultaneously backward & forward, outward & inward, upward & sideways, and on into untold dimensions: their Originator and Creator no longer understandable as simply some super-human, larger

version of ourselves throwing down lightning from clouds explaining "gaps", neatly sewing-up holes in our ragged lack of primitive knowledge;

36 But rather better understood as *Architect, Instigator, Upholder, and ultimate Substance* of fundamental processes, elemental laws, states of being, and means of perception;

37 Reveling and delighting in, perhaps, a complex "Multiverse" and an unknowable Otherness... *amazing permutations extending beyond our known confines*:

38 SPACE-TIME-ENERGY MERE LIMITED WORDS comprising rhymes, riddles, and enigmas of our perceived reality: where God's playground is replete with celestial pearls, rubies, emeralds, and diamonds glittering & spinning, shining & glowing... embedded into spiritual jewels of unimaginable colors; awesome sensations boggling and humbling man's gaze:

39 *Looking out from our ant-sized, skull-constrained, earth-bound brains capturing only a mere hint of what lies beyond speed-of-light chains trapping us within the tiniest little fraction of the Universe*:

40 Preventing us from even creeping the mere smallest distance from here to our nearest star... we remain imprisoned as microscopic specks on microscopic specks on microscopic specks...

41 As sitting on our lonely, spinning tiny rock *we lust after limitless freedom fiercely struggling to break free* of both metaphysical and physically-defined cages:

42 Arrogantly presuming ourselves to be Kings of the Universe ruling the intricate swirl... with galactic space from beginning to end defining the length of our exalted kingdom;

43 WE ARROGATE OURSELVES AS THE DESPOILERS, THE AGGRESSORS, THE DOMINATORS, THE DESTROYERS... ever-hungry for more, never accepting the boundaries of our ephemeral existence:

44 Insisting that our mastery of details negates our infinitesimal size; that our lustful gaze deposits a delicious predatory glaze on the Cosmos: *knowing how good it would be to taste it all and eat it up*!

45 Our greatest sin to forget or never even try to see past that which lies immediately in front of our own eyes...

Lyle 7:1-12

ABSTRACTIONS VERSUS DETAILS

¹ *Romantic love Mother Nature's sweet trick manufacturing babies perpetuating a mad scramble providing token meaning*:

² An equivalent-money necessity for maintaining life... perpetuating a legacy while lessening the fear of old age by growing chubby children... whose own surging hormones drive their own heated frenzies, quickly matured;

³ Delighted conjugaters squirting sperm and dropping eggs... combined, divided, differentiated, and popping-out tiny legs, toes, ears and noses;

⁴ Fingers twitching & grabbing, birthed with demanding brains, sucking & shrieking mouths, robust intestines, soon-ripened testes and ovaries dropping their own products... cycling yet again profound generalities;

⁵ *Details demanding their just due across a frantic spectrum*: eating, showering, kissing, working, praying, and entertaining;

⁶ *Occasionally merging & reforming as useful abstractions*: constructing commerce, law, economics, science, industry, religion, philosophy, art, government, military, medicine, family, tradition, exploration, society, transportation, and many other disciplines:

⁷ *Providing useful, effective, and helpful starting frameworks*... useful as building-blocks, perspectives, justification, comfort, a prevailing sense of order, security, stability, and purpose;

⁸ Built-into waving flags, clever electronic devices, slick magazines, neatly-trimmed lawns, shiny new cars, helpful robots, colorful Christmas tree ornaments, wide-screen super-high-definition TV's, 3-dimensional displays, busy city streets, presidential news conferences, disposable dirtied diapers, plastic recycling bins, blinking store signs, black power lines, faded torn jeans, tasty candy bars, pots of steaming stew, fields of yellow sunflowers, sleek empty caskets, newly-occupied graves, plate glass windows, loaded guns, snow plows, car bombs, voting booths, leather jackets, streaming sunlight, smoggy skies, tiny microphones, and prayer mats for supplicants;

⁹ Looking to acquire sufficient worldly goods to die peacefully at an advanced age; dreamily negotiating difficult choices caught-up in the mo-

ment's cacophony while craving silence; welcoming the final exit while obsessing on not leaving;

[10] *Zealously guarding borders of cherished comfort-zones* randomly ruptured by disturbingly-unavoidable revelations forced by ephemeral, broken, and twisted specifics:

[11] *Requiring more from us than just the minimum payment...* causing peril promoting public good, risking terrible personal injury via rejecting inaction, and jealously building transcendent wisdom shattering "common sense":

[12] DEMANDING THAT WE SHOULD RECOGNIZE THE FOREST WITHIN WHICH WE DWELL as more than just a collection of trees... but as a dynamic collaboration of ecosystems defining our character.

Lyle 7:12-53

STARTLING REVELATIONS

[12] **AND SO LYLE CAME TO TENTATIVE, DISTURBING CONCLUSIONS:**

#1. *That "religion" is largely (and sadly) a conservative security blanket manufactured by man to soften the awareness of impending death*---an artificial Garden of Comfort & Innocence that betrays its noblest goals:

[13] *Enshrining a soothingly-cooperative God blessing comfortable lifestyles* perpetuating easy traditions protecting patriarchal power;

[14] A "god" who demands little but respectful silence to authoritarian lectures or directed-"struggle" securing institutional pillars of command-and-control... rather than exciting exploration for personal spiritual growth...

[15] ---rather than being ideally rooted in tangible, effective, and flexible means of implementation powerfully affirming dynamic Principles by ever-questioning careful actions;

[16] Refining & extending, growing & flexing, strengthening & sharpening, invigorating & expanding non-destructive human potential;

[17] Celebrating Nature, respectful of nonbelievers, helpful to all, liberating the psyche from petty selfishness and unreasonable fear; LOOKING TO REFINE ONE'S OWN SPIRITUAL CHARACTER THROUGH EMBRACING THAT WHICH IS DIFFICULT, COMPLICATED, AND DANGEROUS;

[18] *Instead, sadly, often feeling important and powerful via subjugating others*, looking to an afterlife Paradise to escape present challenges, or celebrating "heaven on earth" forgetting core Principles; institutionalizing and worshiping that which is easy, simple, and safe;

[19] *Gladly embracing the constraints of exclusively-restraining teacher-leaders, when one might otherwise move closer to God by all good means possible*---by being willing to do whatever might *best* please the eternal Creator:

[20] Always studying to learn more and better how to please God even if it is not what I want or what gives me the most pleasure;

21 Without attacking or subjugating any of the Lord's creatures while not denying necessities of biological continuance... or becoming lost in empty repetition or meaningless rituals;

22 Abstractions used as clarifying tools rather than mere smoke screens; exercising edifying interactions focused on honoring the Creator; cherishing His Creation in ways that are specific, ongoing, and tangible;

23 Respecting each individual regardless of sex, race, or status; looking to help the potential good in each person to dominate rather than his or her ever-present faults, weaknesses, and failings;

24 Not imprisoned by society's present-changing-arbitrary standards... but truly liberated in the deep, private recesses of our minds;

25 Inviolate and pure in spirit; given the glorious opportunity to explore a non-chaotic, ordered, and purpose-drive freedom;

26 Exhilarated and engaged as a newborn baby gasping in wonder at each bright, new, marvelous "mundane" everyday thing: life experienced as a continuing Adventure;

27 While respecting lesser awareness by outward conformance; not casually disregarding prevailing religious structures, governmental laws, societal norms, or individual comfort-zones;

28 But still regarding the present state of knowledge as a vehicle for taking the next step upward on one's personal journey: *spiritually driven not by fear but by the joy of careful curiosity merged with an active and personal pride*;

29 The compulsion to create Godly Beauty motivating impatience while simultaneously rejecting dishonor, dreariness, or false fronts.

30 And #2. *That personal insecurity drives most of humanity's decisions ---where profit and innovation are often done only for the personal gain of "feathering the nest" for personal protection and creature-comforts--- man and woman's fondest wish... to be "safe"...*

31 Religions often just cynical "super-life-insurance policies" against if the worst were to actually happen: life after death, where periodic small payments now will satisfy a chit-counting God that calls us to give account of how we lived our lives;

³² Happily avoiding for little cost the rejection of those that refused His higher calling, an eternal separation that denies the reward of rising higher into God's immediate Presence;

³³ Countered, supposedly, by doing just enough here... a modest price: giving only a fraction of my true wealth expended on a "just-in-case" spiritual insurance policy;

³⁴ Not endangering my standard of living... the required price but the soothing bare minimum guarding against terrifying prospects that death might be not just a receding into a dreamless sleep but revelation of a lingering, culpable, conscious soul;

³⁵ Trying to avoid an uncomforted, adrift, lonely nightmare... cast into icy-cold outer blackness: worse even than that fiery, burning-hot, crowded, hectic hell so often preached by fear-mongering evangelists; rather *left alone to float in the silent darkness between tangible realities; where no one can hear one's screams...*

³⁶ *Instead of daring to step out of my safety zone to explore magnificent newly-discovered jewels... happily incorporating them into towering Crystal Cathedrals*; even EMBRACING STRUGGLE TO CLIMB CRUEL MAINTAINS TO STAND AT THEIR PEAKS SEEING BEYOND LIMITED HORIZONS...

³⁷ Escalating rewards & delights extending upward-outward, leaving behind stifling caves; reclaiming deserved limitless space triumphantly embracing the earth, solar system, galaxy, universe, and beyond...

³⁸ Amazing mysteries and puzzles just waiting to be investigated and enjoyed; rejecting personal enslavement by whatever controlling force even should ferocious liberation happen to knock down protecting barriers;

³⁹ While determined not to hurt innocents, nor disturb friends, nor harm oneself---but to celebrate our own God-given Potential rather than bury talents, joys, and aptitudes throwing them away down a deep, dark hole of automatic conformance.

⁴⁰ <u>And #3. *That Limitations are largely society-imposed, not deserved*---hardly one's fate to be born indoctrinated and controlled---where man and woman are trapped in cages of humanity's own making</u>:

⁴¹ Controlled females sequestered by youthful marriage, uninhibited pregnancy, suckling babies, and traditional male dominance;

42 Dominating males likewise ensnaring by heavy familial responsibilities;

43 Couples merrily coupling and uncoupling casually disrespectful of honorable, lasting love;

44 Children tortured in schools beating them down into civility... and then locking them into routine jobs;

45 Even ruthless dictators caged and trapped by their own selfish pride and lusts;

46 Criminals and cads bringing upon their own heads society's defense-mechanisms;

47 Casually accepting legal or illegal drugs as easy, cheap fixes... reveling in quick chemical addictive escaping the pain of the moment;

48 While true valid Needs remain amenable for being selectively met: in ways that are honorable, timely, and respectful of our many overlapping commitments;

49 *Not allowing our present Society to automatically set our boundaries*; keeping alive in our lives that which we most deserve: a responsible Freedom...

50 ---if not total, or allowed in speech or action, then always kept dancing, singing, traveling, painting, or writing within our private, inner, unseen minds;

51 That in this brief, short moment of our fragile physical existence we take as our due the chance to explore, to experience good satisfaction at doing our level-best where it counts the most:

52 Taking the "bull by the horns" and wrestling it down to the ground... or releasing it as we choose; grabbing the "tiger by its tail" and allowing it to drag us on a wild ride; enjoying and delighting in playing the cards God dealt us, whether a good or bad hand; *accepting books, rules, and set-dictates as respected starting points, not ends-unto-themselves*;

53 Daring to write our own stories, sing our own songs, and discover our own talents & abilities resonating with God's Purpose: CREATING SIGNIFICANCE BY LIVING-OUT OUR OWN PRACTICAL & APPLIED, INTERESTING & EXCITING, REFINING & MOTIVATING HOLY PARABLES...

Lyle 8:1-87

PARABLE OF THE WANDERER

[1] *A man woke up hanging face-down,* suspended from a high ceiling, jammed-up hard against cold spikes sticking into his back;

[2] Hurting, stiff, his back bruised, feeling agitated and confused, he stared down at a frighteningly-vast, wide, blue surface; as he grasped frantically at the vegetation around him growing down from that high ceiling, hanging on for dear life:

[3] Wondering if he would soon fall into the deep, deadly waters below... and why it was that he hung so precariously upside down, so far up above;

[4] When he felt something crawling under and over his legs---and tore his gaze from the vast expanse below, petrified to see a long slender animal slithering around his knees;

[5] Its round, slick head aimed straight at his face revealing unblinking, slant-pupiled orange eyes peering intently; its mouth half-opened, revealing sharp *fangs*...

[6] ---as if to silently challenge him: *"Who are you?" "Why are you here?"* and *"Where are you going?"* before nonchalantly crawling off to the side, into a thicket of tall hanging-down plants:

[7] The thickest part of a surrounding, similarly upside-down, wild and leafy meadow that sported gently-swaying bright red, purple, and white flowers;

[8] Feeling a cool, gusting wind fanning his fevered brow, smelling clean & crisp air, and hearing gurgling-flowing water;

[9] Swallowing hard, breathing fast, about to let go and just fall downwards, he consciously slowed his racing heart, and forced himself to calm down;

[10] Shaking his head weakly from side to side, blinking, suddenly realizing that the "ocean" down below was not some watery sea, but rather a high blue dome far *above*!

[11] While off to his side, just emerging over the land, an orb of yellow-red fire cast brilliant light across the strange landscape;

¹² Getting a bit more oriented, things starting to look clearer, he dug his hands into the gravel and stone at his sides and staggered to his "right side up" feet... swaying, trembling, jerking forward, *panicking...*

¹³ ---seeing a narrow, winding path leading into dark woods; he dashed for it, terrified by "cawing" creatures zooming through the air over his head, long-snouted other things "snapping" at him from muddy water, and "croaking" green pod-like things hopping ominously around his feet;

¹⁴ As through his head those maddening questions again arrogantly intruded: *"Who am I?" "Why am I here?" "Where did I come from?"* and *"Where should I go?"*

¹⁵ And so he stumbled into dark woods, sighing with relief to be away from the green scum of the bubbling brook that hid who knows what evil monsters lurking beneath its floating lily pads?

¹⁶ And, slowing to a wobbling walk, he realized that he wore only a simple white robe, made from rough-woven cloth, with hard sandals "clunking" on his feet; as, patting his face with trembling hands, he realized that he was clean-shaven; fingers moving up to his head... stunned to discover that he was also totally bald!

¹⁷ *His flat stomach aching with some strange need he abruptly stumbled out of the woods to see others like himself,* apparently also just waking up; a small village spread out before him...

¹⁸ ---where dogs, chickens, and cats all happily "barked", "clucked", and "meowed" while smiling, chubby women bustled from house to house;

¹⁹ Kids running about doing chores, or walking to a school house, playing and laughing; while grown men carried sharp tools on their shoulders, marching together towards planted fields, singing lustily;

²⁰ Vendors in the main square busily setting up their wares; while at a central building with big wooden columns men and women chanted in unison, arms folded to their chests:

²¹ Together bowing slowly and repeatedly in the direction of the rising yellow orb; bathed in its warm morning glow; they, like him, clad only in simple white robes... their heads also totally bald and gleaming in the sunlight, wearing---as did he---on their feet plain wooden sandals.

²² *"Brother! Welcome!"* an old, wrinkled, bald-headed man called out to him, smiling cheerfully, striding forward out of the praying group to greet

him, arms spread wide, catching the Wanderer up in a strong bear-hug; then stepping back, a big grin on his face, asking: "Where are you from?"

23 "I... don't know..." the Lost Wanderer whimpered, cringing-away from the disconcertingly-intimate attention before sinking down weakly on a stone bench nearby... the old greeter also sitting down next to him.

24 "You don't know where you are from?" the old man laughed pleasantly. "Are you not from the next village over the mountain?"

25 "Perhaps..." the Wanderer sighed, starting to relax a bit. "I don't remember---but my stomach *hurts*!" he bent forward, grabbing his belly with both his arms, groaning.

26 The old man frowned and then hastily motioned for some others to bring over a bowl that was put into the Wanderer's hands: heaped high with a warm, nutty-smelling white mush.

27 "Eat!" the old man encouraged him, motioning for him to lift the bowl to his mouth. "It is freshly-cooked oatmeal! Don't you eat this at your home?"

28 "I DON'T KNOW! I DON'T REMEMBER!" the Wanderer cried-out. But then, more quietly, embarrassed at his outburst: "I... thank you..." he mumbled, with the fingers of one cupped hand scooping up some of the contents into his mouth, chewing carefully, swallowing, amazed at its richness and how it so satisfyingly coated the inside of his stomach: a warm delight that he quickly gulped down, then licked his fingers clean!

29 "Oh... that was *very* good!" he gratefully acknowledged, sighing, sipping now at a delicious cool mug of offered water then intensely marveling: *"What is this place? Who are you people? Why are you here?"* and *"Where are you going?"*

30 The old man's eyes narrowed in sympathetic contemplation as he glanced up at the sky, sighing. His hand went up to his own head, caressing his wrinkled baldness. "Well, my friend... those are good questions! But good answers are not brief. In fact, the best answers require a lifetime of diligent study. It seems, then, there are no easy answers at all---even for me!"

31 "You don't know either?!" the Wanderer gasped, afraid that he would never find answers to the incessantly-nagging Questions.

32 "Oh I know some answers," the old man hastened to reassure him. Then, speaking forcefully: *"But there are things that you can't just hear*

stated and immediately understand! *They must be learned by struggling over extended trials and tribulations...* I think, perhaps, that this is where you are right now my friend---in the midst of trials and tribulations---perhaps by some trauma forced to confront the realities behind what is obvious." He paused, smiling wryly. "But I suspect that you should get some rest before we talk further. You look exhausted!"

33 The Wanderer was vaguely aware of the old man's thin hand lightly touching his forehead:

34 "...and you are burning up!" the old man clucked, taking the Wanderer by the arm and lifting him back to his feet. "You have a fever! You *must* rest!"

35 The Wanderer impatiently pushed the old man away, sinking back down upon the hard stone bench. "I don't want to rest! I just got up... or down... or woke up... or whatever... So you say I am *sick*?"

36 "Well, it does seem to be the case," the old man said, shrugging his slight shoulders. "Perhaps that is why you can't remember. You are ill. Fevered sickness can often cause confusion!"

37 The Wanderer blinked his eyes rapidly, shaking his head from side to side, feeling everything around getting distant and wavy. "Yes... you may be right... I can't see clearly at all... when I woke this morning I thought the world was upside down... hah! But---can you help me to get better? Please?"

38 The old man patted the Wanderer's shoulder comfortingly: "We have some medicines, brother, which might help you. *But your greatest healing comes from within. It is always available to you!*"

39 "What do you mean, 'from within'? And if that's true, then *why*?"

40 "Well, brother, it is *because our greatest sickness comes from our own minds,*" the old man gently replied. "And your own mind often has the power to heal itself, if you wish!"

41 "But if I have medicine in me already," the Wanderer groaned, sharply rapping his forehead with the knuckles of his right hand, "then why must I be sick in the first place?"

42 The old man laughed, clearly enjoying the challenging early-morning conversation. "Perhaps God is *testing* you, brother... or, instead, *punishing* you! Or, God may be *helping you*---in ways you don't recognize as such---in order for you to grow spiritually... Or, hah, maybe the Lord is

just *neglecting* you for a while! After all, you may not be as important as you seem to think you are..."

⁴³ The Wanderer shook his head wearily... then squinting his eyes in pain. *"What is this 'God' of whom you speak? Who is that? And why should he or she care about me? And why should I care what he or she thinks about me?"*

⁴⁴ The old man snickered as if he'd heard a clever joke. He patted the Wanderer again on his trembling shoulder. "Perhaps you should rest, my brother. We'll give you a room with a bed to sleep on. Let your body get a chance to recover from whatever struggle it's been through. Later, we'll have plenty of time to..."

⁴⁵ "NO!" the Wanderer shot-back at him, agitated. "Perhaps I'll not have a 'later'! I don't feel that bad! It's true that I'm tired, confused, and my head spins---but I *have* to know! I want to hear the Answers! Please, talk to me *now*!"

⁴⁶ The old man shrugged agreeably. "Well, maybe talking further right now *will* help you to remember! You are, after all, a Brother..."

⁴⁷ "---and that's another thing!" the Wanderer intensely moaned, interrupting the old man. "What is this 'brother' thing that you keep calling me?! And how is it that you know that I am one of them, whatever it is that they are!??"

⁴⁸ The old man lifted a hand and gestured about the village. "You see around you the people, all looking as do you! Your white robe, sandals, and bald head clearly identify you as one of us. We are all the *true* servants of God!"

⁴⁹ The Wanderer looked down at his own robe, feeling its rough texture on his skin. "Yes," he agreed. "I *am* dressed like you. But I don't feel like a 'servant'... let alone 'the true servants'... and I don't know this 'God'! Is God that bright fire in the sky to which you all bow? Is bowing to it what makes you 'true'?"

⁵⁰ The old man snickered. "No, my friend, the sun is not God. But it *is* a *manifestation* of His magnificent power! He is the Essence, the Initiator, and Supporter of all that is good! And, being the 'true' servants was actually a little joke of mine... I apologize. Actually, there are many groups similar to ours but different in their traditional beliefs and practices that also claim to be the 'true' group of servants to God! Hah! We all like to think that God loves us best! For us to be 'best' makes us more 'safe'... a common motivator of the unenlightened in seeking God. We are actually

a bit more humble than that, my friend, knowing that our little traditions are humorous to God rather than being the Ultimate Good that supposedly elevates us above others! But traditions can be helpful. So we like to bow together to the sun in the morning. If nothing more, it's a nice, easy exercise!"

51 "All of that you just said is... *confusing!*" the Wanderer groaned, shaking his head again from side-to-side. "And what is this 'good,' of which this God is the 'Essence'?" the Wanderer asked, growing more and more puzzled. "You speak to me in riddles! How am I to understand what you explain to me if everything you say adds yet more mystery?"

52 The old man paused, waving a purple-veined hand inclusively-about in the air. "You are correct, my friend," he acknowledged. "In my enthusiasm to help you understand who you are, I am going too fast. I don't mean to confuse you. But it is good that you acknowledge Mystery: which lies at the root of all humility and true religion. Consider this... *that 'good' is the result of God acting through his human servants to inspire them to fulfill their greatest potential*!"

53 "What?" the Wanderer gasped in confusion at the old man's answer... "But that also tells me nothing! 'God is good' and 'good is God!' How does that make the sky-fire shine in the sky?"

54 The old man frowned again, rubbing his chin thoughtfully, staring off into the distance, towards the rising sun.

55 The Wanderer perceived a subtle shift, a deepening of the old man's tone, a slowing of his words, a sobering of his mood...

56 "You are indeed a perceptive person," the old man thoughtfully acknowledged. "It's true I did give you a seemingly circular definition. Many would not have perceived that level of Truth, just accepted my glib explanation! Perhaps... you are here at this moment not just to educate yourself, but to educate me and those reading of us as well! *In this I speak directly to those reading these words in this book! Yes, I can also perceive a deeper Truth, my wandering friend! We are all connected through God through space through time... hi there! I see you!* And I sense there is a bigger issue here than just your own particular confusion... for many others also unexpectedly may 'waken' into an upside-down world where little makes sense and they are abruptly prompted to question everything! These types of people are called *'seekers' who are not satisfied with what is handed to them by their universe or human society. And I love them! You, my Seeker friend, reading these words right now---I love you! God loves you too!* You, see, you Seekers are a wonderful sort... tormented that you don't know everything, indeed can

never do so! It is a marvelous 'curse' from God Himself! But to you and all those in your situation, don't despair, my friends! *In the danger is great Adventure! In the difficulty there is advancement! And though we will never know everything, there is a fascination to discovering what we can!* There's a lot you, my wandering friend, obviously don't know but sense---behind things that most people take for granted and thus don't even think to question! *Be proud of asking Questions! This does not make you an automatic 'heretic' as traditional religions often claim! Quite to the contrary, the true servants of God welcome Questions that lead us to deeper appreciations of Truth!* For instance, God is the Ultimate Reality that initiated, supports, and enforces all the Laws of Nature. It is God that initiated and still governs the magnificent forces that bring forth life formed in his spiritual image: living creatures evolved to the level of self-awareness and God-awareness! The minds of these evolved creatures are developed to the point that they are able to perceive and choose whether to honor or dishonor their Creator---to revel in His great love, beauty, and creativity; or, conversely, to be limited by hate, ugliness, and destruction. They make a conscious choice to embrace the world in which they discover themselves whether as despoilers or protectors. And in their personal and global choices they bring down Judgment upon themselves! So the 'pains' of this life are often simply the results of people attempting to escape from their own responsibilities!"

57 "Ah..." the Wanderer nodded gratefully. "Now you have told me something, old one. You say I can *choose*... whether to acknowledge a responsibility and debt to this 'God' or to depend only upon my own self. But the choice between the two, I am beginning to understand, is not easy or simple, is it? And... who, then, are these 'others' that you are talking to? I only see you and me here! Is my perception still damaged, still seeing things upside down?"

58 The old man clapped his hands together in glee. "Yes! Your perception, my friend, is limited! But in your desire to see further, you are seeing clearer! There is more to be known than you or I can ever know! Our brains are too small! We are but 'two-dimensional' characters in a book about reality within a larger 'book' about reality written by and from God! *You* are from God, my brother---made to be *like* God! Yet we *don't* have to be His true servant if that is our wish! We can blind ourselves at will to that which is uncomfortable and frightening! I choose not to do so, thus can see that which others often laugh at the notion that it might exist! Truly our other friend who reads these words right now has the same attitude! That splendid person---the same as you, dear brother---is willing to contemplate what I call 'spiritual science-fiction'! It is to free one's imagination asking: "What *if*?" As God gives us all life within His infinite imagination, so does our dear reader right now take Lyle's words and

bring them to life! *Thank you, my friend reading these words, for giving us life in your mind! And all this is possible because God gave us all free will to make our own choice as to how we will live our life, either selfishly or gratefully!* You are free to bask in the glory of God or hide from his Presence! You may choose to live only in the moment or also embrace the Eternal! And, as you say, it is not easy or simple because there are terrible Forces constantly trying to drive us from our Heavenly Father! But be assured that you are not alone in this struggle! The invisible 'other' here with us, right now, is a fellow Seekers that you are helping with your present struggles! Many others suffer from the same pains that inflict you---and benefit from the same insights that you perceive because of those struggles!"

59 "That is hard for me to understand when I cannot see those fellow Seekers around me... but you do see further than I, old one! I will take your word for it. But I still don't see why would anyone ever willingly choose to be hateful, ugly, and destructive?" the Wanderer pondered. "And who could be so cruel as to want themselves or us to cower in a cave... when we could go out and dance in the light!?"

60 "No one would," the old man smiled sadly, "---except, of course, if they were *sadly stunted* or *sick*! Some people seek only what is comfortable: meaning that which is easy, safe, and simple! At their core they are motivated by Fear! They are afraid to go out in the true spiritual light that may be from the FIRE of Painful Struggle! In the Light they may find not just inspiration and productivity but also confusion, difficulty, and danger! So they shun that which seems novel or new! For the Children of God that is, indeed, a sickness of their minds! For who is, indeed, the Ultimate Light of our brief lives here in this world if not the Almighty? We should *revel* dancing in the light! In trusting our Great Lord we should find the COURAGE to face the Fire! But, sadly, the Fear can drain the Courage if we allow it! Plus, there exist terrible, ever-present Forces that drive us from our divine heritage! God allows them to exist to test our courage and faith in him! While our Heavenly Father wants us to move into the light, to overcome our animal fears---these affirming-negative Forces aren't bothered by our distress! They just exist! *They have no compassion!* They are not cruel, just uncaring... which is the greatest insult of all!"

61 "So are we doomed?" the Wanderer gasped. "It sounds like you are saying I am under attack both from within and from without! No wonder I am sick! And is my sickness the means of my own death? Is that what is happening to me? Am I dying?"

62 "Well... doomed? I suppose that yes, we all are doomed..." the old man shrugged. "Dying? Yes, certainly! Death is an important part of Life... a

fate that we cannot escape! So, my friend---if that is what you want to hear---you *are* dying! Whether you cower in the cave or dance in the light you will either be crushed in the earthquake or incinerated by the blazing sun! Hah!" he giggled, smiling broadly...

63 "But I *don't* want to hear that! Why do you say I want this?" the Wanderer exclaimed in frustration. "I want to be *saved*, not damned! Why would I want to hear that despite everything I do struggling to survive I must come to an end---that I will be crushed or burned to death!? Why will this 'light', this FIRE from God ultimately consume me?! Why did this 'God' put me here anyway if it's just to be overcome by uncaring 'Forces'? Does this 'God' play cruel jokes on us? Or... does this 'free will' you spoke of give me some personal choice in the means to my own death? Is that it? Despite my words to the contrary, do I deep in my heart *want* to be sick and dying? Is my 'sickness' really of my *own* making...!?"

64 "Sadly... yes," the old man sighed with a rueful smile on his weathered face. He shrugged his thin shoulders.

65 "But why?" the Wanderer asked. "I can see how some super-powerful cruel 'God' might inflict this pain upon me. But *why* would I do this to *myself*?"

66 The old man paused before answering... then carefully spoke each word exactly and distinctly: "Yes, our glorious God *does* allow these things to happen to us. So, ultimately, He is responsible for our suffering. But God does not torture us without purpose. Often, though, the purpose is beyond our comprehension. Yes, I know that sounds like a 'cop-out'... but truly we are tiny creatures with even tinier little brains! Still, even in this life, some of that Purpose is sometimes evident. I assure you, my brother, that our trials and tribulations do not bring pleasure to our Heavenly Father. Rather, *it is our courageous struggle to exercise His magnificent Gift to us even in the face of unavoidable defeat and failure which brings Him great pleasure*! For us to do this requires great personal spiritual character! It is very tempting to try to avoid the Struggle by embracing the illusion of 'comfort'---seeking ease and safety! As you said, to 'cower in one's cave' is to give-in to our animal nature. *Embracing our true spiritual nature REQUIRES us to be uncomfortable: to attempt things that are hard, confusing, and dangerous*! It is much easier to simply pull upon ourselves the comforting delusion of a forgetful fever! Yes! This describes your situation, my friend, exactly! That forgetful fever can even become addictive! That's because in the fever of the illness there can be a wild, exciting *exhilaration*: a feeling of instant, surging pleasure... a self-affirmation at exerting power over ourselves and others; and even the illusion of actually *being* God! But the fever can also be

self-deceptive: a lie we enjoy too much to relinquish! *And so we often, sadly, choose to take the cowardly way out: wrapping ourselves in self-aggrandizement through pitiful resignation, in which we tell ourselves: 'Poor little me, so put-down and oppressed... there's no need to struggle because it is hopeless!'* And so we 'take-control' by giving up! Are we not a magnificent and complex creation!" he giggled again, in amused delight! "IT ALL COMES BACK TO '*WHAT DO YOU WANT?*'" the old man intensely stated, suddenly dead-serious.

67 The Wanderer was deeply troubled, afraid of what more he might find out about himself if he dared to ask further questions to the smart old man. But he *had* to know, no matter the conclusion or consequences... More than anything else, *he wanted to know...*!

68 "So... are you saying..." he gasped, "that *I* am one of those---who *made* himself sick... loving feeling myself greater than others... loving holding destructive power over myself and others... and even loving deriving pleasure from hurting myself and others? Am I then... a *bad* person?"

69 The old man smiled warmly, gripping the Wanderer's arm tightly with a strong, bony hand. "Ah, my friend, I am so happy to hear you ask those questions! It tells me you are not as sick or bad as you think! You *want* to move out of the stinking, dark cave---no matter how comfortable it might seem: rejecting its supposed simplicity, ease, and safety! Also, I see that you *want* to dance in the Light despite of its supposed complexity, difficulty, and danger! But even more than that I see you *want* to MOVE BEYOND ALL OF THAT INTO THE *UNKNOWABLE MYSTERY* THAT CONFOUNDS AND ELEVATES US ALL... where we *transcend* all the limitations of this earthly life!"

70 The Wanderer frowned, perplexed, but oddly excited at the old man's amazing words... "But... if that is true... then why am I here?" he replied. "Your village seems a comfortable retreat from the world... I see no one burning up in the sun! Surely I should not stay here if I really want to move on, as you say! This is all so confusing! I'm so ashamed at bothering you all with my sickness..." he cried, surprised to find himself hanging his head in shame...

71 The old man laughed, patting the Wanderer's forearm comfortingly. "Yes, my friend, many of our order came here because they disgusted themselves and wanted to be healed," he stated firmly, "---ashamed of their own self-imposed limitations. It matters not if nature, others, or you yourself made you sick, my brother. *It only matters that you wish for the fever to be lifted, for clarity to return: so that you can finally go back to where you began---truly safe in the arms of your loving, appre-*

ciative Father, the God of all Creation... the Author of your finest spiritual character!"

72 The Wanderer nodded slowly... "And is this the reason for you and those like you to be set-apart from the others of this world? Are you together moving from the Cave to the Fire to whatever is Beyond...?"

73 "It is indeed part of the work of our particular religious Order," the old man sagely nodded. "We are set-aside with the purpose of providing perspective and healing. We live a simple life. We accept all Wanderers, like you, who come to us *wanting* to find and understand better their place in Creation!"

74 "So you were waiting for me?" the Wanderer whispered in awe. "You *knew* I would come to you, here today? You knew that somehow I'd left behind my own Order that somehow was not satisfying my longing---but still wanted me to join yours? And if I do join, will we together then be more worthy than those who do not bow to the fire in the sky?" he grinned at the sudden realization of being greater than others!

75 "Yes, my friend, to your first question," the old man laughed in return, revealing gaps in yellowed teeth. "God told me you were coming. I *was* waiting for you! But as to your second question, even though we try to enhance our awareness, as I said before we certainly are *not* more 'worthy' than others who do not choose our particular lifestyle, rituals, or doctrines! We are true servants of God, yes---but not 'the' true servants! We only *think* we are!" he laughed again, slapping his thin hand down on a bony knee.

76 "But now you speak again in riddles!" the Wanderer exclaimed in irritation, burying his head down into his arms. "I don't want to be ordinary! I want to be extraordinary! Why would this 'God' want me if I was just one of many others? I want to be *special*!" Then, pausing, he was ashamed of his words that revealed motivations he'd not even realized were within his heart. But... was it a baser motive? Perhaps it was only the truth! Deliberately, he raised his head and said: "So I take it that there are others outside your village *not* praying or chanting, or bowing down together to the rising sun! I supposed, then, that those outside of this village and other villages like it merely go about their business of living: eating, washing clothes, going to school, doing chores, raising their families! *Surely they must be less than we! If all people everywhere were are of equal value in God's sight, then why should people come to this place?* Have I wasted my time to stop here and talk to you? Should I just get up and leave, since you tell me everyone everywhere is 'equal' in God's sight?! Are you just another Order preaching things that don't make sense in the modern world!?"

77 The old man sighed, at once amused and also exasperated with his younger charge. He smiled in a disarmingly-friendly way as he carefully stated: "Each of us in our own way builds our own spiritual characters, creates beauty, and demonstrates gratitude to God," he softly continued. "Each person approaches God from the level of his or her own present awareness and knowledge. Each person is a product of their own particular biological programming, their own parents, their own society, and their own inherited religion or lack thereof. So we all start at different places in our journey, with different resources available to us, and with different capabilities both internal and external. *The Struggle that delights our Heavenly Father is when we, His children, continually strive to be and do better no matter how high or low we started*! In this way *anyone* can learn the most powerful Lessons, whether here or elsewhere... sometimes, yes, even more in the 'everyday' life than here encased and isolated in our pious traditions, rituals, and doctrines!"

78 "If that is true," the Wanderer snapped, pointing an accusing finger at the old man sitting next to him, "then why bother with the different clothes, the carefully-shaven heads, the separate village, or your group that together bows, chants, and prays? It all seems so unnecessary! Surely you are just wasting everyone's time!"

79 The old man gently pushed the Wanderer's accusing finger down, back to the Wanderer's side. Then he spoke with solemn firmness: "By our distinctive differences we remind others that life is more than mere existence. We overtly demonstrate that the instinct for survival does not mandate severing our link with God. We show by collective actions that all humanity is connected together---bound to each other and also to God! By our rituals and traditions we demonstrate the value of diligent Duty: a focusing of the mind beyond immediate rewards or punishments. For instance, our chants and prayers show that we focus our minds beyond the immediate material world. Our traditions also provide predictability and stability in lives otherwise filled with uncertainty, danger, evil-temptations, and fear. Our doctrines provide order and coherence to an unpredictable future. And finally, by our tolerance and friendship to visitors and those of different philosophical or religious persuasions we prove that our Order is built on transparent Meaningfulness rather than just random ideas or superficial emotions. In other words, my friend, WE ARE HELPING EACH OTHER WITH OUR TRADITIONS---just as I wish to help you! The only way this effort is 'wasted' is when Tradition trumps the underlying Principles! This may have happened at your prior Order, sickening your mind! In that case, yes indeed, the mind is sickened when it is required to believe things that are patently untrue!"

⁸⁰ The Wanderer shook his head from side to side, trying to make sense of the old man's gentle but seemingly-contradictory words. He replied in a shaking and fearful voice: "But... *how* can Tradition live happily with Exploration? How can Safety go to bed with Struggle? How can Truth co-exist with the Unknowable? I don't understand!"

⁸¹ The old man's eyes narrowed slyly. He pocked a bony elbow gently into the Wanderer's ribs. "You're funny!" he laughed. "God is extra good to me this morning, sending you to us. But the answer to your question is as simple as it is complex! Sure, the 'impossible' unions you just stated so succinctly seem unattainable. But let me ease your mind! IN GOD ALL IS POSSIBLE! It just depends... *on what you want*!"

⁸² Hearing those firm but loving words, suddenly everything finally "clicked" into place---and the Lost Wanderer suddenly felt at peace...

⁸³ ---the *Reasonableness, Applicability, Respect, Beauty, and Honor of the old man's words striking the Wanderer as a bobbing lifeboat upon a stormy ocean*: lifting him above a bottomless Terror.

⁸⁴ Nodding gratefully, the Wanderer allowed the old man with the help of other brothers and sisters to support his stumbling body as they led him to a small hut. There, the Wanderer sank down in exhaustion upon a hard but comfortable cot. He felt a warm blanket put gently on his trembling body. He pulled it up to his chin, closed his eyes, and sank down toward grateful sleep...

⁸⁵ ---feeling truly safe at last, protected, loved, and appreciated... he drifted down into unconsciousness: enveloped in the strong hand of God:

⁸⁶ *Deliciously dreaming of waking in a peaceful, meadow, beneath a beautiful blue sky, surrounded and embraced by God's Creation...*

⁸⁷ ---now supported and sustained by the many diverse and wondrous creatures all around him, the Wanderer discovered himself *happily embarked on yet another amazing-fresh Adventure*! IT WAS A GOOD DAY TO BE ALIVE...

Lyle 9:1-56

PARABLE OF THE LAST SURVIVOR

[1] *The Creature took a last, tormented scan of a hideous sky... the sun swollen to ten times its normal size, dominating the sky;*

[2] Once a nourishing, energizing, life-giving friend... now that looming sphere was an implacably deadly, torturing *fiend*...

[3] ---having devoured a once-delicious landscape, turning it bitterly-nasty, ugly, decayed, and dead;

[4] Here and there charred tendrils entwined as the last festering remnants of final desperate couplings: lost empty transfers of precious life blueprints... now made futile;

[5] Meant to be joyful rejuggling, invigorating, and refreshment of life... now crushed, shattered, melted, dissolved, and gone... fated soon to become just meaningless blobs of loose atoms;

[6] The blazing heat from above and below violating even spores long protecting the species over countless millennia in periodic swings of the planet too close to the sun;

[7] Soon even those tough protective casings would not endure the last, final, terminal, unstoppable, and brutal insult:

[8] Rapidly-swelling star-power sizzling down, inexorably combining with massive volcanic up-bursts, spewing molten fire;

[9] Bubbling red-hot rivers of liquid magma, belching black soot clouds and volcanically-ejected yellow sulfur;

[10] Bringing to an end the world's once-rainbow surface: once-glittering oceans of waving, liquid-crystalline fungal fields... once-intelligent dispersed-networks reveling in celestial thought... once-producing transcendent science, philosophy, art, and theology:

[11] Singing to their beloved Creator in intricate modes and vibrations circling and oscillating around the entire globe, weaving eons-long symphonies;

[12] Spectacularly-colored continental patterns racing, dynamic fabrics swirling across the face of the planet;

13 Living paintings ever changing, evolving, shining, and honoring the Heavenly Father with glorious praise;

14 A global splendor unique and distinct in the entire universe now reduced to a festering evil: fractured, black, broken crusts floating on hellish lava lakes.

15 *And so the Last Survivor slunk through a quivering crack into a specially-prepared, dark, cool, quiet, smothering vault...* quickly sealing the slit tight, closing behind its last, lingering, reluctantly-retreated tendril;

16 Now protected within many thick polymeric shells of spore secretions transferred across the whole population tip-to-tip over hundreds of years---a hugely thick accumulation lovingly laid down, layer-upon-layer... forming an insulating, nearly-impenetrable barrier;

17 The community of the planet fully realizing that their final life-pod could never be thick enough, wide enough, or durable enough to long stave-off the breaching-shattering-melting supernova blast:

18 But perhaps for just long enough... to persist a few seconds beyond the flickering lick of the exploding star quickly vaporizing all its planets in one massively-hot surge;

19 *All life in that solar system fated to be extinguished and vaporized... yet the pod lingering, the very last organic structure to disappear...* by a few seconds, perhaps a minute... the tiny vault vainly staving off the roiling star-plasma... then gone, no real protection at all... just a short delay of the inevitable;

20 So soon... the supernova would disintegrate all life in the solar system: courageous, defiant, persistent biological units vanquished---on one level the pod a tribute to illogical, angry, ferocious, biological survival-instinct;

21 But on another, higher, more-significant level... the pod was presented as a small burnt-offering, a sacrifice upon the altar of time, humbly summited as a final tribute---a token to the survival instinct's original Instigator;

22 As alone on a sterilized world, the Last Survivor stoically awaited termination, its imminent destruction delayed momentarily to endure beyond the death of everything... as selected and commissioned thousands of years in advance:

²³ Honored by billions of ancestral discrete organizing nodes, the Last Survivor's duty was clear and present: to speak for an extinct biosphere...

²⁴ *---offering a departing, collective statement summarizing millions of years of vibrant, planet-dominating civilization*:

²⁵ Replete with many great scientific discoveries, deep philosophies, and rampant Creativity now reduced to one last stubbornly-persisting individual:

²⁶ The Final Representative, now gathering-in its tendrils to form a disturbingly self-contained, physical ball:

²⁷ Hardened spikes thrusting-out from the forming ball into the ever-warming walls, suspending the sphere in the exact middle of the chamber;

²⁸ Centered on its own meditation, ignoring the warming-stifling air as it gathered all its thoughts together into one pure essence;

²⁹ *Then in one spasm of all its energy, projecting-out a laser-focused, all-consuming, last and conclusive communication*:

³⁰ "MOST-BELOVED, ETERNAL, AND HOLY FATHER... WE YOUR CHILDREN REACH OUT TO YOU WITH ALL OF OUR BEING, ALL OF OUR SUBSTANCE, ALL OF OUR THOUGHTS, ALL OF OUR FORM, AND ALL OUR HEART: HAPPY AND GLAD FOR YOUR MANY GLORIOUS GIFTS.

³¹ *AS WE GLADLY ACCEPTED ANIMATION AND INSPIRATION THROUGH YOUR INFINITE POWER---SO ALSO DO WE ACCEPT EXTINGUISHING TERMINATION... YOUR WILL BE DONE.*

³² *HERE AS IN HEAVEN, WE COMPLETELY ACCEPT OUR PLACE... BE IT TO DELIGHT IN LIFE OR SUFFER IN DEATH---IF IT FULFILLS YOUR HIGHER PURPOSE. USE US AS YOU WILL.*

³³ *WE COMMEND UNTO YOU OUR ENTIRE COLLECTIVE SPIRIT, BEYOND OUR INDIVIDUAL SOULS, THE SUM OF OUR ENTIRE EXISTENCE.*

³⁴ *WE HOPE THAT IN LIFE WE GAVE DUE AND PROPER REFERENCE, RESPECT, AND LOVE TO YOUR NAME; THAT IN SOME SMALL WAY WE PLEASED YOU DURING OUR BRIEF TENURE IN THIS PHYSICAL UNIVERSE.*

35 *THE PAIN, THE DESTRUCTION, THE HORRORS OF THIS ENDING PALE TO NOTHING NEXT TO OUR TRANSCENDENT, ETERNAL JOY:*

36 *BECAUSE YOU EXHILARATED AND EDIFIED OUR SOULS; YOU LET US EXPERIENCE YOUR INDESCRIBABLE BEAUTY; YOU INSTILLED IN US INEXPRESSIBLE EXCITEMENT TEMPERED BY COMPASSION AND MERCY;*

37 *YOU ALLOWED US TO BE AWARE... OF OURSELVES AND OF YOU; AND YOU GAVE US THE ABILITY TO CHOOSE ADVENTURE PARTAKING IN A SMALL WAY OF YOUR MAGNIFICENT DIVINE CREATIVITY;*

38 *AND SO WE BASKED IN THE LIGHT OF YOUR GLORY; EVEN AS NOW WE FREELY ACCEPT YOUR PURIFICATION BY FIRE; THAT WE MIGHT BE LIBERATED FROM THE CONSTRAINTS OF PHYSICAL LAWS, FINALLY AS INDIVIDUALS AND A SPECIES TO BE SET FREE;*

39 *BIOLOGICAL FORMS NO LONGER LIMITING US VIA CLUNKING CHEMICAL REACTIONS; NOR SLOWING THOUGHTS TRAPPED IN SYNAPSING NEURONS... ALL LEFT BEHIND;*

40 *THROWING OFF THOSE WEIGHTS WE TRANSCEND, RISING HIGHER, SEEKING YOUR ULTIMATE PURITY, POWER, LOVE, AND GRACE.*

41 *TAKE US, DEAR GOD, IF IT BE YOUR WILL, INTO YOUR INNER HOLINESS; YOUR IMMEDIATE PRESENCE OUR COMFORT; MERGED BACK AT LAST, FULLY UNITED, INTO YOUR SPIRITUAL SUBSTANCE.*

42 *FOR ALL THAT WE HAVE BEEN AND ALL THAT WE WILL BE... WE SAY 'THANK YOU'!"*

43 ---as in a *bright red flash*, the hot-glowing walls burst inward and the Last Survivor was incinerated...

44 ---reduced to constituent atoms, blown-outward into the Universe, together with the stuff of the super-nova, an expanding substrate:

45 Eventually combining with the detritus of other exploded stars to coalesce and condense into newly-lighted stars with fresh planets suitable for hosting the special characteristics of God's Nature:

46 Unique life-forms emerging, swarming, swimming, creeping... transmitting accumulated information from one generation to the next;

⁴⁷ Self-replicating systems quickly reproducing, sexually scrambling, a spectrum of many dynamic-spreading nodes... perception sparked, organizing;

⁴⁸ Reacting and evolving, analyzing, thinking radically-different yet all the same; some discovering an engrained capability to recognize and honor their Creator:

⁴⁹ Feeling Love despite persistent pain, choosing to accept or reject God's magnificent great Gifts; finding their own distinctly special place:

⁵⁰ In harmonious cosmic symphony singing-out throughout the vast expanding space of the Universe: whether from nebulas of drifting gas, or from volcanic rifts beneath frozen oceans, or basking in radiant energy from brilliant stars, or by even more-radical means:

⁵¹ Billions of billions of billions of permissive configurations expressing self-and-God awareness; elevated consciousness both blessed and cursed with "start" and "stop" signals of a personal beginning and an impersonal end;

⁵² Until, turning at last to the side, they all meet in the middle... embracing joyful growth, leaping forward happily together: conquering the limitations of space, energy, matter, and time.

⁵³ All of this allowing the beginning of yet another furious cycle filled with hope; yet again forming other thriving worlds built on fire, explosions, and cosmic death;

⁵⁴ Yet another opportunity for global struggle, discovery, and great Adventure: exercising a Divine Creativity... seeing everything through new eyes, time set-back to zero, all situations made totally different and amazing!

⁵⁵ Filled with the potential for awful pain or exhilarating delights, reflected in the blinking light-receptors of each new self-aware unit:

⁵⁶ Born to some progenitor creature in each unimaginably bizarre place: A CURIOUS, LAUGHING, REACHING-OUT BABY...

Lyle 10:1-39

PARABLE OF THE SICK CHILD

¹ *He was orphaned at an early age, torn from safety; the security of a poor but loving family shattered*:

² Cast out upon mean streets; made to fight or die; aged far beyond his brief lifespan by awful circumstance;

³ Rescued by ineffectual state agencies to shuffle between sets of bare-subsistence foster parents, kind but distant;

⁴ Until, finally, too old to be passed on again, yet too young to succeed by himself, he unexpectedly took quite sick;

⁵ *Struck down by deadly childhood leukemia, he wound up lying on a bare cot, in an impoverished hospital*;

⁶ In the absence of sophisticated cancer therapies or even simple medications, there was no way to relieve the crushing weakness, raging fevers, and nausea;

⁷ The critical act of breathing becoming more and more difficult, his wheezing gasps pitiful to hear as he lay dying; his nurses only able to cool his brow with a wet rag; not even oxygen to ease his ragged gasps;

⁸ *And so he sank into an expanding, all-consuming, depressive gloom: thrown far beyond the point of suicidal thoughts, knowing his end was near...*

⁹ But he was also painfully aware that throughout the world, in richer societies, there would have been hope: where he might have had a family with the means to survive hard times, to not be destroyed by the cruelties that took his father and mother;

¹⁰ There might even have been effective help for him when he was struck down---early diagnosis, good treatments leading perhaps to remission---greatly extending his life---perhaps even a complete and total cure;

¹¹ He might then have grown to full maturity, attended school, gotten a job, had a nice career, along the way met a pretty girl, gotten married, made for himself a loving family, and been successful in the game of life;

12 Then, finally "passing away" at a ripe old age, wrapped in comfort, warm drugs pushing off the pain, surrounded by close friends, with children carrying on his legacy into the future---all cruelly *denied* to him now...

13 *---as in his last few miserable hours of lingering existence he surrendered to either a cold, heartless, Godless universe or to a sadistic realm where gods torture mankind for their own amusement*;

14 When into his blurred vision there came a humble man claiming deity not as a ruthless dictator or cosmic clown but as comforter, supporter, admirer, and sympathetic friend:

15 Sinking to his knees, a big strong hand reaching out to gently take the boy's trembling thin hand in his own comforting grip;

16 The visitor closing his eyes, bowing his head, speaking words of reverence and assurance... sending cooling rivers of peace into the sick child's panicked mind;

17 *The boy suddenly realizing beyond a doubt that even though no hope remained and his time was short, his tormented and tragic life had not been in vain*:

18 That everyone he'd ever touched in any way was now enlivened and sobered by his example in facing his own impending fate;

19 Cutting-through the facades of smug complacency, superficial comforts, and wealth---all dissolved-away revealing to the more fortunate their *own* impending fates:

20 *Terrible endings looming for each and every one of them... giving pause to reconsider insufficient self-sufficiency despite every medication or medical treatment known to man being readily available and utilized*;

21 Scientific-research into new treatments and all of modern technology all doomed to fail... the Grim Reaper triumphantly gathering-in his inescapable, required due:

22 Facing imminent eternity, shaking the cold bony hand of death---whether by disease, accident, or old age---hearing the final ticks of the winding-down clock...

23 *---as time implacably moves on, leaving everyone swamped in its wake... their painful last hours, their last minutes, and their last seconds*

all floating away... everything that came before the present moment collapsing-backward into history:

24 Be it ten seconds or ten-times-ten years---each a mere cosmic flicker, all people taken to the same final point wondering in the last instant... *where did it all go?*

25 The dying child's clawed death-grip on life loosened, relaxed, and withdrew---while the gentle Man of God kept his firm grasp in place:

26 The offered prayer neither mindless ritual nor senseless repetition, but shared sympathy and grim experience... a mutual awareness:

27 *Bespeaking not a horrible, pathetic, empty ending... but a new beginning beyond our ability to even conceive or imagine*:

28 As the child stepped across the threshold into a different world, far beyond fear---leaving behind a shed mortality of sickness, hurt, weakness, and decay;

29 The awful pain and terrible loss now a thing of the past, a fading memory interesting but no longer paramount... as closing his eyes the sick child freely gave it all up:

30 *His true self now loosened, freed, rising upwards---flying at the speed of thought, he found himself adrift in a bright void filled with amazing new colors*;

31 Stunned by the impact of indescribable beauty---a blazing power surrounding and infusing his spirit---his mind happily expanded:

32 Floating weightless in the crackling, sparkling, limitless expanse he sensed the presence of others such as himself and reached out...

33 ---touching and connecting with glittering tendrils of spiritual energy welcoming him back into their midst he was greeted warmly: as they clamored to hear of his time in the finite land of rigid boundaries;

34 So he told them all about his earthly childhood of loving family-life crushed by tragedy---his flight, his savage struggles surviving on tough, dirty streets... then rescued by the inept state;

35 New homes of many strange personalities, hard encounter with others... then abruptly knocked-down by excruciatingly-painful illness, finding himself lost in despair:

³⁶ The metastasizing, awful sickness sucking him down, torturing him as he tried to fight against the terminal pain and misery; but finding in the end not empty hope but powerful awareness from a servant of the Almighty...

³⁷ *---as they all marveled and thanked him for sharing his vivid secondhand danger, uncertainty, challenges, earthy adventures, and desperate puzzles;*

³⁸ *Congratulating him on the blessing of such a searing experience*---so different from the blissful, ever-joyful, unbreakable connection to the all-powerful Lord---then everyone settling-back into their continued, unending peace...

³⁹ ...again facing the vast expanse of eternity---FROM WHICH HE'D JUST EXPERIENCED SUCH A POWERFUL AND WONDERFUL VACATION.

Lyle 11:1-45

WISE SAYINGS

¹ *A wise person does not speak in smug absolutes, inflexibilities closing the mind to further learning...*

² ---but in humble tentative conclusions moving forward one careful step at a time... ready to alter direction, even retreat, if greater knowledge demands change; more comfortable in asking Questions than giving pat Answers...

³ A solid foundation built upon respectful curiosity as to how to "be" and "do" even better than now, a continual upward progression;

⁴ Never arriving at a state of perfection---*ever-seeking the Deeper, Wider, Higher, More-Complex, and More-Substantial*;

⁵ Without rejecting "truth" as understood from one's present position, yet eager to expand one's vision into a broader perspective;

⁶ Knowing that at the center of everything---though deliberately set-off at a small distance from us---resides *an unknowable Mystery that we label as "God": at once unattainable but also underlying and supporting everything we know...*

⁷ ---never far away, an Essence always within our grasp: there ready to help lift the cloud of doubt and confusion by instilling irrational Hope;

⁸ ---at the vortex of enlightened confusion... an uncertainty that motivates, propels, and forces true Learning: a considered decision not to trust in temporary security, but let-loose and anchor ourselves in the unknowable Divine.

⁹ *So Lyle discerned that the highest, boldest wisdom is not just "the effective use of accumulated knowledge" but rather a basic attitude to-wards living life*:

¹⁰ Where superficial, set-answers to questions---whether grounded in science or religion or some other faith---are but a false security blanket covering-over an ocean's depth of deeper uncertainty of which there is no bottom ever to be humanly reached or attained;

[11] Where every "definitively-proven" final conclusion is misleading: true honesty requiring us to acknowledge at least ten new yet even-harder questions newly revealed!

[12] *And for each agreed-upon, absolute, established "fact" the underlying Assumptions expose increasing degrees of arrogance*:

[13] Short-sighted beliefs that our brains are even capable of knowing the full extent of reality, smugly assuming that we can discern all that exists and is knowable;

[14] Subsuming entire cosmos where we may actually be but lowly amoeba squirming and reacting, eating and excreting, happily replicating our engrained mindset:

[15] TOTALLY CONVINCED THAT WE ARE INDEED THE MASTERS OF ALL THAT WE SEE, WE UNCONSCIOUSLY LIMIT "REALITY" conveniently to its superficialities reconfigured into our own image: not realizing that we may be even *less* than amoeba in the cosmic intellectual scheme... perhaps mere bacteria not seeing beyond the grossest characteristics of reality, the inner edge of our manufactured "petri-dish" home.

[16] *Thus Lyle discovered he was smarter than most smart people in that he knew without a doubt how dumb he was*: confused, only vaguely understanding the depth of his own ignorance, floundering in the morass of his own unconscious assumptions, and trying like so many others to put God into some easily-manipulated box...

[17] ---contrawise, learning to happily and carefully listen to other people, gain fresh insights not as guru but rather continuing student of life;

[18] Teaching not by smug lectures but by tweaking receptive imaginations: offering tidbits, tools, facilitation, "O.J.T." stimulation, and attentive listening;

[19] Confident that a fully-informed small group finds solutions better than any one individual could reach on his or her own;

[20] *A synergism not distressed that parables don't resolve all issues; rather, intrigued that they set the stage for further "add-on" stories*: expanding from set stage-plays into complex societies... from tentative answers to discovering ever-deeper questions;

[21] Scratching the nagging itch of intelligence... making us truly wise beyond dictators or legislators, scholars or mystics, sinners or saints, scientists or Popes;

22 Fueled by a raging humility eagerly searching for super-human insight beyond inflexibly-absolute doctrines: munching-down tasty nuggets of mental invigoration enlivening one's soul.

23 *And in embracing a Godly Wisdom, Lyle was amused at inherent contradictions*: obsessing to find time when one wants it all right now; pursuing happiness though the very process makes people unhappy; discovering unhappiness rooted in satisfying our dominant survival instinct:

24 Our engrained, programmed emotions driving us like "mooing" cattle; where stress is more motivating than spirit; and most of us are compulsed to dig safer, deeper caves out of genetically-mandated fear...

25 ---popping-out periodically to snatch an apple or subdue a suitable mate; trying to make transient motivators permanent; speeding ever more quickly into self-perpetuating downward spirals:

26 Frustration forcing even more unwise actions causing additional hurt that winds up greater than the initial pain---resulting in more loss than gain, a sadly-accelerating terminal self-destruction;

27 *Such that in the midst of a huge banquet we starve ourselves skinny, sucking-out our own viability supposedly to augment our vitality*;

28 Resulting in skeletal feeble characters grotesquely staggering about... attempting to dance while falling to pieces---bare bones scattering, pale skulls grimacing:

29 Bouncing and rolling, grinning toothily, empty eye sockets glaring blindly---to finally crumble into dry dust... aspirations of generations vanished;

30 Only the wind carrying the remnants of their dreams, a warning informing the next set of like-minded young people:

31 Who, determined to build their own solid fortresses of security and joy, reap---in the end---sum totals of sadness, terror, and loss;

32 The careful accumulations of lifetimes of work dissipated, gone, squandered, lost, taxed-away, eaten by greedy scavengers, or melted into fetid pools;

33 Careers of sterling achievement taken for granted, caricatured, subsumed into historical footnotes, discarded, or just plain forgotten;

34 Individual efforts blurred for even the largest of creative legacies: proud of whom we are rather than where we came from... vague notions of continuance discontinued;

35 Heritage lost on genealogical trees where all of a person's existence melts into amorphous twigs or leaves: the real person long vanished into recombined DNA virtually identical from one generation to the next... familial differences merging, blurring, then lost;

36 Emotional satiety leaving the psyche flat; easy answers subtracting thrill; societal acceptance rejecting uniqueness; empty rituals abandoning purpose; meaningless traditions wasting time; authoritative dictates shrugged-off or ignored;

37 Subsuming the zest of all the rest of one's life in gaining and insuring comfortable non-heroic deaths... uninstructive, wasteful, and negating of what was notable;

38 *Yet in all the negatives, Lyle saw reason to be proud of humanity: here and there a few people rising above the blind pursuit of security and happiness...*

39 ---REJECTING ROTE WORSHIP OF THEIR OWN SURVIVAL INSTINCTS... dedicated beyond material accumulation to obey more than just engrained genetic imperatives;

40 Uncomfortable with the bland satisfaction of superficial answers... seeking dancing-to-tunes greater than only those of one's immediate society;

41 Purposeful actions not traded for empty rituals or meaningless traditions... faithfully working to achieve more than just comfortable deaths;

42 Honorably acknowledging personal responsibility beyond just self... seeing Connectivity to not only friends and family but even strangers, flowers, coral reefs, vanishing animal species, future generations, divinity, trees, and destiny;

43 Realizing hurting others, nature, or God is a knife to one's own throat;

44 DARING TO SAY "WHAT IF?" braving even continual failure to follow waking dreams...

45 ---*transcending one's own limitations not by knowing more but by knowing less.*

Lyle 12:1-49

SCHOOL & LEARNING

[1] *Having an awareness of logic, rationality, and the scientific method as good learning tools when coupled with nagging curiosity... Lyle determined to also apply Godly Wisdom to figuring things out*:

[2] Puzzling through each of life's many intertwined aspects, seeking if not "the" Meaning of Life... then perhaps just hints of Lasting Significance;

[3] Learning not just "things" and "places" but the PURPOSE behind actions, the CONSEQUENCES of processes, and the REACTIONS of dynamic systems... the gears behind the watch-face;

[4] In other words, *how* to effectively move known or unrecognized core objectives worthy of being AIMed at places located at the heart of a VISION:

[5] New realities, fresh vistas applauded or rejected by the Almighty... or cast adrift by internal illogic and inertia, sadly-colliding with each other, mutual destruction assured;

[6] *Choices possible if we understand where we distinctly stand versus where we want to go... but impossible if blindly-drifting on random currents or fickle winds*:

[7] The unexamined life allowing fate to drop us to die where we never anticipated or desired... a precious, quick-vanished interlude of freedom wasted, lost, and gone;

[8] Or, conversely, well-used in educating not just our minds but also our souls... lifting up our spirits, honoring and pleasing our kind and attentive Heavenly Instructor:

[9] The process of real learning found *not* just by the accumulation of competing facts nor ranking of clashing rewards nor by muting the Joy of Discovery;

[10] Where civilizing "carrots and sticks" externally prod and tickle: competence deemed "ok" as the main requirement for certifying grudging survival;

[11] *Rather, mandating awareness of crisp, useful "take-home messages" summing up main Significances where details drive meaningful Projects*:

[12] Where people benefit from focused diligence; where everyone gets an "A" grade whatever the results of an honest, careful, and sustained Effort---or an "incomplete" if clear parameters are violated---but certification is withheld if specific customers are not pleased;

[13] Where formal schooling ideally teaches useful tools, applicable methods, and self-teaching techniques: a dynamic capability unencumbered by required mastery of non-useful details;

[14] *Where school teaches Enabling Competencies that truly equip youngsters for life-long Adventure: from learning HOW to apply-innovate, attack problems, and challenge-accept*;

[15] Producing gleeful encounters with books, mentors, coworkers, computers, group interactions, and individual real-work tasks leaving students hungering eagerly for more... unhappy to have to move on to a new topic, sad that it's time to go home at the end of the day;

[16] Knowing the "how" to find necessary information either slow or fast---laying aside that which is not useful while applying that which is;

[17] Combining-discarding until newly-formed innovations or inventions satisfy true needs: not having to wait for a course, an instructor, or a boss to give direction;

[18] *Able, willing, trained, equipped, and eager to engage either difficulties or opportunities: skilled at critical thinking, prioritization, self-motivation, and "turning lemons into lemonade"*!

[19] WHAT IF THIS WERE THE NORM RATHER THAN THE RARE EXCEPTION IN FORMAL SCHOOLING?

[20] ---where it would be an oxymoron to say: *"There's nothing to do, I'm so bored!"* when all around us are libraries, sports, eager tutors & mentors, unmet needs, unused resources, music, art, churches, synagogues, temples, community-initiatives, family responsibilities, little brothers, little sisters, zoos, computers, games, and puzzles enough to fully engage one's mind, body, spirit, and soul well-occupied for a *thousand* lifetimes!

[21] Any single day only containing a tenth of the time to do what's necessary... that only being a tenth of the time to do what one really wants... and that only being a tenth of the time to satisfy one's full potential!

22 *If 24 hours could be expanded to 24,00 hours for each day, then perhaps we could truthfully say: "I've done all I can do in one day: my talents & abilities are exhausted!"*

23 Speaking not just of the rich and privileged in wealthy societies being blessed with rampant opportunity... but even the poorest and lowliest people of us all being set-into a spectrum of choices filled with fascinating arrays of curiosity-stimulating self-education:

24 ---seen as crawling bugs, sung as songs, glittering as rainbows, chanted-prayed as tribal rituals, and masquerading as "work": all aspects of true learning and creativity possible in all situations!

25 Heard in snarling survival-struggles or crying newborn babies; made visible as colors lovingly placed on dry cave walls; there to be grasped or sadly ignored... but often, sadly, to be disregarded, dishonored, and cast aside!

26 *It is so easy to allow society, problems, and heavy responsibilities to destroy our innate love of true learning... leaving it* SMASHED, CONTROLLED, and BOTTLED-UP:

27 Fermented into bitter vinegar only useful to spice up the glee, satisfaction, and comfort of *other* people... allowing them a smug happiness at our own subjugation, deference, obedience, and validation of their supposed superiority or "authority" over us;

28 *As safely contained, directed, chained, harnessed, and constrained... we slink through the school of life groaning, cursing, and controlled;*

29 Certain that we have the worst of all fates, condemned to live miserably, looking forward to the end, happy to leave it all behind, denying any lasting zest to Life.

30 Yes it is a choice. It is my choice. I make it every day, every minute, every second.

31 Yes it is a choice. It is your choice. You make it all the time.

32 Do you or I allow the heavy hand of restraining forces to smash us down? Or, conversely, do we dodge aside on nimble legs, scampering away?

33 Is our waking time drudgery or play? Are our eyes wide with amazement or squinted in fear? Do we welcome the rising sun or dread the dawn?

34 Or are we between the two extremes---neither hot nor cold, but lukewarm... content to warm ourselves at the crackling fireplace of acceptable comfort---drifting along, neither asking nor questioning, accepting societal-supplied answers;

35 Meekly conforming to settled precedence as the final word, the ultimate truth: choosing neither "yes" nor "no"---pliable and moldable---a clay for anyone to fondle, amenable to whatever our society imposes upon us;

36 *Not lacking imagination or intelligence, but missing that bouncy "spunk"... choosing to take the wide, easy, downward path rather than embracing the challenge-struggle of climbing up the mountain;*

37 And then wondering why God would "spit such from his mouth" as tasteless and neutral, of no real substance, merely barely existing!

38 *This, then, is the true challenge to us: not in finding "the" Final Answer, but in exercising our brains, spirits, and emotions daring to seek a religious reality that's larger than "Sunday School"... reaching ever-higher than traditional church sermons or established "authority";*

39 EVEN THE TALLEST PHYSICAL CATHEDRAL MADE INSIGNIFICANT BY US RISING BEYOND OUR ANIMAL INSTINCTS, reveling in learning ever more: stretching ourselves reaching up to our ever-encouraging Lord.

40 *So Lyle found the best, highest, and most powerful mode of learning... not from authoritative lectures or doctrines, nor repeated study of detailed manuals no matter how sacred or esteemed;*

41 Nor continual reading of accepted texts, nor artificial practice, nor unfocused exams, nor rote repetition: finding them mostly as poor uses of his precious time. Even facilitated small-group discussions, fun as they might be, were a lesser mode of true learning.

42 *Rather, Lyle gradually recognized the value of rapidly going beyond the introductory concepts and materials, advancing by careful progression actually "doing", honed to the point:*

[43] As efficient military-jargon "O.J.T." (*on-the-job-training*): where the major mode of true learning is real, meaningful, important work acquiring skill accomplishing interesting, customer-pleasing tasks...

[44] ---immediately at hand, a personal application with one's own fingers, feet, hands, and minds burning "take-home messages" indelibly into one's muscles and long-term memory;

[45] ---*where spiritual deeply-engrained validity is acquired and built-up always the same*: where the best learning process is identical to that used to master doing clinical tests in a hospital laboratory:

[46] Much like Lyle's military "O.J.T." job (during his obligatory stint in the U.S. Air Force) assisting physicians, nurses, and pharmacists in helping injured or ill people to heal by providing laboratory test results used in diagnoses and treatment:

[47] Blood the main test substrate---ugly spilled, but beautiful examined---composed of varied magnificent cells swirling and flowing... the fluid of living humans revealing inner workings of the body healthy or sick; imbalance revealing sickness when the body cannot accomplish the brain's goals;

[48] Much like formal schools---whether religious or secular---that too-often neglect or forget lasting skill-building... leaving nothing behind upon graduation except fuzzy memories of having studied something, such a sad waste of time;

[49] *Where the effort might have been much more effective and meaningful with well-designed, targeted, customer-driven, exciting tangibles*: WHEN INTERESTING, SATISFYING, AND MUTUALLY-VALUED "ON-THE-JOB-TRAINING (O.J.T.)" PRODUCES THE TRUE LEARNING. LEARNING.

Lyle 13:1-21

WORK, BUSINESS, & COMMERCE

¹ *And so Lyle further observed that mankind perpetuated its fatal flaws by knifing itself in the heart: needlessly separating Work from Fun from Learning...*

² Without further questioning, accepting artificial partitioning: a slicing and chopping of life divided into neat, small, disconnected, or even competing compartments;

³ So that our psyches are fragmented into disjointed "blurps" hiccupping along: jumping from cars stressfully commuting to hectic, grinding work to boring classes to yelling kids to giddy parties to grinding tasks to quick sex;

⁴ Regularly bouncing from drudgery to droning lectures to interesting TV shows, to tasteful treats, to basketballs, to required shopping;

⁵ Buying ourselves some relaxation after long days spent earning pay after finally having graduated from the dreadful struggle of awful school;

⁶ Resigning ourselves to the sad reality that to be given money we must provide fair value in return; doling out our precious time mainly in sleep and doing jobs and taking care of familial responsibilities: jealous of the tiny space left "in between" to finally get just a little bit of enjoyment.

⁷ Having grown up and been firmly embedded within societies based on the flow of money, we can't conceive life possible in other modes: where the profit and loss of materialism is not a total requirement;

⁸ *And yet we try to fool ourselves with illusions that we're independent: pretending to float above the need for toothpaste, hamburgers, houses... somehow not pawns to our paychecks, but masters of our income;*

⁹ In an economical swirl of services and goods that circle the planet in competing chess-moves: trading, profiting, investing, and accruing... terrified that the economy won't grow the expected percentage each and every year...

¹⁰ *OTHERS* might be slaves to the all-mighty dollar, but somehow we are still free: smugly thinking we can walk away any time we wish; that proper "principles" keep us firmly in the saddle, keeping up with the grind, and willingly trapped in the work-a-day world;

11 Knowing that even secluded monks still grow grapes to make wine to sell for needed cash, right?---*pushing-back the dread that underneath the hassle of our fragmented lives there is nothing...*

12 That without a job, a salary or career we are lost, empty, and crushed: looking into an empty void where we thought our soul would thrive; finding instead an "I.O.U." saying our check has bounced, so sorry!

13 Occasional attempts by a few to form self-sufficient communes inevitably overwhelmed by the pervasive power of lacking necessary money;

14 Most of human existence subsumed and consumed in earning & acquiring... if not precious gold, jewels, or paper-currency, then barter;

15 *All to get that which I don't already own, not realizing it's here already all around me... on me and in me---richly, fully, and supremely tasty*:

16 Nourishing, enlivening, satisfying, and pleasuring beyond big bank accounts, stocks & bonds, investments, or nest eggs... that which I don't have to leave behind for others to dissipate when I die: the very best of all;

17 *Adventures, cherished Memories, human Relationships, and true Learning---all wrapped up inside my spirit, stuck safely down deep in my soul*;

18 Nodding politely to honorable labor giving value for value received: certainly agreeing to my responsibility to take care of myself, help others, and not be a drag on the spirits of friends-family-society... pulling my own weight!

19 But not allowing my financial obligations to become the "all-in-all" taking up all my time, thought, obedience, substance, and self-worth;

20 *Fooling the Grim Reaper by deliberately melding Work & Fun & Learning together---reclaiming the confused jumble of a fragmented life, defiant!*

21 Refusing to waste my time... not one precious moment ceded to senseless compartmentalization: making <u>everything</u> support a continuous hunt to understand and apply a Godly Creativity fueled by a God-given Curiosity: PRODUCING A WEALTH BEYOND MEASURE...

- -

Lyle 13:22-48

MONEY & SUCCESS

[22] *Acclaimed success!--- is often but an accident of having the right talents and/or products in the right place at the right time*: a lucky business "blip" which if transplanted just a few years forward or back in time... would be rejected outright!

[23] Society ignoring, not needing, or not even recognizing the otherwise "superstar" which slightly offset in time or space or presentation could have been a Noble Prize-winning acclaimed scientist, a Pulitzer Prize-winning rich novelist, a famous inventor, an renowned artist, or respected politician;

[24] Dynamically-swirling technological levels, economies, and cultural sensitivities herding group mentalities: defining standards and novelty, capriciously;

[25] *As men and women find self-worth and affirmation in the eyes of others: temporary humans existing merely to satisfy the transient likes and preferences briefly imbedded in the psyches of other ephemeral humans, confused and random;*

[26] Applauded by the masses, enduring for a moment... but which a few years on wouldn't even make it through the "slush pile" of publishers, not even find a penny from investors, music-movie producers laughing and jeering;

[27] Peers scoffing and dismissing out-of-hand trashed proposals: which in another time, place, or society would have become icons of success... now not even recognized as having any worth at all---missing by just a few years, future or past, illusive permissive conditions.

[28] Even un-acclaimed, general successes are also an accident of time and space: occurring if born to the right family with the right opportunities and favorable conditions; while denied to the exact same genetically-endowed newborn having to compete with, say, twelve siblings...

[29] Presented to the world within a poverty-trapped rural existence, scrabbling just to find one's next meal in a hand-to-mouth struggle; far different than might have been in a one or two-child, secure, "middle-class" well-off family whose parents are professionals with access to healthcare, good schools, societal connections, and avenues for advancement;

30 And yet the very same exact genetics in a permissive condition *also* may be cursed by divorce, disfavor, accidents, disease, or other intervening misfortunes:

31 *Such that even a budding genius can be cut-off at the roots, withered, his/her potential squashed and lost: despite one's best efforts... unable to advance at all!*

32 Of course there is merit in the many examples of stubborn persistence where dogged determination somehow manages to overcome the heartaches and roadblocks of life:

33 Managing to scrabble to the pinnacle of highest distinction in business, art, invention, accumulation, or social institutions... admired and respected!

34 Yet often envied and attacked on the basis of being successful, briefly having clawed to the top of the heap to then be savagely overtaken, overcome, and destroyed by the very forces they'd fought so hard to defeat--- laid into their graves like anyone else... a defeated corpse:

35 *Dead and disappeared into the swirl of history, with others eager to step up, fighting to take their previous place as "the best", standing tall and proud before they, in turn, are likewise quickly cut down and thrown aside...*

36 And so---reluctantly accepting the brutal, brief terms of human existence---we agree to modify our definition of success to fit the framework... deliberately forgetting the final, terrible ending as we choose to focus on the immediate moment;

37 Defining progress by the accumulation of tangible and intangible goods adding-up both material and nonmaterial achievements on our "authoritative" list of Significance: a good job, a solid family, reasonable satisfaction, comfortable shelter, tasty food, security, money in the bank, retirement, meaningful accomplishments in one's field of interest, children surviving into the future to perpetuate our legacy with shared genetics, good health lasting into a long and productive old age still respected by others;

38 Until, finally, the best one can hope for occurs: a comfortable and peaceful ending among good friends and loving relatives, fading-away without too much pain.

39 All well and good... but how many really achieve that definition of success? *God, fortunately, values the EFFORT far more than the results---*

indeed, our best achievements next to His of no weight, vanished into nothing!

40 So small... our entire planet in the vast universe but a tiny invisible speck; where our entire galaxy is just one pinpoint dot on the vast canvas of God's Creation...

41 ---such that things we daily hold to be so critical actually matter nothing in terms of Cosmic Significance: those "achievements" not even having the tiny impact of a feather falling down upon a concrete slab;

42 ---as if we'd never been... even the sacrifice of our entire world as a stellar flare would not be noted across the span of just our own Milky Way;

43 *Where true value and affirmation is only possible in the sight of the Almighty: the intent and determination of our hearts to please Him in the best way possible by exercising His greatest Gift to us carries more weight than all the wealth and achievements of mankind across all of time summed together;*

44 WHERE EXERCISING HIS HIGHER ENGRAINED SENSIBILITIES DELIGHTS THE CREATOR more than sculpting the mountains of earth into mighty physical cathedrals piercing the clouds... rather, far better to form personal spiritual Crystal Cathedrals:

45 Where stretching our minds and spirits attempting to fill empty voids---working to create tangible, real objects & thoughts & systems & structures heavy with utility, sensibility, and beauty... completed or not... glows brighter than the largest supernovas:

46 As a throbbing, resonating Harmony making the true "music of the spheres"---louder than smashed-together galaxies or collapsing black holes:

47 Tickling God's ears to nod in affirmation, labeling us "successful" regardless of our time, place, opportunities, handicaps, strengths, disabilities, societal-approval or disregard thereby, genetic talents many or few, abilities or lack thereof, tangible achievements or long line of bitter failures... WE *TRIED!*

48 *---honoring our Great Creator by exercising His Divine Creativity...* which, in the end, is more than enough: AN ELIXIR MORE DELIGHTFUL THAN ANY TASTY TREAT OR ADDICTIVE DRUG.

Lyle 14:1-27

FOOD & DRUGS

¹ *Lyle observed that humanity stands at the pinnacle of earthly biology, honed by millennia of gradual development, crowned as the planet's top Predator;*

² Since humans are incapable of biologically directly transferring sunlight into chemical energy, men and women to exist must kill and consume other living creatures;

³ Whether plant or animal, the devoured cell products are biochemically burned: internal chemical fires transforming energetic molecules into muscles, neurons, metabolism, growth, and reproduction--- which all require *protein, carbohydrates, and lipids chewed, swallowed, digested, and extracted;*

⁴ Their basic chemical units sucked into the blood while the leavings are deposited on the ground as substrate adding to the cycle of life--- providing nourishment to plants and microbes, that they might again capture and tame yet more power from the circling-sustaining ball of fire;

⁵ Brains frantic to not lose their critical supply of blood glucose, nor be endangered by constant external threats: an engrained lustful longing for quick hot fuel from simple sugary, fruity sweets;

⁶ Likewise craving the potent fuel of power-packed fat... commerce cooperating by perverting modern-day foods, loading them down with processed sugar and artery-clogging excess fat;

⁷ Blood vessels predictably shutting-down from resultant strokes and heart attacks, people killing themselves with the very items necessary to life and vitality...

⁸ *---or mindlessly pursuing instant pleasure in exchange for horrible death: taking that which is good and wholesome in proportioned balance and turning it into slow poisons...* even healthy foods often laced with compulsive or addictive drugs;

⁹ Dependency-causing chemicals from nasty, foul substances spiked with fat, sugar, and other tasty ingredients producing something tolerable to chew, eat, smoke, drink, or inject: all for a pain-escaping, temporary "high";

¹⁰ Delighting in killing physiologically-critical feedback mechanisms; replacing positive biochemical triggers with artificial, harmful ones... *allowing tiny little molecules to rule one's life*:

¹¹ ---REVEALING HOMO-SAPIENS AS A SPECIES SELF-ABSORBED, STUPID, SHORT-SIGHTED, DISRESPECTFUL OF NATURE, OBLIVIOUS TO THE TRUE GOD, AND IMMINENTLY WORTHY OF EXTINCTION.

¹² *If it were only about food, perhaps there would be an argument for leniency*:

¹³ Certainly to lust after sugar and fat is a natural hunger, a wise biological attraction facilitating survival in times of great famine or immediate danger.

¹⁴ *But Lyle observed that food is only the most visible indicator of the very same attitudes and actions in many other pursuits of humanity*:

¹⁵ Where supposedly for the well-being of one's own family and children, a cozy house is stuffed to overflowing with many electrified gadgets... with comforts richly warmed and powered, dandy cars racing along by the millions...

¹⁶ ---while largely ignoring abject poverty in the rest of the world, assuring one's own luxury: as if one were a dictator wallowing in a vast pleasure-palace gorging on the finest food, hosting lavish feasts for the privileged few, while the rest of the people in one's kingdom *starve*...

¹⁷ ---not caring or even noting the effect of one's actions on others, or even on one's own society! *Casually shrugging and stating*: "*If my own people are impoverished because of my own selfish actions... so what?*" What does it matter if a few starving babies barely survive to perpetuate making even more starving babies? Life goes on...

¹⁸ ---where male sexual dominance of females is a sad insurance policy in impoverished societies hoping a few of one's kids will survive to adulthood to take care of the parents in old age: that the majority of the babies die a miserable death seems to them an acceptable price to pay...

¹⁹ *And yet the worship of one's own survival instinct to the exclusion of all else is the common default position of seemingly everyone*---where nations rise up against nations, groups against groups, and sects fervently lash-out with blind zeal---all to perpetuate what... the ambitions of a few powerful individuals?

20 ---raping and broiling the planet, plundering the future of one's children, and savaging the beauty and diversity of nature... all for what? All of that evil done to protect the short-term security of not just a powerful few, but with assent-complicity of many individuals, families, religions, or countries...

21 ---*all happy to create their own compliant "gods" in their own image*: cooperative idols soothingly making things better even if things go totally wrong; fixing up a happy heaven to ease the fear of dying; elevating the masses to, in the "great by-and-by", reign on high; subservient "deities" with the sole purpose of serving us now;

22 ---CONFIRMING THAT MANKIND STANDS CONDEMNED BY ITS OWN LONG, UGLY TRACK-RECORD of gladly destroying itself, nature, and the beauty of God;

23 If humans were merely smart animals ignorantly proliferating to fill maximal territory, they would be innocent of wrong. But, *having been given the great blessing of elevated consciousness capable of projecting both forward and sideways---it is their culpable choice to ignore the wider and long-term effects of one's own abject selfishness*;

24 Not chained to reacting by instinct, like the lower animals, but in all of our conscious decisions capable (if we wished) of respecting others, nature, and God... instead placing Personal Security number one, *deliberately taking our pleasure by inflicting a wider pain*:

25 Setting priorities based on personal comfort; demanding whatever it takes to succeed and get ahead; tolerating laws, rulers, societies, and world-interests imbedded in immediate convenience;

26 *Fixating on food & drugs for eating & enjoyment,* stuck like monkeys on seeing only what it takes to live in the "now"... largely ignoring the day ahead:

27 HARDLY DESERVING ANYTHING---LET ALONE THE HIGHER INTELLECT, BROADER PERSPECTIVE, VISION, AND ELEVATED CONSCIOUSNESS OF SELF-AND-GOD-AWARE MINDS---choosing instead to cast it all aside in favor of drugged sensitivities voluntarily dulled and subverted... *killing Godly Creativity with cruel pleasure...*

Lyle 14:28-49

SEX, LOVE, & MARRIAGE

[28] *Lyle further observed that the delivery or receipt of sperm preoccupies many---especially the young---whose hormone-saturated bodies squirm*:

[29] Eager to fulfill their biological mandate, smitten by obsession seeking ones "true love" or to find one's "soul-mate" they greedily clutch for eternally-blissful happiness...

[30] *---shocked to discover that sperm and eggs make babies, bills, painful huge responsibilities, and bizarre changes to once athletically-cut & handsome, young & sexy bodies*:

[31] Now sagging, fattening, bloating, and wrinkling from the many traumas, demands, and stress of working-breeding-nurturing fresh & helpless humans;

[32] *Mother Nature successful, yet again, in her grand deception, her sweet trap producing the desired results*: perpetuating the species with tired, strained, and exhausted parents now re-evaluating their partners... finding him/her bewilderingly unattractive, frail, and irritatingly fault-ridden... their "true love" or "soul-mate" no longer the handsome Prince Charming nor slender Cinderella Princess that they'd thought they'd married...

[33] ---the cute and cuddly young "honey" or "darling" somehow fundamentally contorted: inexplicably, strangely, bizarrely, and incomprehensively transmuted into just mere grubby human beings scratching, snuffling, and intruding:

[34] Dearly-held comfort zones violated by snapping, snarling, and shouting; convincing themselves that they've just made a terrible mistake, somehow having missed the mark...

[35] ---and that their *real* True Love, who will bring endless Joy, is still out there... waiting... mandating looking beyond the present entanglements, recasting one's vision, and setting one's sights anew:

[36] *Finally and disdainfully casting-aside the old hag or dirt bag, they often set out yet anew... older now and seemingly wiser... looking again for the one who will finally make their life blissfully completed*:

37 Not realizing that the mating urge still drives their emotions, sadly self-deluded that the right intimacy will bring Paradise on earth...

38 ---and in their feverish search to find that total satisfaction often missing the highest relationship of all... *not a live-in, doting Lover*;

39 ---neither eternally-bonded Mate exotically-extruding soulful narcotics... but RATHER A "TRUE FRIEND", THE RAREST OF ALL FINDS, *much different than a "friend" or even a "good friend"*: instead, a relationship that each person is fortunate if they find just a few times in an entire lifetime:

40 *Perhaps a maximum of five or less... two often taken totally for granted, one's very own mother and father*: they who are concerned & devoted for always; hanging in there through whatever troubles, heartaches, disappointments, struggles, and let-downs that inevitably occur; still unfailingly supporting and encouraging, sympathetic to our weaknesses & failings; demanding little or nothing in return;

41 Not dependent on physical appearance or sexiness, but finding a deeper connection, whether genetic or harmonic: resonating on a deeper level than mere alignment of mutual needs;

42 *Other than one's parents, a True Friend is often found in the oddest of places, sometimes as a partner for life*: a person who likes you because you are you... not just for what you can give to them; a person who is not willing to cause you harm even when you deserve punishment;

43 Hurt if you are hurt; happy if you are happy; even willing to endure your rejection hoping you will see the error of your ways... keeping an eye on the horizon after you walk away, hoping that you will repent and return; and should you finally stagger back, they are happy to run to you and greet you with a warm hug---despite your guilt and decadence;

44 Willing to overlook evil, pain, disappointment, abuse, silliness, and stupidity that you've done to them; remaining when all others would just shrug and angrily walk away...

45 *A True Friend: very hard to find amongst us hormone-driven, selfish, short-sighted critters; where the norm is, contrawise, to be spiteful and ungrateful, focused only on our own immediate needs*;

46 Where the normal "friend" arrogantly demands perfection, impatient with weighing out the good versus the bad, unsatisfied with only a slight tilt of the scales to the plus over the minus, ruthlessly seeking to hammer down your negatives rather than build-up your positives;

⁴⁷ Where the process of nurturing improvements is much too slow, long, and difficult; where considering changing themselves to have better positive effect on others is too hard for most people to even attempt, let alone contemplate;

⁴⁸ But not instantaneous, RATHER A PROCESS OF MATURITY NEEDING TO BE LEARNED---exemplified by many parents with rebellious offspring where compassion comes too late: patience, lasting-concern, protecting faith, and deep unshakable affection---sadly, often *not* made-complete by meaningful actions;

⁴⁹ And even when done perfectly by parents, the kids themselves are often too young and immature to appreciate *the immense gift of a True Friend*: *as perfected in the Divine, Holy, and Steadfast God of our universe--- our own heavenly Father.*

Lyle 15:1-24

FAMILY, COMMUNITY, & CHURCH

¹ And yet through all the fighting, squabbling, and breakups cracking like thunder through the fabric of society---heedlessly fracturing relationships and damaging souls---Lyle observed some hope scattered amongst the carnage of smashed and mutilated psyches:

² Where families somehow manage to pull together, broken bonds reform, dripping blood congeals, festering wounds close, and sick spirits somehow manage to heal;

³ *Finding lasting ties beyond death---reflected in churches when they function at their best---where synergy of like-minded believers continually supports and encourages each other:*

⁴ With mutually-enlightening effective teaching drawing people together... then reaching out, touching, soothing, calming, and inspiring even some nonbelievers;

⁵ Communities knitted comfortably together as multicolored, beautiful quilts combining work, play, church, restaurants, music halls, malls, school, and families;

⁶ *Respecting each other enough to learn from each other's differences; instead of just fearing and rejecting different beliefs & backgrounds,* delighting in enhancing life:

⁷ Happy that we are not all exactly the same boring cookie-cutter duplicate identical clones all thinking, feeling, saying, and doing exactly the same; but rather continually enriching our experiences & thoughts by new & fresh perspectives;

⁸ Challenging our assumptions with a wealth of varying possibilities filling-in our blind spots; improving present conclusions that are often initially made in error which *need* to be corrected or expanded!

⁹ DELIGHTING IN FINDING DEEPER APPRECIATION OF TRUTH, BEAUTY, AND SIGNIFICANCE---discovered by eyes deliberately kept wide open;

¹⁰ *But, unfortunately, Lyle also saw the converse: where small-minded people rebelled against nonconformity, determined to make themselves*

big by needlessly cutting others down---insisting on subjugating women, hating minorities, outlawing dissent, and demonizing "sinners";

[11] Legitimized by a supposed exclusive connection to the Almighty God of the Universe: serenely and self-righteously beating up wives, abusing and mutilating children, lambasting designated scapegoats, and taking revenge against supposed enemies; where minorities blame the system, preachers damn sinners, fundamentalists attack modernists, conservatives ridicule progressives, liberals dismiss rejectionists, moderates reject extremists, and zealots beat up conformists; epitomized when ranchers shoot squatters, bosses destroy unions, customers sneer at corporations, and competitors punish profiteers... *all in a perpetual state of angry conflict*:

[12] Squabbling and struggling looking after one's own narrow interests, angry that others should do better, not willing to cut anyone any slack, and insisting that no one be given any help that hasn't been properly and fully earned in advance; continually ripping at the cohesiveness of society, law, family, and religion:

[13] *Their seething & bubbling emotions exploding-outward not understanding stable dynamic systems functioning to benefit everyone*: where total chaos is undesired...

[14] ---but, just as important, where complacency, easy-acceptance, and conformance are *also* capable of collapsing the dynamic tension that keeps everything in a working, reasonable balance:

[15] ---*where inherent contradictions are necessary between Conflict and Comfort for the system to be productive*... irritation and balm the two sides of the same glittering, valuable coin;

[16] Without which, loving relations are perverted... healing religion is turned to hate... and mutually-profitable cooperative business is soured and destroyed;

[17] Friendships twisted and tarnished; solid marriages broken and shattered; great works of art defaced and destroyed; and cooperation collapsed...

[18] ---as classes, social-strata, and fraternities narrow, excluding the "unwanted"; distracted from mutually-beneficial networking, short-sighted people stab-out the eyes of their fellow humans so that everyone can likewise stumble blindly in the dark;

[19] Not realizing that knifing the other person slices-out one's own beating heart... that shooting my enemy fires hot lead through my own body;

[20] That poisoning the wells of neighbors insures the death of one's own children; while labeling others as "fools" puts a pox on one's own soul.

[21] *Still, few go off to live in actual caves; even less to be lonely isolated wolves howling in the wilderness; and the approval and respect of others is rarely distained.*

[22] Pets are very nice as nonjudgmental companions but can't take the place of interested fathers, mothers, brothers, sisters, children, grandchildren, grandfathers, grandmothers, uncles, aunts, coworkers, teachers, students, supporters, lovers, close friends, husbands, wives, like-minded thinkers, ancestors, or descendants:

[23] *Giving a sense of a larger presence, continuity, power, stability, and significance---all denied if we obsess only on one's own existence*: resulting in lives void of meaning divorced from community, family, or congregation;

[24] A taste and explicit hint of greater kinship beyond humanity: WHERE ALL OF LIFE, NATURE, THE COSMOS, AND THE DIVINE---ARE CONNECTED!

Lyle 16:1-17

FORMAL RELIGION

¹ *Lyle observed that formats, structures, and the rules of formal religion built up over centuries are cherished by many of their adherents... whether or not those constraints make any sense in the present society:*

² Systems of belief codified in teachings embraced by billions, while adapted and evolved into many offshoots... offering a kaleidoscope of security, authority, comfort, refuge, hope, and even transcendence;

³ Accepted and practiced in many different but linked forms, seen in their best light seem capable of lifting many people above their day-to-day struggles... offering inspiring visions in place of the decay of the tomb;

⁴ *But also are very easily mutated into stifling prisons run by careless dictators, inflicting crushing boredom, and devolving into suffocating traps---where the spirit is equally likely to be stifled as liberated;*

⁵ Places where confusion runs side-by-side with certitude, snarling and barking at each other: the members of that religious group contesting, fighting, and even dying as they happily attempt to tear each other apart;

⁶ The goal, seemingly, being to climb to the top of a heap of twitching, slaughtered bodies: there in victory to wave a blood-drenched flag celebrating a "God" loving mankind enough to punish, torture, and kill all who disagree or dare to disobey any particular dogma of men:

⁷ Thinking that all those who dare disrespect God by not doing everything that particular religious group dictates deserve nothing less than the worst torture; as "righteous" judgment wrecks brutal punishment upon "wicked" transgressors... exercising the most extreme hatred and coercion in the name of the Almighty.

⁸ *But the same Creator that instilled within each person "free will" deliberately did not make identical robots thinking, feeling, doing, and prioritizing exactly the same;*

⁹ Neither required them to march in lockstep, mirroring each other: nor all men to have the same exact length of beard, nor set times one can pray, nor single place of worship;

10 Instead, it is us humans that insist on absolute moral answers---"the" answer to any particular situation---thus *subverting* the will of the Almighty!

11 Some religious leaders so intent on using God as their personal vehicle to personal glory that they zealously bend everyone else to their own conclusions---seeking compliance rather than empowerment;

12 Even forbidding careful, sincere, personal exploration as a mode of learning; demonizing finding the best answer to solving any specific problem;

13 *Where solid guidelines, Holy Texts, doctrines and traditions are best used as helpful frameworks for people making personal decisions as to what particulars in their life are Reasonable, Useful, Respectful, Beautiful, and Honorable*:

14 Traditional Restrictions which can be helpful---in that we do not have to figure it all out from scratch each time we face a problem or opportunity... but we can benefit from centuries and eons of prior struggles, explorations, advances, and conclusions;

15 *At their very best offering time-honored and tested flexible Principles of earlier times offering clear value*: the potential to see a bit higher, an opportunity to advance a bit closer to Divinity... assuming they don't crush the very things they claim to support!

16 In our brief, short lifespans seeking by whatever means works... to better understand our place, duty, potential, and capability at attaining *a Holy Joyfulness*:

17 ---A DYNAMIC WORLD-OUTLOOK THAT'S FUN, EXCITING, INTERESTING, PRODUCTIVE, AND TOTALLY CAPTIVATING: a "cage" from which no one would ever want release!

- -

Lyle 16:18-44

SPIRITUALITY

[18] *A vague notion of a connection with God is like "rock soup": hard and hot, appearing substantial but offering no nutritive value;*

[19] Where the supposed nourishment and fuel for one's body are mere bubble and froth---lacking real meat, potatoes, vegetables, spices, rice, or noodles---just a flat dry picture of a hearty, filling sandwich;

[20] *Spirit an underlying substrate upon which we all rest*: our matter-energy-time-space existence built upon it, held together by it, networked and enlivened by it---whether we recognize it or not:

[21] *Our choice to ignore it or celebrate it beyond the constraints of our visible cage...* the conscious awareness of our own limitations being a necessary condition for proceeding with active enlightenment;

[22] No more important or different from critically acknowledging the ground beneath our feet, the blue sky above our heads, or the warm sun shining down on our skin;

[23] *Where actions honoring and applying this reality are what matter the most*---expressed through individual commitment or group endeavors;

[24] The opposite of lying motionless and flat on the ground, or insisting on a green sky, or being content with the sun as a mere light obediently circling the earth;

[25] Instead, we use spiritual reality as a bright guiding path upon which we run super-powered caught up in its gleeful flow... *happily linking hands with like-minded fellow seekers running up the Golden Path*:

[26] *Encouraging and helping each other build and decorate vast interlocking Crystal Cathedrals shaped from its substance*---Inspiring! Glittering! Gleaming! Sparkling! And floating right beside us as we run steadily forward;

[27] INDEED, IT IS BOTH OUR LIFE PORTFOLIO AND CRUISE SHIP: ever with us on our journey, a refuge to which we retire whenever needing rest or energy, and a repository of the most valuable parts of our lives:

28 *Carrying inside all our most important treasures, preserving our most meaningful achievements, populated with all manner of Godly Creativity*: novel ideas, towering synergisms, practical applications, careful improvement-experiments, and holy behavior;

29 Protecting and facilitating targeted sacrifice, mutual empowerment, supportive love, and respectful worship... ever new and exciting not as plodding Duty but as gleeful Celebration!

30 Destinations merely vectors orienting each fun step forward on the journey; WHERE RESULTS ARE SECONDARY TO EFFORT... attempting to climb the cliff more meaningful than standing on its top;

31 Where the thrill of winning is but icing on the cake... running the race more rewarding than donning the victory crown;

32 Where challenges and problems are but opportunities for introspection and growth... a sweeping-out of the dirt, dust, and grime of our minds, ever-liberating;

33 With well-greased joints smoothly swinging into thoughtful action painting, hammering, lifting, moving, smoothing, and building... resulting in spanking-new terraces, halls, rooms, stairs, chandeliers, and towers all gracing the ever-expanding living edifice;

34 Moving and dancing with a vitality of its own, the richly endowed translucent chambers warmly encircling us with vibrant hugs... welcoming both us and fellow travelers triumphantly entering the ever-widening and growing structure;

35 Comfortably stretching to contain a small group, a congregation, nations, species, galaxy-collectives, or universal conglomerates... or just a single soul in quiet meditation, serenely communing in a cosmic mansion teaming with trillions of other self-and-God-aware Creatures;

36 Where we remain individuals as we are captured and subsumed in deafening cacophony of fresh Creation... yet are not lost to the demands of productive cooperation: enhanced and clarified with each atom, molecule, cell, tissue, neuronal net, twitching finger, and vibrating hair magnified a billion times:

37 *Triggering thoughts and revelations---seemingly from nowhere--- arriving full-blown and startling; almost scary in their stunning impact, those "Ah-Hah" moments!*

38 Not just the fruit of aligning, resonating, and overlapping brain pathways... but planted also from beyond the physical-temporal plane, from beneath the spatial-vibrational floor: inspired from the conductive substrate flowing out of the endowing Origin.

39 *Spirituality, then, must be attained not presumed: earned by purposeful Seeking aimed at the heart of our Vision... an ever-upward progression;*

40 Requiring many individual directed steps on a long and challenging journey: building us up as we simultaneously advance, a substantial edifice growing around each of us, composed of the very substance upon which we tread, a living monument to our efforts and existence;

41 Encompassing not just one's own struggle, learning, and accomplishments... but also that of like-minded fellow travelers who choose to synergize together with us:

42 Producing a holy offering pleasing to the Almighty beyond just me---as we link hands together to encourage, energize, and supplement each other's talents, abilities, and skills---filling-in, facilitating, and mutually-empowering everyone;

43 *Desiring to rise above mere evolving molecular aggregations... we reach up, down, and outward to the real substance behind everything!*

44 Embracing, absorbing, and expressing its inherent power and Creativity in all types of formal and informal dynamic structures and frameworks---WE GRADUALLY ADVANCE BEYOND BEING JUST SMART ANIMALS... honoring and delighting our Ultimate Source.

Lyle 17:1-39

CHARITY & COMPASSION

¹ *A different and sometimes conflicting path to the spiritual is physical: realistically starting out making our first priority the comfort and safety of our flesh... to do what it takes to survive!*

² But rather than continuing onward---striving to advance---many choose a leveling that draws-inward: attempting to hide, safe and secure... cowering behind solid, high, and impenetrable barriers or secured boundaries;

³ Set firmly upon known-expected quantities or results, well-codified rules of society, laws, traditions, repeated rituals, and paid protectors warding off unexpected dangers, missteps, or stumbling falls;

⁴ *Such that should those threats ever be encountered, strong defenses are ready to spring into action: the biggest being a cooperative "God" whose job we expect is to make our lives peaceful, happy, long, and comfortable*;

⁵ Taking away our troubles, solving our problems, easing our pain... *at the best reflected in sincere believers doing the same for others, expressing a true Godly Love*:

⁶ A genuine concern that extends a strong helping hand to others---lifting them up out of poverty, misery, sickness, deprivation, and terrible fear;

⁷ Willing even to shoulder their burdens, give assistance, provide aid, and edge them towards an easier, happier, healthier, and safer existence;

⁸ *Seemingly aimed at bringing everyone into a ubiquitous "middle class" so that everyone can be warmly dressed, well fed, have good jobs, and look forward to a peaceful retirement*;

⁹ But the stimulation of souls and the building-up spirits are often mere after-thoughts: small luxuries layered around the main objectives of obtaining work, providing for a family, having hobbies, and enjoying our time of relaxation;

¹⁰ While token times are studiously sacrificed on the Sabbath or Sunday, enduring solemnly-articulated prayers, lengthy monologue stand-up lectures, classes going yet again through the same set of well-known holy

texts, saying or singing chants or songs already long since burned into one's memory past the point of enlightenment or "Ah-hah!" inspiration;

[11] *Such that sometimes it seems that mere boring, plodding duty is more important that enlightenment: fresh, delicious, intriguing treats for the mind forgotten... in order to run in circles going nowhere;*

[12] *Counting as distractions or heresy anything that pricks or disturbs the mental substrates of emotion, instinct, intuition, and speculative thought;*

[13] Worshiping instead of a vibrant Creator our own poorly-formed idols: images of dead golden calves that conveniently and automatically assent to, certify, and authorize anything we wish to do or be:

[14] Putting our faith in the pavement under the tires of our cars, concrete sidewalks under our feet, chairs under our butts, beds under our backs, pillows under our heads... the Lord there just to soothe our minds, lessen our physical ills, calm our fears, help with our problems, and meekly offer us a heaven complete with streets of gold where our new indestructible bodies will prance;

[15] A God who looks just like us only bigger, whose ruling angels flutter on fluffy wings, fixing up a nicer-kinder-better and more-durable earth patiently awaiting our arrival;

[16] A paradise rising above the screams of cast-off sinners burning forever, tortured by evil surrogates---who gleefully wring tons of sweat, howls of pain, excruciatingly-bulged eyes, writhing limbs... perpetuating other horrors too terrible to name...

[17] ---containing, condemning, punishing, and revenging-upon those wretched ones who did bad things to us in our life upon the earth;

[18] *Happy to be motivated here by carrots and sticks, many of the faithful make themselves into obedient-but-stupid donkeys resigned to carry heavy loads for supposed future vastly-larger pleasures;*

[19] Plodding forward in lockstep bent on mutual herd-protection---no matter how boring---content that ultimate survival and comfort await us at the end of the day:

[20] An eternal bliss forevermore, safe at last, no more tears, claiming our just due when we invoke the "great insurance policy" should the worst actually happen:

21 If discovering to our surprise that God is real, life after death exists, and karma must be appeased... then relieved that the small periodic payments "to God" we made in life will reap a grand "windfall" reward after all!

22 *True, a few enlightened humans offer charity seasoned with spirit, religion deeper than ritual, and humility enlivened by joyfulness*:

23 All while, yes, realizing the necessity of sustaining all aspects of our personal life---not burdening others with our own responsibilities, maintaining a healthy balance both physically and mentally;

24 *But also recognizing deprivation, starvation, and sickness as deep challenges offensive to our mutual connectivity*: seeing ourselves in the eyes of other sufferers;

25 Looking beyond mere selfish comfort and security to a grander motivation, a nobler endeavor, and a higher purpose:

26 Still constrained and contained by the physical parameters surrounding mental computation, bodily movement, and mechanical manipulation;

27 Our energy-driven biochemical "robots" a medium of expression for representing and mediating our allotted portions of spirit;

28 *With actual events, interactions, and consequences comprising our Crystal Cathedrals---where vague meditations or withdrawals from real world events are seen as trivializing rather than empowering*;

29 And, yes, dreams of feeding starving souls put to the lie when their bodies shrivel---smashed, wounded, and brutalized... screams emanating from ripped-apart, hurting flesh;

30 Simultaneously shattering so-called high principles, grand schemes, or lofty ideals---towering castles tottering, falling off the Golden Path, and left behind in flaming ruins...

31 ---as we spin out of control, bouncing and crashing into obsidian walls, descending into a dark pit of lightless silence, freezing in an icy void...

32 A fate from which we may never escape should we ignore critical needs... choosing to suppress sad cries ringing-out all around us; shutting-off the torments of our society, nature, and old age;

33 *But at the same time, neither trapped nor caged by the never-ending riptide of human suffering*: a Constant always present throughout human history... choosing, again, to look yet further:

34 Seeing that which exists even in the deepest recess of the most evil heart... that *spark* never quite extinguished as long as we draw breath into our lungs;

35 NURTURED IN OURSELVES AND OTHERS, A FERVENT DESIRE TO GO HIGHER, if only by hand-carved spires placed at the tip of already-looming towers, reaching up *beyond*...

36 ---going on past that which has gone before: a personal mark drawn on a cave wall in coal-mud-blood... forming a saber-toothed tiger caught leaping up on the woolly back of a huge mammoth... howling down past centuries, millennia... immortalizing an unknown ancient artist;

37 ---reaching on past temporary ego or fleeting vanity... inspiring many with a sense of awe, bringing an unexpected order amongst disorder, tweaking our collective curiosity/imagination;

38 ---REACHING ON PAST THE LIMITATIONS OF OUR OWN GENETIC CODE, enlarging our candle lighting-up a dark house, igniting and exploding our spiritual base into fresh colors & forms;

39 ---*delighting and pleasing our heavenly Creator facilitating others beyond just attaining a comfortable life: seeking eternal transcendence in the infinite joy of Godly Creativity*!

Lyle 17:40-74

THE HUMAN CONDITION

⁴⁰ *And so Lyle was introduced to the study of human interactions: Sociology on a grand scale, the self-organization of millions and billions of humans*;

⁴¹ Fast interactions---collisions, wars---versus slower cooperation codified by trade pacts and alliances; all simultaneously merging & diverging, attracting & repulsing, dominating & resisting;

⁴² *Economics* documenting the ceaseless flow of goods, services, and money... trying to understand and make sense of what and why we do what we do;

⁴³ Helpful *Philosophy* unfettered by rigid limits: encouraging introspection, thinking "out-of-the-box" speculations, wondering "What if?" imaginations and fanciful dreams;

⁴⁴ *Expressed in all forms of creativity*: bombs falling as classical concerts rise, land mines blowing off legs as lives lost are eulogized in countless ballads, folk songs, jazz, blues, pop, and rock & roll themes; gently picking up the traumatized remains to display as high Art...

⁴⁵ ---*zombies* staggering from killing fields returning to a gentler time... where former enemies embrace, knowing they did their utmost duty, in service to some larger cause, by accident winding up on opposite sides caught up in the sticky spider web of national pride;

⁴⁶ ---*protestors* risking everything... conscientiously-rejecting imposed rules departed, withdrawn, intent on having their own single-minded way;

⁴⁷ ---uneasy *compromises* blanketing the land with stifling laws totally-acceptable to no one... vigilant police, regulatory agencies, and armies enforcing the will of country-state-county-religion-family bending individuals to reluctantly obey;

⁴⁸ Slight shifts of public tolerance & standards complacently mirrored in hair-clothe-mannerisms-styles tied to what's current or not in shifting peer-group fickle pressures;

⁴⁹ Enthusiastic idealists determined to make a difference subdued, stopped by dictates of physics---where the protruding nail gets ham-

mered down---actions provoking reactions... for every good improvement a worsening or loss of something else; negatives in every desirable condition irrevocably imbedded with positives;

50 Dirty selfish pride paid for by horrible atrocities, mutilations, petty violence, and short-sightedness: repelling apart even dedicated lovers, driven away by the very same forces that drew them initially magnetically together;

51 *Such that they stumble through an acid-yellow chocking fog... groping blindly, searching not for solutions but a handy exit sign... hoping not for rescue but just messy escape*;

52 Glad to manage to stumble to the end, embracing a welcomed relief from worries and strain... willing to stop and smell the roses, but shocked at being impaled on wickedly-sharp thorns;

53 SCREAMING WITHOUT RESERVATION: *"WHERE IS THE FUN?"*---the excitement, the wonder, the thrill promised to each newborn baby---when the entire world started all over yet again, time set back to zero, with fresh-shining vistas stretching out endlessly across the horizon...

54 ---but soon to be broken down, limited, made ordinary by constraining society draining the joy out of learning; celebrating success through yet-more-difficult demands; requiring that all pleasures be paid for by equal pain; accepting smooth transactions paid for by cemented traditional boundaries;

55 *Where reasonable contentedness is measured in access, possession, and control of natural resources: oil-gas-water-crops the new ancient coin of civilization*;

56 "Duty" degraded and normalized into a 4-letter word; sad conformance masked by false-fronts of supposed individuality... against which they feebly rebel:

57 Thinking slight differences equal affirming significant achievement; strange hair-dress-mannerisms specified and blessed by peer groups ready to lop off heads of those who differ from their differing by a mere degree;

58 *Paradoxically seeking safety by blending-in, dancing to whatever tune is played, superficially complying with barked orders*:

59 Snarled commands demanding that everyone acknowledge the dictator's name, a bully's plea to be seen, heard, felt, and made-real;

⁶⁰ Temporal ghosts flashing briefly into sharp focus as they zip past, swept away by shimmering sheets of space/time rolling ever onward...

⁶¹ *Leaving behind each little wide-eyed baby, teenager, adult then corpse... caught-up in dry desert winds... shredded, crumbled, and turned into dust;*

⁶² In their last few seconds of pain-wracked consciousness wondering why his/her life suddenly seems so empty, meaningless, futile, and brief... plaintively pleading: *"Dear God... if there is a God... take my soul... if I have a soul..."*

⁶³ Seeing backwards a grand evolution, turmoil, and trauma---a blood-bath rushing forward, with arrogant progeny rising up quickly in turn:

⁶⁴ Immediately falling backwards under the weight of their own advancing age, the Grim Reaper towering over the sweep of history savagely cutting-down each generation as fast as it joyfully arises... slicing heedlessly into animated bone and guts;

⁶⁵ Its silver blade rippling through the retreating waves of leaping children, harvesting them like fields of rusty wheat... their bloodied husks thrown to the ground without pause or pity;

⁶⁶ As---seemingly oblivious to their impending fate---the little humans fight and argue to the last moment as to which of them is the greatest, the most worthy-noble-true-dominant... *fighting to rise above others by happily cutting all the rest around them down... such a sad irony;*

⁶⁷ Rarely seeking power by giving the same mutually-energizing force; psychic vampires thriving by sucking and draining the vitality of others: eating tasty self-respect, pride-of-achievement, and unique discovery;

⁶⁸ Erecting second-hand barriers vainly attempting to block the Reaper's deadly advance: cowering behind settled institutions, solid & reliable conventions, international treaties, negotiated contracts, dependable jobs, accessible health care, reliable police, decent retirement, and comfortable established religion protecting sanctified moments;

⁶⁹ *Blindly obeying genetic imperatives---dutifully elevating personal-family-species survival as unquestioned top priority now and for all eternity---we unconsciously allow our existence to be ruled by deeply-embedded FEAR setting our limits, dictating our thoughts, and controlling our actions;*

⁷⁰ Occasionally soothing our conscience when security seems assured by devoting a fraction of our time to unselfishly helping others attain the same standards:

⁷¹ Not just "look at me" but "I look to your positives and give to you encouragement-support, helpful-feedback, and admiration" evidence affirming that we are not just smart monkeys scrabbling hand-to-mouth fighting Darwinian battles of bestial fitness;

⁷² Neither outwardly desiring to be seen as religious fanatics distaining flesh for undefined spirit; but seeking to realistically merge God-sensibility with our present potential; balancing conquest with consequences;

⁷³ *Relishing the challenge of rising above our genetic programming while still honoring and appreciating our engrained awareness & abilities... ceaselessly yearning*:

⁷⁴ GRAND AND GLORIOUS CANVASES EAGERLY AWAITING OUR SPREADING PAINT forming amazing pictures dynamically merging, shifting, and altering our very natures... as empowered and molded by Reason, Utility, Respect, Beauty, and Honor---*delighting God while elevating and growing up our collective spirit!*

Lyle 18:1-23

SCIENCE & MEDICINE

¹ *Early on, Lyle became interested in science... yes, those overwhelming factual revelations expanding complexity behind even the simplest thing*:

² Ever-deeper levels of understanding revealing yet richer and wider vistas pregnant with many vibrant new concepts, relationships, and mechanisms---themselves but additional windows into even deeper, more-amazing realms;

³ Taking us to the very edge of our ability to comprehend: rocks transformed into glittering collections of inter-connected atoms, themselves but collections of subatomic particles & waves;

⁴ Down to fundamental energies and inflexible cosmic laws fixed yet strangely fluid...

⁵ *Forbidden knowledge fueling technological insights: progressive advances challenging orthodoxy, exploding the rigid boundaries of narrow minds and stunted thinking*;

⁶ Defining biology ever-better paradoxically altering society: disconnecting man from nature with insulating barriers while the unseen horizons continue to expand;

⁷ Resulting in cultures of plenty plundering and despoiling the world... invoking new religions of self-worship, complacency, settled-sufficiency, and circular justifications;

⁸ Lowly ants puffed-up with pride at knowing everything there is to know: recognizing the elements of their cage---light, heat, water, sugar, pebbles, plants, fibers, air, space, barriers---sufficient to illuminate, warm, feed, protect, and support living creatures;

⁹ Defined by their constituents, unknown mechanisms claim emergent ants, flowers, dogs, and babies as self-contained, biological constructs:

¹⁰ Solid, defined forms resolve down into tissues, cells, molecules, genes, inter-signaling dynamic systems conscripted to incessant communication;

¹¹ *Life a mere containment barrier replicating deliberately-imperfectly; external forces driving adaptive improvements, progressively competing;*

¹² Upward, downward, backward, and forward accidental or chosen paths diligently studied in refined, defined experiments: where credible data hides leaps of faith beyond what is humanly knowable;

¹³ *Humanity driven to continually explore while cowering within accepted limits: choosing to accept one's own glass "ant cage" as the total reality;*

¹⁴ Or, conversely, viewing incomprehensible images as evidence of a larger place within which our universe with its particular set of defined laws and restrictions is but a part:

¹⁵ Perhaps a relatively-small box outside of which we cannot even perceive; our greater knowledge-capabilities beyond the lower animals tempered with expanding humility...

¹⁶ *Medicine a good example as a subset of science, providing the means to intervene, a God-given intellect exercised to help sick or injured people recover functionality;*

¹⁷ Preventing terrible disintegration, restoring futures, fighting pain & suffering & misery all seen as a tribute to the Almighty;

¹⁸ Realizing that the purpose to illness, accidents, and death is not to force us into believing beyond immediate evidence in a supernatural salvation... rather that *in the uncertainty of the moment lies that "humility" to acknowledge Laws operating seamlessly and flawlessly;*

¹⁹ Where as a Creation is certainly subject to its Creator, *we can trust beyond fragile flesh without requiring undeserved miracles---simply by marveling in the smooth operation of the physical universe we can discover that which we label as "God";*

²⁰ AND IN THAT KNOWN UNCERTAINTY FINDING A DELIBERATE SPACE IN WHICH TO EXPRESS A GODLY CREATIVITY: grandly bringing health where there was disease, joy where there was unhappiness, strength where there was terrible weakness, and beauty where there was ugliness;

²¹ Truly a fine and noble application of Godly-sensibilities easily lost in the superficial conclusion of "Never mind Lord, your help wasn't needed

because we saved ourselves" silly words spoken by the inexorably damned:

[22] Where despite our best efforts we live but a flicker in the ongoing movie---cut-down naked, alone, helpless, smashed, and destroyed by brutal death;

[23] *All of our medicine and science insufficient to soothe our inflamed souls... yet properly applied becomes a great boost to sagging spirits*: PROVIDING THE SPACE TO LIFT OURSELVES ABOVE OUR ANIMAL NATURE.

Lyle 18:24-40

ANIMALS & NATURE

[24] *Over eons of time, countless combinations---replicating molecules blue-printing in slight error their own macrostructures---competing immensely-fiercely*:

[25] Furiously dividing, multiplying, devouring resources, expanding to the limits of their environment protected and defined within containing microscopic, selective bags-barriers... learning ever better how to survive and thrive;

[26] Power derived from the sun driving biochemical reactions, or from inside the earth, and even from active chemicals: *eating each other discovering cooperation, specialization, and distribution of tasks as multicellular life; arising in splendiferous variety, ever-devouring and dominating*;

[27] But continually under attack and defending from past colonizing microbes forcing ever-evolving protective strategies: striving for each individual to be unique and different, less venerable to the deadly swarms...

[28] ---as sex swept the world in a heated fever, staying just one step ahead of the microbial hordes, immunity an arms-race protecting species survival;

[29] Bombarded from the sky and baked by volcanoes, swamped by climate changes and resultant mass extinctions... *ever-selecting more-capable and cleverer top predators, the most vicious and savage emerging*: Man.

[30] The culmination of eons-long processes of permissive conditions, chemical evolution, and blind luck... all supported and directed by predetermined established universal physical Laws dictating a progression of simple to more complex living creatures:

[31] In itself little more than a thin glaze on the surface of huge cosmic spheres... gracing dead deserts and black boulders with sheens of green, red, orange, blue, tan, purple, yellow, white---displayed as living fungus, leaves, fins, wings, scales, tentacles, vines, fur, and skin exalting & thriving & spreading ever onward...

³² All of it contained within a tenuously-thin layer of atmosphere, a precious skin of air, held within a gravitational curtain pushing back the vast vacuum of outer space;

³³ *The human race proliferating wildly, intent on dominating the planet, striving mightily to occupy all ecosystems, threatening everything with its weight of presence, seemingly intent on taming Mother Nature herself, paving over the very ground beneath its feet;*

³⁴ POISED TO HEEDLESSLY CONSUME EVERY OTHER SPECIES... triumphantly sprouting middle-class tract homes, freeways, fast-food chains, and strip malls attempting at last to conquer its slime-mediated chemical origins by a thriving "middle-class" meritocracy;

³⁵ *But in its heedless rush smashing up against implacable limits*: running out of room, food, power, water... all greatly escalating Man's natural anger and greed---exploding tribal conflict, starvation, disease, chaos, greed, fear, and war;

³⁶ Where brutal warlords find ready opportunity to drain the heat, substance, and riches from dying masses turned to fanaticism & selfishness & rage: *the masses looking to find some answer larger than the sum of its milling, snarling, mutually-devouring parts;*

³⁷ As the heartaches of life brew a deadly reality dragging down the higher aspirations of humans back into sluggish savagery;

³⁸ IN THE MIDST OF WHICH ONE UNIFYING FORCE BECKONS WITH BRILLIANTLY-FOCUSED LASER BEAMS---not the faint glows of man-made deities, but a deeper-sighted awareness beyond the gritty struggle for everyday survival---*a longing for lasting Significance that makes sense of squirming scum reaching up for life-giving light*:

³⁹ An inbred yearning not just to survive, nor temporarily thrive, but to find connection & purpose, worthiness & love, even Meaning beyond the stark physical;

⁴⁰ In a warmth that will not stop even when all the stars flicker out---*continuing even as our universe finally goes cold, dissipated, its energy depleted, no longer capable of initiating or supporting biological life forms, its lights burned out*---progressing undaunted into the welcoming Presence of the one true Source BEFORE WHICH WE ALL FINALLY BOW DOWN IN UNQUESTIONED SUBMISSION.

Lyle 18:41-61

COMPETITION & WAR

[41] *And so Lyle observed the obvious lesson that Competition underlies evolving Quality*: whether in the rise of biological intelligence, or commercial excellence, or good societal governance, or rapidly-advancing scientific achievement, or viable family structures, or vibrant religions, or spiritual growth;

[42] More than just benchmarking, A CERTAINTY OF BEING DRAGGED DOWN, LEFT BEHIND, TOSSED ASIDE, AND EVEN IGNORED... *if customers are ill-served*;

[43] As such, a positive force making us think twice about our actions---weigh all possible consequences, challenge assumptions, and review alternatives---before making rash or hasty decisions:

[44] Lest other biological entities thrive while we languish and perish, or others dominate markets while we shrink or go-out-of-business, or another candidate with better track record and clearer promises bump us out of contention;

[45] Or different laboratory makes a key breakthrough first, our own years of parallel effort gone for naught but unnoted replication; or that most-desired potential wife/husband accepts someone else; or places of worship lose members, decline, and then are forced to close their doors; or individuals lose heart, settling for tattered tents that might otherwise have been noble cathedrals;

[46] An apparent contradiction to genius jump-starting success, one-against-the-mob's vaunted individualism often a formula for being casually brushed aside and crushed; while others form alliances & friendships---partnerships solidifying & protecting & enlarging---taking advantage of many opportunities one cannot reach alone;

[47] *Principled, respectful, civilized Competition moving us all forward expanding pies rather than fighting for dwindling, shrinking, ever-more-pitifully-small slices*;

[48] ACTUALLY FINDING HAPPINESS IN THE SUCCESS OF OTHERS that boosts and expands our own fitness!

[49] Reflecting multicellular organization, specialization, and synergy in our society & group: an interactive division of labor & talents & niches where

the goal is not utter destruction of any and all opposition; but rather a forging of mutually-beneficial, friendly, sharing relationships;

50 *A more enlightened approach to evolution, business, politics, science, family, religion, or spirituality... that's eager to benefit from the strengths of others*: where differences in perspective fuel learning; where success of competitors is not a defeat but an inspiration to do and be even better;

51 *Conflict, however, has no such ennobling constraints... built as it is on selfishness, short-sightedness, winning-at-any-cost, pride, and intolerance*:

52 Using all means possible to dominate and rule; not reluctant to take up the sword-gun-knife-bomb-club to insure survival by just killing one's rivals;

53 Glad to demonize the opposition, dehumanize them, and convert them into mere ignorant brutes deserving nothing more than quick deaths... or a preferred revengeful slow torture if possible;

54 Seeing the "other" as dirty, disease-carrying cockroaches... or poisonous vicious snakes fit only to be trampled, stabbed, bludgeoned, and dismembered... utterly without mercy or regret!

55 No longer fellow men, women, or children... just rabid animals who along with all their livestock and pets are mere subhuman savages---contaminated beasts lacking any intelligence---vile vermin worthy only of well-deserved, pitiless extermination:

56 Disgusting creatures that foul and desecrate their own possessions, rot their own lives, and despoil their immediate environment; where the "righteous" actually do them a favor ending their wretched existence; where it is actually commendable to "recover" their ill-used land & food & water---taking their possessions back into "sanctified" hands---winning a great "godly" victory by subjecting them to rape, plunder, murder, and purging fire;

57 *And the true God weeps as his children write their own history... claiming divine mandate to slaughter their own brothers, knife their own mothers, fight their own sons or fathers---unleashing a "supreme" bloodlust*;

58 Happy and eager to spread their conflict into all-out War: breaking any binding connections, losing themselves in their own lusts---each person cast adrift as a single screaming soul;

⁵⁹ *Not seeing in the other's eyes their own self looking back in fear... just an imagined evil threatening deadly danger, begging to be crushed;*

⁶⁰ But, in the end, that very fury against the "other" destroying not just the enemy, but collapsing-inward the "defender" shattering his or her own sensibilities: perverting Quality into a twisted horror where dungeons hold trapped sensibilities stinking of death and decay;

⁶¹ AND THE GOLDEN PATH IS RIPPED-UP AND TOSSED-ASIDE... *as the despoilers are shocked to find their own selves tumbling down a slippery slope into darkness...* forever lost in an icy Abyss: a fitting fate for all those who ignored themselves seen in others.

- -

Lyle 19:1-14

DEVOTIONS & OBSESSIONS

¹ *There is a thin red line between Devotion and Obsession: drawn in blood separating honor from dishonor, respect from distain, obligation from disregard, and service from suicide*;

² *Seemingly motivated by extreme sacrifice, in fact often an unholy betrayal subverting the very principles upon which one claims to stand*:

³ In the name of a holy, creative, loving God mutilating innocents while destroying one's own potential to do worthy deeds;

⁴ Supposedly justified by a necessary reaction to overwhelming evil... in fact the lazy tyrant's unwitting pawn violently forcing compliance;

⁵ Not a ceaseless sequence of good deeds patiently building upward... but rather THE WHINING TANTRUM OF A SPOILED CHILD violently trashing his own room;

⁶ *Embracing the ethos of conflict and war, an attitude repugnant to the Lord*: forcing one's affections upon unwilling suitors; committing psychic rape; demanding superficial conversion at the point of a sword or the muzzle of a gun; children compelled into trauma living out fantasies forced on them by parents miserable at their own failures; destroying congregants of the faithful in blind obedience to heedless pursuit of "truth"; or allowing any idea or concept or goal to take total control of one's life...

⁷ A VOLUNTARY FORM OF ADDICTION, AN INSIDIOUS CONVICTION OR PURPOSE... stealing one's own balance, leveled thought, compassion, curiosity, ability to realistically analyze, or capacity to learn and improve---all sadly lost;

⁸ *Disguised demons leading us prancing merrily along easy, safe, simple, downward-sloping, rose-strewn paths*... studded with hidden traps into which we stumble, break through thin camouflage coverings, and fall into deep, black pits;

⁹ *Where we might have otherwise chosen to climb up the difficult, dangerous, demanding Golden Path leading to higher vistas and true acclaim...we miss the best way*;

[10] Sustaining a strong long-term positive effort hijacked, twisted, and perverted... WE END UP MISGUIDED, CONFUSED, AND HURT;

[11] But, fortunately, not necessarily stuck in our mistakes forever---having the ever-present option to change our minds, refocus our viewpoints, open our closed minds, widen our tunnel-vision eyes, melt our hardened hearts, and find Meaning in Connection instead of withdrawal;

[12] Carefully weighing out the best return to the Almighty on His investment in our lives... with gratitude, thankfulness, and joy---a shining tribute of deeply-enjoyable service;

[13] *Resisting the temptation to stop at easy, safe, and simple answers*: where superficial set conclusions exclude debate; where rigid doctrines stop possible enhancement of religion or faith; where meaningless tradition restricts our ability to worship in truth and in spirit...

[14] ---instead *showing love to our heavenly Father in the best way possible*: not by tunnel-vision obsession but by TRUE, LEVEL-HEADED, SOLID, STRENGTHENING-AND-ENLIGHTENING DEVOTION.

- -

Lyle 19:15-30

INSPIRATION & CREATIVITY

[15] *From nowhere definable come new ideas, concepts, and dreams not content with the way things appear, but yearning...*

[16] *---if indeed it might occur... what could possibly be changed, built-up, improved, or created...* as constructions, institutions, movements, art, music, science, politics, and even religion!

[17] Supposedly merely the inner workings of mental neural-nets adapting, strengthening, forming new connections, and sprouting new pathways;

[18] But perhaps undergirded by something more: *an active Divinity present long before our universe exploded from a dot*, a warm Intention...

[19] A purposeful determination forming a vast and growing panorama pregnant with trillions of trillions of trillions of possibilities:

[20] *Creative nodes---elemental-atomic-energetic-cosmic-biological---producing many sons and daughters of source-enlightenment*;

[21] ENDOWED WITH THE ABILITY TO LOOK UP AT HIGH STARS AND SEE NOT JUST TWINKLING LIGHTS BUT ULTIMATE DESTINATIONS;

[22] Even though the laws of physics may make that an impossible dream, primitive man/woman still looked up, held up his/her hands, and tried to grasp that which he/she could not reach... all the time wondering *"Why?"* ---and even more profoundly: *"Why not?"*

[23] And inscribing that uncommon Vision into the tangible form of theories, tests, data, songs, paintings, poetry, devices, and stories with heavenly-beings abounding and prodding:

[24] As earth-bound humans artificially constructed their own wings... leaping up off the ground to soar in the sky like lofty birds!

[25] Then blasted up out of the atmosphere, journeying into outer space, landing on the moon, sending robots to other planets, venturing further away from the sun;

[26] *Imagining and then doing all manner of things that are Reasonable, Useful, Respectful, Beautiful, and Honorable---demonstrating Godly*

Creativity: reflected not just in the mental sparkle of far-away pinpricks in the night sky, but as a Cosmic Constant;

[27] Easily ignored or devalued, arrogantly ascribed to one's own merit, or horded into oneself as a means of gaining power over others---making "little old me" seem big by suppressing the good yearnings of others: insuring that the talents of other people are neatly tied up, constrained, limited, and controlled; fostering a cold conservatism afraid of what might be, should be, could be; embracing FEAR aggressively rejecting any Change no matter how worthy the goal might be...

[28] ---or, conversely, accepting with a deep gratitude, enthusiasm, and joy that which takes us beyond just being smart monkeys... happy to connect back to the start in full circle, complete;

[29] *Embracing our origin and purpose, recognizing the Golden Path with humility, accepting a supernatural mandate to synergize together*:

[30] CONSTRUCTING OUR OWN INTERRELATED PERSONAL CRYSTAL CATHEDRALS not of human success but of spirit-endorsed, energized, and informed Effort: finding therein a deep contentment, delight, and reward unlike mere survival... in which our true selves *thrive*.

Lyle 20:1-18

BALANCE & HEALTH

¹ *A sick body or spirit is both empowered and limited by Creativity*: rather than contentedly basking in a warm sun, it is the spur of blistering heat or numbing cold;

² Whipped by an intolerable status quo, it must seek better conditions... and in its thrashings to escape pain may create great art: music, songs, writings, innovations, inventions, fresh thinking, and even Quality;

³ *With some of the finest paintings, stories, and songs of all time depicting war, death, illness, hideous suffering, and even torture...* sometimes driving societal improvements, birthing helpful organizations, or even institutionalizing better governments;

⁴ Whereas the opposite can occur when times are pleasant, settling back into a blissful complacency: *comfort and security often stagnating rather than lifting aspirations*; forgetting initial dreams we settle, unaware, for far less, happily drifting downward...

⁵ WHERE GOOD TIMES AND GOOD HEALTH MAY INHIBIT CREATIVE IMPULSES with no need for improving that which is already perceived as dandy, sweet, happy, serene, pretty, plentiful, and perfect;

⁶ BUT TOO MUCH ILLNESS---particularly that which is self-induced---CAN DRAIN, SLOW, AND EVEN KILL THE URGE TO SURVIVE AND THRIVE... where suppressing the pain dulls and slurs both our speech and our thought;

⁷ *And alcohol/drugs can become the bane of excellent artists; seemingly permissive to creativity at first... but (without fail) in the end destructive* to the very neurons-muscles-lungs necessary for manipulating and enhancing our physical environments;

⁸ *Such that self-induced sickness withers our spirits*, twists our perspective, and perverts precisely-moving expert limbs-hands-fingers into twitching caricatures;

⁹ Causing a trembling-jerking-dropping-breaking destruction... a shameful falling-short of one's true potential all for the sake of momentary superficial pleasure... feeding the beast of addiction with deceptively-pleasurable, mind-numbing drugs;

¹⁰ Leaving a nagging itch of dissatisfaction, a touch of depression, a blue mood... not, however, condemned to be eternal curses, *but actually capable of prodding us to not get too comfortable, too satisfied, too happy with the status quo*... rather to be shaken-up, pensive, looking to expunge the negatives while building up the positives;

¹¹ *Such that our hardships, problems, sufferings, set-backs, and failures can become unexpected gifts that open up new opportunities-spaces-introspections* for something different, bigger, better, higher, wider, deeper, and more beautiful than if we'd not gone through that trauma;

¹² Not giving-in to terror or heartache... because we are fighting back: *consciously allowing our creative & curious nature to drag us back from the grim brink*;

¹³ Not sinking forever down the inevitable slide of time, but bouncing back up: *outwardly allowing our souls to seek a healthy balance, neither giddy nor suicidal*;

¹⁴ *Where stability is found in hanging onto the Golden Path*: its momentum always insuring movement forward-upward-higher-brighter-better; walking in its pull whether outwardly we crawl or creep; centered by our spiritual tightrope that's always there to grab onto; always there to draw strength from; and from which we take our true "north star" bearings;

¹⁵ Manic-activity seemingly promising a cauldron of energy: but its flaming explosions resulting in little other than smoke and fire;

¹⁶ *And, yes, that tight-woven rope is there pulling us back into focus by calmly reminding us to as*: "What's next?" ---as we orient our panicked mind, take the next shaky step forward, grab the next handhold, and once again are able to recognize what is practical... anchoring ourselves in the doable, the reasonable, and the possible;

¹⁷ Lost not in dreamy illusions, but with a firm grasp on reality: *taking advantage of our present circumstance---whether deadening pain or surging energy---poised to pounce!*

¹⁸ GLIDING GLEEFULLY IN THE EYE OF THE STORM... floating on the hurricane, or harnessing the tornado's powerful cone: our Crystal Cathedral remains safe and secure in dynamic, healthy balance... PRODUCTIVELY SUSPENDED IN THE SPACE BETWEEN PLEASURE AND PAIN!

Lyle 20:19-39

PAIN, INJUSTICE, & SUFFERING

[19] *One of the biggest arguments against there being a loving God is the undeniable presence of pain, injustice, and terrible suffering:*

[20] Where innocent little babies are hideously deformed, hurt, or killed; societies are stuck under the thumb of evil-oppressive dictators; or populations are decimated by sweeping pandemics, deprivation, and starvation;

[21] Why would this "loving" God allow such awful pain and torture? As one person said to Lyle: *"There's no answer to explain it away!"*

[22] And certainly that is correct: those horrendous things do indeed exist, smearing the Golden Path with a poisonous, putrid, stinking slime;

[23] Festering, eroding, devouring, destroying... mind, body, spirit, and souls withered... *giving solid evidence to those who wish to write-off responsibility to some deity or to fellow creatures*;

[24] If, indeed, the very Creator puts so little worth in our well-being then why should we agonize over the fate of the less fortunate?

[25] If chance happens to favor our own life above other people, it's not some divine blessing---rather just the luck of the draw to have a few more laughs before the tides of time inevitably turn against us;

[26] Even as we are thrown down upon the nails of cancer, accidents, and old age crippling & tearing & ripping us apart---yes, we end up tortured like all the rest---screaming in horror in a hellish chorus;

[27] BUT ALSO, UNDENIABLY, "PAIN" IS OUR DEAR FRIEND: always there alert and ready at any instant to warn us of danger, motivate us to take positive action, and constantly report back to us on our attempts at remediation...

[28] ---without whom we'd soon be dead, the human race never taken root at all, the status quo crumbled, abandoning a fruitless struggle for improvement!

29 *But exquisitely-magnificent Godly Creativity is often initiated by pain, injustice, and brutality*! ---especially where innocents are savagely struck down:

30 Not as the result of an inattentive or absent deity, but from the laws of physics embedded in the fabric of our reality... dictating that complex systems eventually break down, that nothing is immune from destruction:

31 Where entire worlds lose their water or atmosphere (such as our neighbor Mars), suns die, galaxies collide, and even the universe itself is running down to an inevitable end;

32 And us little human "ants" crawling on the surface of our rock fare no different: *all of us humans subject at any time to being damaged, crushed, diseased, attacked on all fronts, battered, broken-apart, fall ill, or crumble from old age*;

33 Where the Queen of the hive is as susceptible as a newly-hatched baby ant; worker or soldier likewise vulnerable---stark reality insisting that no safety is 100%, no defense impregnable;

34 EVEN OUR GOOD FRIEND PAIN CAPABLE OF DYSFUNCTION---pathologically doing more harm than good, producing hideous suffering where agony goes on and on---like a sword hung by a thread above each of our heads;

35 *Yes, it is a price we must pay for the gift of physical life... and is also a challenge to us to not give-in to despair, fatigue, or fear* by retreating, hiding, or attempting suicide:

36 RATHER, WE CAN CHOOSE TO "CHARGE THE BULLET" AND TURN THE NEGATIVES OF OUR LIVES TO OUR ADVANTAGE... in an imperfect world building up our own collective place of ultimate refuge:

37 *Not in retreat, but in rapid advancement attacking problems, crafting diamond-hard transparent walls*---clear, friendly, intriguing---inviting our friends to come on in and participate in our grand campaign!

38 *In an ugly empty marsh of stinking dead mud to grow an oasis of vibrant life*: verdant with flowering plants, sparkling waterfalls, fluttering birds, insects, frogs, lizards, fish... all forms of life abundant and thriving:

39 Supporting, strengthening, and healing each other in flesh and spirit; *concentrating mutually-edifying, synergistic, lasting pleasure crafting masterpieces even from dreary rocks, stinking sludge, and searing lava*

as marvelous spires rising upward; driving back the dread---making the uncertain struggle of life worthwhile.

Lyle 21:1-26

SOCIETY, ART, & BEAUTY

¹ *From family groups arose tribes, states, and countries---often formed by vicious conflict*, where warlords consolidated their power in their quest for influence, control, and wealth:

² Culminating in vast empires built on the subjugation of "others" by rape, pillage, murder, and plunder: wantonly slaughtering the men, impregnating the women, stealing all their treasures, and carrying away crying children into slavery... *as fitting tribute to mankind's innate brutality and savagery*;

³ *But eventually rounding off enough of the rough edges and excesses to become "civilized"*: where good governance replaced despots, rule of law subsumed luck-of-the-draw "justice", respect for individuals softened bribery, fine arts substituted for thievery, and well-controlled sports for wanton butchery;

⁴ *Such that relative safety & security expanded far beyond the family's local cave*: where everyone with a stake in having reasonable order would (at least grudgingly) obey the immediate traffic lights and laws;

⁵ With public education, accessible health care, job training, mobility, and affordable housing fueling thriving economies---*seemingly freeing up the creative potential of millions of people*;

⁶ *However, to the contrary, stable societies often enslave many to the mundane weight of complex responsibilities*: rents, mortgages, jobs, child-care, utility bills, car payments, taxes, and many other obligations...

⁷ *Ensnaring us in the many requirements of moderately-successful life*, making "leisure time" a precious luxury that's very jealously guarded;

⁸ Hardly able to find the space to think, purposeful existence suffers... where "just making it through the day" often becomes an exhausting struggle overwhelming all else, even in the wealthiest societies!

⁹ When the magnificent benefits of settled civilization might promise a vast outpouring of human creativity... actually only a tiny minority is able to rise to serious, sustained effort:

¹⁰ Powerful songs, probing writings, useful inventions, athletic beauty---all scintillating performances or products to be witnessed/purchased rather than produced by the efforts of most individuals;

¹¹ With daily duties & demands leaving little energy to explore or search... pat-answers, set careers, delivery of service & goods, and conformance to accepted norms are sufficient to cement our brief place in the world---but often leave us vaguely dissatisfied;

¹² *Where unfulfilled deep inner yearnings to be more than just a temporary cog in a machine are not met: confirming the nagging suspicion that I as an individual do not matter...* gone tomorrow by accident, few would even notice, leaving hardly a ripple in society's splashing pond;

¹³ The complex fabric of human interactions swirling globally onward... as even the most famous or acclaimed or successful or powerful amongst us fall from their lofty positions with nary a pause in the collective stomp of mankind; except for those behind previously queued up eager to grab that acclaim spot happily advancing one step nearer their goal;

¹⁴ And the hundreds behind the queues racing up, clamoring themselves to get in line... perhaps one or two with personal connection to the deceased bothering even to shed a tear at that person's passing;

¹⁵ *Such that the most renown amongst us, if remembered at all by history, become just a caricatured sketch*---the true self swept away, snuffed-out, and lost to succeeding generations;

¹⁶ This "wondrous" fabrication of human civilization enshrining not the fulfillment of highest aspirations... but rather: 1) fitting-in by not rocking the boat; 2) meekly going along with the flow; and 3) finding contentment in just keeping one's nose above water...

¹⁷ *Until, at long last, a few fortunate may get the tremendous reward of an honorable retirement* finally taking pleasure from pursuits missed in the rush and crush of a demanding career... and, if not possible to have a retirement, then the continued fight to survive for just another day, to breathe a few more breaths!

¹⁸ Yes, we are all awash in a torrent of magnificent Art of the highest sort---every kind and manner... for a small price, to access incredible masterpieces---a true benefit!

¹⁹ *Stable societies offering a refuge and market for great creation*: music, books, movies, paintings, electronic inventions all mass-produced,

widely distributed, and *available to almost anyone... yet in the mass enlightenment also comes a marked inhibition*:

[20] That---although the hearing-feeling-reading-seeing-using of creation by an audience is necessary and noble---still, being the recipient is of far less benefit versus being the originator!

[21] *"But,"* you might ask, *"why should I bother putting in all the time, effort, and work to 'make my own music' when so much of the best is already there complete, cheap, and available to grab?"* What could I or you do that would even compare to those genius works & productions?

[22] Surely there's no need for you or me to even try---just relax, sit back, and sigh... too much effort, too little need---who'd even listen to, read my thing, sing my song, use my gadget, or watch me at all??

[23] In unthinking, casual acceptance of near-perfection, idyllic superstars are worshipped... while me with a mole or chubby-tummy or crooked nose or twisted teeth or less-than-perfect final production... I seem but a freakish afterthought: *where the best rise to the top and the normal slink unnoticed underfoot, what have I to offer in a parade of seeming Giants?*

[24] Where success, after all, is counted in numbers---books sold, audiences viewing, price paid---*"few"* or *"none"* proves only one thing: FAILURE... and who wants that?

[25] *Better, then, to just not try at all...* than to be laughed at, rejected, or publicly humiliated---certified in front of everyone as an ugly, untalented, unprofessional misfit; even if untrue, that's too hard of a public flogging to endure!

[26] SO WHY EVEN ATTEMPT ANYTHING? It's too difficult... much better to not even try---just settle back in my easy chair... what's on T.V.?---*if, indeed, our worth is determined in the eyes and minds of fickle fellow men and women... giving them the power to judge the value of our own lives*!

Lyle 22:1-19

POLITICS & POWER

¹ *Many people crave the ability to move things, either directly or indirectly*---from the earliest of prehistoric times humans throwing rocks or hurtling spears; not just for fun, but to survive... one's skill at manipulation often making the difference between feast or famine, living or dying;

² Killing animals for food, taking prized women, fending off deadly rivals, protecting from feared predators, building safe barriers, forcing others to make one's own life easier, or helping favored individuals to meet their needs that they might in turn help us meet ours:

³ *The more capable you are at manipulating the world, the better chance for happier families, a prospering tribe, or for dominating those around you*---perpetuating a strong belief in the usefulness of pure, raw, useful Power;

⁴ "Civilized" society no different from cavemen... the most successful people on the planet often adept at purposeful manipulation: grabbing hold of the horse's reins, directing the course of the swaying wagon, securing safe "comfort zones"---expressed as riches, acclaim, political punch, or altruistic influence;

⁵ *Seen historically as a choice between polar opposites*: good governance or plunder; improving the public good or raping one's own country; easing hurt or taking pleasure from causing pain; rewarding good workers or exploiting them; giving value in one's services-goods or draining the "suckers" dry; providing Quality versus demanding bribes; facilitating rather than demanding obedience...

⁶ Beyond receiving a fair compensation, it's a hunger to have it all! ---at whatever cost! ---willing even to lose the war in order to win some short-term battle... giving up the most important things for feeling good now!

⁷ An aching temptation that can indeed be controlled by strategic thinking: transparency, accountability, cooperation, checks-and-balances, competition, reporting, and just plain holding-back the evil;

⁸ *But natural impulses for domination, barking unquestioned orders, being recognized as "the Authority" exercising iron control can be moderated*---turning potential tyrants into actual servant-leaders, who truly earn their pay!

⁹ *As it can also occur in the realm of spirituality & religion…. where the best leadership is not a right but a privilege---with the mutualistic goal of helping thinking individuals succeed---where merit comes not through bluff but in achievement:*

¹⁰ Happily accepting limited terms of office that are revocable, open, and justified; working with others to empower them with recognized responsibility; distributing opportunity along with responsibility; insuring productive competition based on the best viable alternatives bubbling to the top from the bottom; encouraging transparent reporting of problems; insisting on real results based on the level-headed pursuit of clear AIMs; mandating that Purpose trumps procedure;

¹¹ *Not swept-away by fanatical obsessions that ignore resultant harm, nor so arrogant as to claim sole linkage to the Almighty, the Divine:*

¹² ---THE ULTIMATE BRAG OF MANY A TIN-PLATED DICTATOR; a demand for worship soothing a huge ego by compulsed torrents of bowing adoration; an excuse for sinking into depravity, drug-addiction, cruelty, and even madness; an arrogance common to many rulers, so-called "messiahs", musicians, parents, bosses, ministers, or anyone else in a position of authority; a lie loved by all hypocrites…

¹³ *---saying all the right things but then acting as if those words weren't spoken at all…* as if the person did not even hear the words coming from his or her own lips!

¹⁴ Not just weakness, short-comings, or failings present in every person… but rising to heights of arrogance acquiring power insisting that others live up to the "letter of the law" while denying one's own dictates with opposite actions; a blithely-embraced inconsistency often not made from callous disregard… but cloaked in subtle deception:

¹⁵ *Seeking to control, direct, and move other people by manipulating their minds*; looking to control prized resources with clever slight-of-hand; thriving on staying at the center of attention while betraying holy callings; embracing superficial outrage, intellectual thievery, and sly sneakiness:

¹⁶ *Staining the reputations not only of themselves but also that of their decent and sincere followers; misdirecting those who honestly seek the Light of the Lord; and worst of all, suppressing those willing to become not just "leaders" but true servant-leader Facilitators!*

[17] *Seeking Power counterintuitively by giving it away*: loosening arbitrary dictates; consciously striving to be life-long learners rather than dictators; flexible in what Means to use in best achieving worthy Purposes; lifting others up rather than pushing them down; being an Encourager rather than a Critic; not reluctant to say "thank you" when good is done; helping others discover and use their own talents; and eager to find new ways for us all together to move closer to the Almighty;

[18] HAPPY TO LEARN BETTER EVEN FROM HARD FAILURE OR CRITICISM: how to be helpers instead of bosses, listeners rather than orators, and builders of enabling & channeling boundaries rather than guards of exclusionary walls;

[19] *Leading others to the Golden Path by example and shared good deeds*: excelling at recognizing and nurturing in oneself and others a Godly Beauty---a rare Quality that can be developed by anyone, if they wish...

Lyle 23:1-22

QUALITY RELATIONSHIPS

¹ *Precious indeed is that rarest and highest relationship of all, a True Friend...* in one's lifetime each individual privileged to have but a few, if any at all:

² ---that person who hearing that you'd been untimely killed would actually shed a tear, not just a few shocked gasps; rather than a shaky self-check with relief at finding oneself still being alive, discovering a deep sadness at an empty gap that will never be filled; experiencing a gash in one's heart that will never be completely healed;

³ *Though time softens the edges of the wound, a True Friend remembers you as a person who was a big part of their world*; your loss to them is shattering... a cracking, marring of reality---forcing acknowledgement of the black void beyond;

⁴ Dividing time into a "before" and an "after"... making me different---the me that was before and someone else after;

⁵ Perhaps now a bit wiser, with illusions of living "happily-ever-after" popped like a bubble---but grimmer and a bit sadder, the glitter in one's smile faded...

⁶ Thinking of consequences, inevitabilities, accidents, and fate... rather than just taking happy action experimenting: *the urge to drive forward heedless of direction now tempered by a mystic maturity*;

⁷ Not giving up, surely... just keenly aware of potential high costs---as taught by your friend's ultimate sacrifice that some things just aren't worth the cost;

⁸ Contemplating... if given one's own death sentence---to be executed on the marrow---what would be missed? What regrets would there be? What not done would be mourned? In other words, *what really was the most important thing in our whole life?*

⁹ Certainly not acquiring a new car, a sleek boat, a big house... but perhaps what should have been said, might have been done with other people, connections broken that could have been mended if one had tried---or perhaps never been lost at all with a little understanding and sympathy;

¹⁰ *And what were the regrets, the pains, the sad losses of one's life?* --- perhaps the less-than-optimal, the drifting apart, the selfishness, the needless fears, the stupid greed, the careless killing of Quality, and the broken friendships... a drifting lonely soul looking back shocked that no tears were shed when torrents were justified;

¹¹ One's life summed up as an impersonal, legal "death certificate" single page... or in scattered consumptions tossed in the trash or taken by others who value little of what you prized---the leavings of your life snatched-up and carried away by others---one's whole life settling and disappearing as if it never were... hardly a ripple left to mark its passing on the surface of the surging ocean of life;

¹² In a generation or two... often no continuing loving connections remaining to either past or future; perhaps a picture in an old photo album that no one recognizes... *so sad if one's forgotten soul is left bereft and tumbling in the icy black void with no way to make it back to the Creator*:

¹³ *The Golden Path never enjoined, never grasped or trod*... just a discarded mentality left shrieking in agony, whose soundless screams are blanketed in a black vacuum... stunned that so many interactions across so many years dealing with so many other scrambling-grasping humans should leave behind so little... now lost in the void... realizing that most of one's existence on the earth was just superficial squirms of briefly-solidified, transient energy;

¹⁴ *If of little note other than consumption, or mutual mind-rapes, or just lesser transactions trading my needs for your needs... then nothing at all is left behind or beyond*:

¹⁵ ---except for mentally-cackling, shrieking laughter: "YOU GOT WHAT YOU PAID FOR, DIDN'T YOU? WHAT MORE DO YOU WANT?" ...moving on, horrified to realize that one's best "relationships" were just mutual-transactions...

¹⁶ ---*unless, perhaps, we were trying to behave in a Godly fashion consciously seeking Reason, Utility, Respect, Beauty, and Honor in all our thoughts, words, and actions*... deliberately, proactively, and carefully experimenting & refining & building love-out-of-gratitude for what others have already done for us; making each of them a part of me into a real "we"...

¹⁷ DARING TO MOVE PAST OUR GENETIC ANIMAL HERITAGE where frantic copulation drives brief spurts of pleasure, maternal instinct, or unanticipated obligations;

[18] Brave enough to look into each other's souls, past the frailties & stupidities & sickness & accidents & death... giving each other everything one can within the constraints of law, societal norms, and a sense of Godliness:

[19] Tolerant---"cutting each other some slack" from the strictest of standards---forging forgiveness in spite of inevitable faults; seeing myself in you, as you see yourself in me... *where all of us reflect together in the Light of the Almighty*:

[20] A powerful illumination revealing the Golden Path rising above us, stretching from beneath our feet to beyond the material world into an endless eternity:

[21] The best way out of the black pit, hands joined together, *constructing linked Crystal Cathedrals set firmly upon the warmly-glowing Golden Path*:

[22] WHERE LIVES SO VICIOUSLY TORN APART BY DEATH ARE NEVER REALLY SEPARATED---just stretched---their elastic Connection helping pull those left behind onward and ever upward... to meet again at the heart of their Creator.

Lyle 24:1-27

SICKNESS, ILLNESS, & INJURY

¹ *Even worse than chronic physical illness is the sapping of the spirit that drains joy from life: forcing us to cower & run & hide in fear, poisoning our relationships, and breaking our connection to God*;

² Not necessarily just chemical imbalances of the brain---a clinical depression where many folks outwardly appear healthy, happy and successful while still groaning inwardly---but a festering of their essence... producing virtual skeletal skin-on-bones zombies spotted with ugly, oozing sores:

³ Diseased, crippled, starving, dying, and *tumbling backward into the Black Pit, away from the healthy exuberance of the Golden Path*...

⁴ ---and even though it's receding away overhead, yet it's always still within reach: a dangling, slender cord that trembling fingers can grasp, slow the headlong plunge, stop the tumbling, and begin the long climb back up...

⁵ *A life-line to reverse our fall, rescuing us from all terrible sickness*--- immediately available until the very last moment of your life;

⁶ Steady, strong, and supporting... an electrified line crackling with life-giving energy, capable of infusing even the driest husk of tortured spirit with fresh vitality;

⁷ THERE TO BE GRASPED BY ANY WHO DESIRE... but not forced on anyone... then with dedicated, focused, enjoyable effort expanding, spreading, and *growing into awesomely-towering Crystal Cathedrals*:

⁸ Formed from the substance of the Golden Path combining with our own tangible efforts... collective structures transporting & renovating our very souls, carrying us in style as gleaming health-spa spiritual cruise ships;

⁹ *Housing not just those recovering from religious rot, but all other humble self-and-God-aware creatures*: any Godly-creative Seeker, Thinker, Leader, Artist, Scientist, Philosophizer, Mother, Father, Politician, Soldier, Brick-Layer, Maid, Bus Driver, King, Child, Baby, Farmer... and all other manner of humans joined in worthy efforts;

¹⁰ Their pooled imaginations merging, swirling-about each other; dancing and striking-up a SPARKLE greater than millions of night-time stars:

¹¹ Causing a TWINKLE in God's eye, overcoming the trials and tribulations of life... brightening the darkest depression whether of mind, body, or spirit;

¹² *Ennobling even the most horrible illness, transforming the worst injuries, gathering-in all that is good or bad, heightening the sensations of this physical existence by augmenting & transforming & radicalizing & metamorphing & transcending;*

¹³ Banal traffic lights turned into glowing, blinking, living giant jewels; a moment's exhausted rest becoming a wondrous cleansing vacation; sitting in a rocking bus commuting to work no longer just a chore, but transformed into a magical carpet-ride:

¹⁴ Accelerating, decelerating, swaying side-to-side in sensational vibration; an exquisite experience embracing the rhythms of a pulsating universe;

¹⁵ *Becoming one with the fabric of reality; a "mindfulness" feeling & appreciating all surrounding beauty where even the most mundane & ordinary & lowly objects-events are enlivened:*

¹⁶ Blades of grass of a field streaming past outside the bus window swaying in the wind resolved into pulsating patterns playing with sun and shadows... a green tide of oxygenating placid life opening a window into the vast complexities of nature, the cosmos, and us;

¹⁷ *An antidote to insidious poisons of the spirit sickening, injuring, and killing us...* those ubiquitous "downers" all around us---whether real or imagined---that hover as malignant clouds poised to surround, choke, and suffocate us;

¹⁸ Taking us often unaware and unprepared in honest mistakes of bad prioritization... limiting our own potential by not empowering those around us;

¹⁹ Missing the point as to why we're doing what we are trying to do; mistaking form for substance; confusing fiction with facts;

²⁰ Refusing to understand that everyone may not think the same as us; wasting our substance acquiring things of little lasting value; making bad bargains giving away our futures for one-time pots of tasty stew;

²¹ Not taking the time or effort to connect the dots; jumping heedlessly instead of carefully plodding; unconcerned if meaningful progress isn't

produced daily; careless about proactively delighting and helping those we care the most about;

22 Taking pleasure even if the means discomfort or pain those around us; forgetting that character is demonstrated mostly by unseen actions;

23 Not valuing intangibles the same or greater than tangibles; allowing trivial irritants to hijack our joy; forgetting Purpose for aimless meanderings;

24 Wandering away from the Golden Path thinking all methods are equally good; not evaluating & refining Quality as seen through the eyes of our customers; content to drift on the tide rather than paddle against the current;

25 Insisting on getting what we're due; intolerant of weakness or faults in others; willing to sacrifice even our own children for our own comfort, pride, and "rights"; following instinct & biological-imperatives without caring where they originate;

26 Thinking that the Almighty God owes us something; substituting anger for gratitude; losing the great gifts of life pigging-out in the moment instead of relishing a slow, healthy savoring; thinking that success lies in not failing rather than in making an honest effort; refusing to see Purpose behind even time-institutionalized religious rituals; putting one's faith in ceremony rather than celebration; seeking comfortable-drifting rather than difficult, dangerous Exploration;

27 Bewildered and astonished that our soul might be eternally lost: *not believing that we can be voluntarily withered, shriveled, twisted, crushed, crippled, spiritually-diseased, smashed, squashed, ripped-apart, shredded, and subsequently cast into the Black Void as worthless*---WHEN WE NEVER DID ANYTHING ALL THAT BAD...! Just frowning when we should have laughed...?

Lyle 25:1-22

FUN, HUMOR, & JOY

¹ *God has a tremendous sense of humor... and expects us to have the same!*

² Moving beyond just the release of stress-fear-pain when facing or contemplating horrible situations... instead lifting our mood by a deep appreciation of the gift of Life;

³ Neither ungrounded exuberance nor giddy partying... rather *a playfulness that savors the positives of everyday things & events: a fluid "mindfulness"*:

⁴ WHERE NEWBORN BABIES MARVEL AT EVERYTHING... their big eyes stretched wide in amazement at a puppy stumbling across a carpet;

⁵ Or the baby's greedy mouth filling with warm milk--- torrents of delicious sensory input---that, with repetition, form-resolve into objects, concepts, and emotions;

⁶ Sadly, too often left behind once we've settled on rigid definitions... quickly forgetting viable alternatives, now faded-into dull backgrounds, solitude, or sameness;

⁷ *And thus we lose our lust for Adventure... maturing into a sour cynicism*: familiarity killing gratitude; fixating on what we don't have rather than our many magnificent everyday treasures; choosing to snidely criticize rather than applaud;

⁸ Sour, dour, angry pouting... attitudes that are displeasing to the Lord; likewise insincere drugged, superficial, or incongruous-cackling deemed by God an ugly noise;

⁹ *The Almighty contrawise desiring from us ready smiles, friendly hugs, hopeful anticipation, and a balanced equilibrium*---positive reactions that are spontaneous and appropriate to the circumstance... biased toward encouraging potential good;

¹⁰ In every bad situation seeing the positive that might be generated; celebrating Life in the best way possible by embracing God-defined beauty;

11 Ever-eager to sing praises to what is reasonable, preserves helpful connections, and brings joy to one's own efforts---producing lasting satisfaction and pride;

12 *Taking one's greatest fun all the time in exercising one's own God-given Creativity...* becoming so engrossed in fascinating activities that we lose track of time;

13 SWEPT-UP INTO THE GOLDEN PATH DEVELOPING AND USING OUR MANY GOD-GIVEN TALENT; sometimes in isolation, but often arm-in-arm with like-minded travelers supplementing and complementing each other's knowledge and abilities.

14 Building our interconnected Crystal Cathedrals into a mighty city where dwells, excels, soars and delights the true Spirit of the Lord;

15 FINDING HUMOR INSTEAD OF HORROR AT THE ONGOING STUPIDIES OF US FRAIL LITTLE HUMANS; a tolerant amusement that's often without reservation bestowed by the Lord upon bumbling babies;

16 Where mature parents love their "little monsters" in spite of the kids' abundant frailties & faults... more prone to give a comforting hug than a chiding slap;

17 Nurturing, uplifting, encouraging, and supporting the good to drive out the bad; demonstrating a serene, contagious happiness that draws others to us rather than hatefully drives us apart;

18 *Choosing to laugh even at ourselves*: joining with others to see humor in our own shortcomings, dissipating cruel derision with hopeful commonality, and pulling ourselves together rather than allowing angry pettiness to drive us apart; shrugging our shoulders to let trivial things past by that otherwise might cause us to ball our fists and fight;

19 *Looking to nurture our ever-present positives rather than condemn the ever-present negatives; concentrating on what we are "for" rather than what we are against;*

20 MAKING EVERYDAY EXISTENCE SOMETHING EXCITING AND DEEPLY ENJOYABLE; eager to find excuse for uplifting humor; happy to see the dawning of a fresh, new day; celebrating learning-better---even if via biting criticism---over safe intellectual boredom;

21 *Helping us to challenge soul-sickening bad thinking*: arguing against ugly self-talk, dismissing irrational and hurtful obsessions, sidestepping sickening-stagnation with practical action by asking *"WHAT'S*

NEXT?"...our happy Mantra focusing our minds and jarring us to move forward;

[22] *Advancing our journey one small step at a time*: fully savoring and enjoying all the delightful aspects of being alive... wherever and whenever prompted to do our best out of a profound gratitude for the magnificent daily Gifts given to us by our smiling Lord; *not obsessing on inevitable terrible endings, but laughing at our futile caskets...* CHOOSING GRATITUDE OVER REGRET!

Lyle 25:23-35

ENDINGS & DEATH

[23] *Nothing in this existence lasts forever---for every start a finish... for every new birth a lingering death---yet we pretend that we are secure and stable... such a sad illusion;*

[24] But if that be our goal, why not pray to be turned into a stone? Perhaps we could be a large bolder, sitting on a hillside, impervious to it all...

[25] ---blasted by wind, attacked by rain, baked by the sun... yet oblivious to everything, since there's no danger at all---yet what utter boredom to never change, never advance, never experience Adventures;

[26] Yet also, to be fair---no fear, no loss, no pain, and no sorrow... most threats vanished... irritatingly-disturbing excitement, thought, imagination, growth, and learning... all happily forgotten!

[27] Yes, a final sad ending is a price we must pay for our quickening... our survival-instinct properly prompting FEAR at the final prospect; but to live in terror of our ultimate demise is surely a waste of our time, no matter how brief or long that life might be;

[28] *How much better it might be to "grab the bull by the horns" and "charge the bullet" accepting the inevitable, yet determined to fully live until we die; stepping up to the plate risking uncertain & scary Adventure; to take a chance that everything might not turn out exactly right; not afraid to dance on the blade's sharp edge taking calculated risks;*

[29] SO THAT WHEN THE GRIM REAPER APPROACHES---looming above us, his sharpened sword held firmly in skeletal bony hands---WE CAN SPIT INTO HIS SKULL'S EMPTY EYE-SOCKETS, knowing that in spite of his little victory we've won overall!

[30] ---our past very real, tangible, and quantifiable... the gain greater than the cost, having done our best under the prevailing circumstance... *content at last to fly away:*

[31] Launched from this mortal plane by the impacting scythe of the Reaper, our existing Crystal Cathedral becomes a protecting spaceship... carrying our soul higher-wider-deeper-further & more-complex than anything we've experienced before!

32 *Knowing that the uncertainty of life made each and every second precious; motivating us to accomplish in our brief earthly existence a lot...* indeed, far more than those seemingly-eternal hard rocks sitting unmoving, thinking and doing nothing;

33 Forging prodigious collaborations accomplished in a mere cosmic microsecond... us & others & nature & God the four engines of our golden super-rocket!

34 *Blasting us up into the cosmos on a dazzling fiery column*: where we are displayed not as a decaying corpse buried underground in a dark, tight box... but as *LIVING FIREWORKS* LIGHTING UP THE SPIRITUAL UNIVERSE WITH BLAZING COLORS:

35 ---*expanding waves rippling through space-time-&-beyond* in silver, yellow, orange, blue, green and white spectra... punctuating our triumphant and glorious delightfully-powerful Passage onward... the ultimate affirmation of self-worth! CELEBRATING NOT JUST A LIFE WELL-LIVED BUT FULLY APPRECIATED...

Lyle 26:1-18

CONNECTIONS & HUMILITY

¹ *It is quite natural for me to think that I am the center of the universe, for after all does not everyone and everything revolve around me?*

² AND DID NOT THE WORLD BEGIN WITH MY BIRTH---AND WILL LIKELY END WITH MY DEATH?

³ Of course there is a theoretical prehistory and a hypothetically-continuing future... but aren't they just logical scaffoldings helping support *my* existence?

⁴ And, as such, surely there is none as important as the "great" Daniel Basil Lyle? Or, tables turned, *you* as you read my words right now? Come on, let's be honest. Look around you! Are you not at the center of everything!?

⁵ *Yes, yet another of the costs we pay for our Miraculous Quickening is a Grand Arrogance shared equally by us with the smallest microscopic amoeba or the largest, thrashing whale*: an integral part of our engrained survival instinct is our unquestioned conviction of our own self-worth;

⁶ Even behind the most pathological self-abuse or loathing is the *boiling anger* that the world does not recognize our "true position" which deserves (since we are foremost of everyone) nothing less than unreserved respect, deference, gifts, and obedience!

⁷ ---shocked to discover that predators love us only for our meat! "Delicious" they say! "Tastes just like chicken!" Viewed by them we are only a means to *their* survival, forcing us to "flee or fight"... hardly the abject worship we instinctively know which should be showered down upon us (that is, upon both you and me)!!!

⁸ Those ignorant, stupid, and blind fools! How dare they give such disrespect, even trying to *eat* us? How can they refuse to recognize or just disregard our obvious superiority! Certainly their own action (or lack thereof) qualifies them to richly deserve their own sad fates of me/you using and consuming *them*!!! *Hah*!

⁹ ...that is, until I realize that they are not just making my world a bit more complete by their presence, but in every sense are quite similar to me---indeed almost replicates of me---and may even be *extensions of me*

crystallized at a little distance from me: endowing on "them" an immense Worthiness equal in weight to me!

¹⁰ Pausing in my rampaging anger at being so badly used by others to actually look hard into their eyes, I see looking back out of their eyes... me! Such that my mind moves away from the dividing paradigm of "I" versus "You" to "We"... to where causing you harm, pain, or dishonor hurts me *equally* bad!!

¹¹ Explained on a deeper level not just by a superficial resemblance, nor membership in the same species, nor a common humanity, nor abstractly being valued by the same loving deity---but by *an actual Connection: my distinct soul an up-pushed nodule of spiritual substance where the very same up-welling also makes you:*

¹² JOINED-AT-THE-HIPS "SIAMESE TWINS" SADLY CHOOSING TO FIGHT EACH OTHER with fists & words unaware that the intense discomfort-unease-pain we receive from the battle comes as much from a bruised connection as from visible blows...

¹³ So how then can we justify attacking, using, or manipulating other people?? When it's actually ourselves that we are abusing... it is just plain wrong!

¹⁴ *Faults, weaknesses, and irritations (in this new paradigm) calling-out for understanding, sympathy, and forgiveness---to help them to get better, not worse*;

¹⁵ And when our twins turn into actual evil demons, sure... cut them off, as painful as that may be! Reject them, escape from them, or use justifiable defense---but in many cases, unfortunately, the "demons" are just us sadly over-reacting:

¹⁶ Not at all what we'd like done to us when we stumble and fall, goof-up, and deliberately do wrong things... *a humbling thought that I am actually not as unique as I'd thought*!

¹⁷ One amongst many, surely... but yet not without some special worth: especially when visibly-distinct hands are joined together in friendship, work, and brotherhood:

¹⁸ Overtly acknowledging and nurturing real spiritual ties we find true religion beyond just sharing a pew, ideology, doctrines, or rituals---*as enlightened self-interest truly advances and empowers ourselves in others*... sympathetic to the failings in others all the more so because it's a

reflection of what's in me... REDIFINING EVIL NOT IN TERMS OF WHAT'S DONE TO ME BUT WHAT I FAIL TO GIVE TO OTHERS!

Lyle 26:19-37

SIN, EVIL, & PUNISHMENT

[19] *So Lyle observed that forgetting and denying our Connection by erecting walls, winning-making-others-lose, and emphasizing differences is the true "root of all evil"*: in which we stay alive by making others die, deliberately taking pleasure inflicting others with pain;

[20] *Where hurting us, others, God, and Nature---whether intended or not ---is the true definition of "sin"*;

[21] THOSE PATHS TO SIN MADE MUCH MORE DIFFICULT TO JUSTIFY OR DO WHEN I RESPECT MY MIND BY GIVING EVERY OTHER SENTIENT SELF-AND-GOD-AWARE BEING THE EXACT SAME COURTESY AND KINDNESS I WANT FOR MYSELF... treating them not only as if they were me, but as true extensions of myself;

[22] Motivated in a practical way by me seeing in them my own displaced self... knowing without doubt that to hurt them, hurts me;

[23] Only sick, confused, and ignorant people deliberately hurt their own flesh... and as such are objects of pity, needing help to better understand their own valid self-interest!

[24] But why bother with such painful and restrictive self-evaluation if, indeed, the suffering of others has no impact on me at all? Under that situation, why should I care if others live in misery, hunger, disease, pain, or depression?

[25] *They who are not me, if disconnected, can easily be dismissed as less than me: as subhuman beasts deserving only to be used for my own selfish pleasure*---mere "cattle" to be slaughtered into tasty hamburgers---or inconsequential irritations to be casually brushed aside... or even extinguished without concern;

[26] After all, those disconnected pests are just taking up room! So let's kick them off of "our" territory, casually kill them without remorse, and wipe them out as worthless distractions from our own far more important needs!

[27] Knowing that no court in the land would convict us for stepping on mere ants---squashing their bellies, breaking their legs, twisting their antennae---which are, after all, simply beneath our notice!

²⁸ This evil attitude stems from our own spirits made-manifest in isolation where connection is not obvious: a selfish justification always lurking deep down within each of us that's ready to spring up whenever the suppression of spiritual networking is lost;

²⁹ Such that noxious fumes readily bubble-up, flare, and mentally-rear ugly & deformed heads; attempting to percolate throughout our minds, usurp our nobler instincts, and poison all our relationships;

³⁰ *Risking a dreadful punishment in which those twisted & festered nodules are flung into the Black Void located between the pearly-white wrappings of universes*:

³¹ And should our souls be dragged along with those discarded pustules... then we may find ourselves alone, cold, slowly tumbling in blackness... a lingering exile that may last many times the lifespans of universes... an awful fate... until the eventual evaporative-purging is finished:

³² Culminating in the total and final loss of individuality, awareness, and soul... our spiritual substance taken out like water evaporated from dried-up stagnation; the spirit cleansed, purified, and returned to its Creator with all the evil contamination removed;

³³ *The lost soul is without excuse, having consciously allowed that self-exclusive inward evil to dominate*; seduced by its promised thrills; thinking we could control it to our benefit; eager to drink deeply from its seductive power; but clearly chock-full of warning even inside the most fanatical and cruel dictator's mind... a gathering red cloud warning each individual:

³⁴ A huge "STOP" sign there at the back of all hateful minds... an unwanted warning festering & spreading & burning; torturing one's pleasure with pounding rams slammed repeatedly into the city's fortified gates; such that the fortress finally crumbles from a constant bombardment of boiling, pent-up *rage*;

³⁵ *Where victims---seemingly safely-dominated and exiled---instead, via their unalterable connection, send back wave upon wave of savage revenge*: as ever-closer draws the Reaper, sharpening his ebony black blade ready to dispatch diseased souls into the yawning Icy Void;

³⁶ *God's abject displeasure shown by His withdrawal, denial, absence, and rejection*: banning the deceased rejects from the Celestial Light---for them, all of the Lord's Glory and Magnificence extinguished and gone...

37 In a twinkling, *towering Warlords changed from absolute Dictators to tiny nothings of no consequence at all*---THE WORST PUNISHMENT OF ALL, TO BE UTTERLY CAST ASIDE, FORGOTTEN, AND *IGNORED*---when it all could have easily been so much better...

- -

Lyle 27:1–34

CREATIVE-THEOLOGY®

¹ *So then is our ultimate AIM in seeking God to avoid eternal damnation---to not be irreconcilably rejected, cast into an eternally black & icy void?*

² If that were true, what a sad and fearful existence it would be here: no dancing lest we trip, no exploring lest we get lost, no attempts at improvement lest we fail... continually-cringing beneath a heavy & dangling sword, held tenuously above each of our heads by a fraying thread, a slender & fragile reminder of our own selfish animal nature;

³ Terrified that we've got just a wee bit too much inner evil left in us; swinging perpetually back and forth above the "discard" bin or the "saved" container; desperately hoping that a taint of spiritual poison won't doom us to be kicked-out into the cold vacuum beyond God's warm heart;

⁴ Seeing God not as an infinitely compassionate, caring Father... rather as a mean-spirited Enforcer obsessed with our every fault, eager to casually crumple up and toss-away His own handiwork:

⁵ Having spent untold eons in crafting every tiny detail, intimately endowing us with spiritual knowledge, instilling a spark of His Divine Creativity into every person...

⁶ ---raising-up and setting into place each self-and-God-aware individual as His cherished son or daughter: allowing them powerful mandates and high hopes;

⁷ *Surely such a loving Initiator and Maintainer would not with a shrug of disdain cast His beloved children into the cosmic sewer like soiled pieces of toilet paper;*

⁸ But, on the other hand, is God's purpose concerning our universe perhaps to produce just a mere handful of self-and-God-aware masterpieces? ---and thus a part of the price of such divine creativity might be to throw away many less-than-perfect rejects? Would the discards then be repulsive to His shining gaze? As such, might even the slightest of imperfections justify our eternal banishment, as an affront to His Greatness?

⁹ *Yet we observe in the larger Creation that the seeds of mighty trees often germinate from within rotting fruits*: where decay & corruption feeds and nourishes struggling sprouts;

¹⁰ Or, seeds likewise robustly sprouting up after fruit has been eaten, processed, and dropped from the intestines of animals... where stinking feces, rich with nutrients, help the fledging plants to take root and flourish;

¹¹ Such that dung-fed saplings spring up to become great branching Giants supporting and sheltering entire ecosystems of insects, birds, and mammals!

¹² Themselves in turn also attacking, eating, consuming, excreting, and breeding... so that the "vileness" which from one perspective is atrocious savagery is yet, from another viewpoint, merely a required phase of a larger lifecycle;

¹³ No hatching of cute & fluffy baby birds done without the death of many insects or other food-animals or living plant cells; no reproducing, thinking, aspiring humans birthed except for the top predator's (human's) successful predation!

¹⁴ *As such, all life forms thrive from a selfish urge to survive at whatever cost*; the advancement of creatures from simple to complex driven by survival-of-the-fittest passing on new characteristics to progeny; not only in genetics but also a path for progress in thought, society, art and spirit---where a required component of advancement is beating out competitors;

¹⁵ And a keen awareness of "saved" versus "damned" does indeed heighten our awareness of what's good and what's bad: an ingrained compulsion helping us avoid premature termination, keeping us doggedly "keeping-on keeping on";

¹⁶ *A biological negative-imperative that transforms the notion of "Quality" where the quantity of achievements over time matter little*;

¹⁷ *Asking the question*: "Should experience be a bland, drab, stifling, suffocating, depressing balance between the effects of 'carrots' and 'sticks'?" And is that balance sufficient to drive the behavior of immature or even mature creatures?

¹⁸ Indeed, odious as it may seem at times, immature children often *do* need appropriate bribes or threats, their developing brains unable to comprehend more abstract, future, and lofty concepts; the helpless little critters necessarily born with short-sighted blinders:

[19] Where compelling self-interest broadens only as the baby matures; finally acquiring the realization (often sadly too late to avoid short-term-optimizing negative consequences with family or friends) that *survival is impacted by indirect and diffuse awareness in addition to responding to immediate threats or benefits*:

[20] Where we learn to appreciate the strains of violins in the overall cacophony; or grace expressed in traffic-flow patterns; or my place in a smoothly-functioning harmonious society; or shades of difference widening our perspectives...

[21] ---enjoying conversations that take us to new places... loving a honking-"V" of Canadian geese flapping high across a deep-blue sky;

[22] ---eager to use one's own abilities & talents attempting to make good things happen... whether easy or hard, short or long, paid or unpaid, recognized or not!

[23] ---*deriving a deep satisfaction, a lasting enjoyment, and great Significance beyond the narrow & constrained question of immediate personal survival or loss*;

[24] *In prolonged Creative activity feeling a profound connection to God*: folded into His cradling arms, immersed into His heart, profoundly altered;

[25] Not just there as a humble, chastened petitioner bowing-down at the Lord's feet... but rather lifted up by infinitely powerful yet gentle hands as an Honored Participant:

[26] Standing rather than bowing; active rather than passive; learning by doing rather than by just listening or observing... not an unquestioning robotic servant meekly obeying each dictate of the Lord out of slavish fear; neither excluded from the conversation afraid to differ in one's opinion... rather offered the Ultimate Divine Respect of proffered freedom in both thinking and acting;

[27] *Enabled and cradled within the constraints of Godly Connectivity*; happily exercising our imaginations by experimenting, testing, refining, adapting, and advancing;

[28] *Doing so deliberately and carefully---constantly measuring our efforts against flexible standards of rationality, usefulness, respectfulness, aesthetics, and self-worth (the metrics of "RURBAH")*---guiding us into the best, most joyful and meaningful religion:

²⁹ *Discovering Life as an ever-challenging, spiritual, continuing Adventure*---struggling to understand and make meaningful progress through tangible efforts... trying to put Art in the place of nothing, extending mutual and courteous help & inspiration to those around us, *together forging our Crystal Cathedrals*;

³⁰ LINKING ARMS HAPPILY GIVING BACK THE BEST TRIBUTE GLORIFYING OUR CREATOR, moving far beyond any thought or worry of being tossed-aside by our delighted Mentor;

³¹ Knowing without doubt that ingrained faults & fears do serve as purposeful kick-starts for seeking God, fueling a divine curiosity & exploration:

³² Firing-up indignation and repulsion at that in our lives which is unreasonable, destructive, disdainful-of-its-effect-upon-others, ugly, or dishonorable... the *opposite* to that which fuels true spiritual growth:

³³ PROVIDING DEEP PERSPECTIVE AND A DOUBLE-EDGED PURPOSE---*from which we persist not in a quest for unobtainable perfection... but for the joy of putting a smile on God's lips*:

³⁴ As He pats us on our little heads, gives us a hug, and draws us deeper into his infinitely-complex warm heart... causing our own hearts to sing!

Lyle 28:1-20

MUSIC, DANCE, & SINGING

¹ *And so we exult not just in achieving excellent results, but in serious attempts... making the effort---whether resulting in stunning success or utter failure---all the same in the eyes of God: the key component of vibrant Creative-Theology®;*

² Not just rote repetition of the same thing over and over---ritual prayers using the same words, singing the same set of well-known songs, preaching the same concepts & passages perpetually, or going through identical motions like an army of pre-programmed robots---NOT interesting or exciting to God when we take pride in being boring!

³ Hardly of divine note---often just a waste of time honoring tradition and ritual for the sake of honoring tradition and ritual---leaving audiences dazed, tired, glad-it's-over, not eager to return, and demotivated... a "religion" often an unproductive chore;

⁴ Reading, singing, or saying again and again the same ritualistic words... until their meaning is instantly forgotten---ignoring intent for the sake of saying "we've done our duty";

⁵ *But Godly inspiration compels us to move beyond the fundamental "milk" guidance to quickly focusing on the "meat" of the teachings: taking considered action attempting to apply lofty Principles to immediate needs!*

⁶ Where spiritual instruction manuals ("Holy Texts") do not become ends unto themselves, but serve as critical initial orientation for doing specific jobs: now and then referred back to, for sure, but not in meaningless ritualistic repetition;

⁷ And the "application" of those Holy Words is not painful "make-work" but exercising our unique talents together with like-interested folks---especially when expertly facilitated by trained leadership---doing exciting things of real importance:

⁸ *Converting formal religion from a dutiful chore into a delightful challenge: where in one's area of intense interest the leadership helps me use my talents together with other like-minded people; growing ever greater through applying my particular set of abilities serving actual customers: where I am caught-up and involved to the point of losing all track of time... surprised and unhappy when it's time to have to stop and leave;*

looking forward to getting back together to continue the grand Adventure!

9 Experiencing not just superficial emotional "highs" which dissipate rapidly away---providing no greater significance than hearing a good concert or going to a fun party---but ENJOYING AN INTENSE EAGERNESS WHICH COMES FROM ATTEMPTING THE MOST-MEANINGFUL CREATIVITY;

10 *Doing so not just as an observer to someone else's performance, but as personal participants*: where a project can't be finished without your focused contribution which synergizes with the efforts of others... producing magnificent efforts attempting to accomplish important things:

11 Possibly great Art of various sorts, of clear usefulness impacting all areas of human endeavor; building, advancing, enhancing and elevating our knowledge-awareness-understanding beyond what it was before; lifting our gaze to see fresh horizons; triggering those amazing "ah-hah!" moments;

12 BUT NEVER ARRIVING AT THE POINT WHERE WE THINK WE KNOW IT ALL OR HAVE DONE IT ALL; ever curious, searching, and reaching for a higher level of attainment;

13 *Always ready & eager to go deeper, wider, higher, more-substantial, and more-complex: where "truth" is a fascinating multi-layered "onion" offering ever-more revelations as we peel back each successive layer*;

14 DISCOVERING THAT A CONTINUED, CAREFUL EXPLORATION RATHER THAN BORED CONFORMITY IS DEEPLY SATISFYING: filled with reasonableness, usefulness, respectfulness, beauty, and honor;

15 Where our efforts---whether successful or not---are honored by being regularly put before the congregation: efforts aimed at creating new songs, fresh words, unexpected insights... learning not just by hearing, seeing, and doing but by "on-the-job-training (O.J.T)" with real, delighted Customers;

16 *The main mode of most-effective instruction & learning done by quality small-groups or true teams well-supported by Facilitative Leadership*: finding effective solutions to pressing problems; taking advantage of each new opportunity for thinking, being, and doing ever-better; accepting challenges as intriguing puzzles demanding all our talents working together;

[17] *Carefully imagining, planning, executing, analyzing, and continually improving*: not afraid to make mistakes, learning from failures how to be better, and eagerly supporting other people as they support me;

[18] Not limited to traditional religious ideas of "service" but engaged in all inspirational and edification efforts: ready to accept, embrace, and expand worthy projects from a few people to millions or billions;

[19] While not daunted if only a handful choose the active dance giving glory to God with new music, fresh words, or different steps...

[20] *Embracing an ever-interesting, delightful, challenging, stretching, and productive festival: the highest, most substantial, and worthiest form of true Celebration!*

Lyle 29:1-95

SONGS & PRAYERS

The Most Courageous and Dangerous Prayer:

[1] DEAR GOD IN HEAVEN: THANK YOU FOR ALL YOUR MANY BLESSINGS---*HELP ME TO APPRECIATE THEM MORE!*

[2] PLEASE FORGIVE ME MY MANY STUPIDITIES, WEAKNESSES, AND FAILURES---*BEYOND JUST MY LOWLY STATE, WHEN I SHOULD HAVE KNOWN BETTER!*

[3] I'M ESPECIALLY SORRY FOR HURTING MYSELF, OTHERS, NATURE, AND YOU---*BRINGING DISHONOR, CONFUSION, AND SHAME!*

[4] HELP ME TO BETTER UNDERSTAND WHAT YOU WANT ME TO UNDERSTAND---*TO REALLY SEE THE THINGS YOU WANT ME TO SEE, TO VALUE WHAT'S GOOD AND REJECT WHAT'S BAD, AND TO NOT PUT FIRST THE COST TO ME PERSONALLY!*

[5] SO THAT IN SOME WAY, IN WHATEVER TIME REMAINS TO ME HERE IN THIS WORLD, I CAN MAKE YOU HAPPY---*RIGHT NOW, TO BE PLEASING TO YOU!*

[6] HELP ME THINK THOUGHTS THAT DELIGHT YOU---*NOT JUST WHAT MY MIND FINDS IMMEDIATELY SATISFYING!*

[7] ENCOURAGE ME TO SPEAK THE WORDS YOU WANT ME TO SAY---*NOT JUST THOSE THAT I FIND COMFORTING!*

[8] GUIDE ME IN THE DIRECTION THAT YOU WANT ME TO GO---*EVEN IF IT'S NOT WHERE I WANT TO GO!*

[9] CONTROL MY HANDS, FEET, MOUTH, ARMS, MIND, TALENTS, ABILITIES, AND RESOURCES---*USING THEM HOWEVER YOU FIND BEST, NO MATTER MY PERSONAL WANTS OR DESIRES; WHETHER IT'S FUN, EXCITING, AND PLEASURABLE... OR DIFFICULT, FRIGHTENING, AND PAINFUL!*

[10] THAT WHEN THIS LIFE IS FINISHED, IF IT BE YOUR WILL, I CAN BE WITH YOU---*IN YOUR DIRECT PRESENCE, BASKING IN YOUR GLORY!*

[11] AMEN.
. . . .

Song of Personal Godly Creativity:

[12] I AM A PIECE OF GOD, GIVEN DIVINE CURIOSITY;

[13] NOT JUST A BAG OF PUMPING BLOOD BUT THINKING, FEELING, AND CREATING;

[14] HOW CAN I MAKE BETTER SENSE SINCE "GOD DON'T LOVE NO DELIBERATE FOOLS"?

[15] HOW CAN I SERVE OTHERS MORE, EXTENDING OUT A HEAVENLY BLISS?

[16] KEEP ME LORD FROM BEING CRUEL; AND HELP ME LORD DO WHICH MAKES YOU PROUD:

[17] PUTTING WHERE THERE WAS NOTHING SOMETHING REASONABLE, USEFUL, RESPECTFUL, BEAUTIFUL, AND HON-ORABLE;

[18] SPEAKING WISDOM RIGHT OUT LOUD WEAVING A WEB OF VERBAL TRUTH;

[19] ALWAYS LOOKING TO LEARN BETTER EXERCISING-STRETCHING THE TALENTS YOU'VE PUT IN ME;

[20] FINDING IN MY ABILITIES: PROOF OF MY LOVING CREATOR.

. . . .

Trapped in Tradition/Ritual:

[21] FREE MY MIND DEAR LORD...

[22] HELP ME FLY UP INTO THE SKY LEAVING BEHIND EARTHLY LIMITS:

[23] OUT PAST THE MOON AND PLANETS LOOKING BACK ON A SHRINKING SUN;

[24] ONE WITH THE BRILLIANT STARS STARTING FROM SCRATCH, IMAGINING WHAT MIGHT, SHOULD, AND COULD BE DONE;

[25] WITHOUT WORRY OF PROBABILITY, ONLY THINKING GOOD-POSSIBILITIES:

[26] FOR MYSELF, FAMILY, FRIENDS SOCIETY, NATURE, AND YOUR-SELF;

[27] WHAT CAN I REALISTICALLY DO TO TAKE JUST ONE SMALL STEP FORWARD?

[28] NOTHING DRASTIC OR FOOLISH, WELL-WITHIN YOUR ENABLING CONSTRAINING FRAMEWORK:

[29] MOVING EVER SO SLOWLY & CAREFULLY, HAVING DEEPLY-ENJOYABLE FUN GENTLY, NON-THREATENINGLY...

[30] ---ACCEPTABLY SHIFTING MY STANCE: IN THAT VERY WORTHY DIRECTION.

. . . .

Valuing Working with Others:

31 IF I COULD DO IT COMPLETELY ON MY OWN, I'D KNOW ALL OF CONSTRUCTION & BUILDING;

32 NOT JUST WOOD, ROCK, GLASS, AND PLASTICS BUT CREATING FROM EVERY DISCIPLINE;

33 IMPOSSIBLE FOR JUST ONE MAN OR WOMAN, THERE'S TOO MUCH TO GRASP BUT A THIN SLICE;

34 "TAKE-HOME" MESSAGES THE BEST I CAN RETAIN, HUMBLING MYSELF GRATEFUL FOR HELP;

35 SEEING GAPS AND LIMITS OF MY OWN MIND WHICH OTHERS CAN FILL-IN AND EXTEND:

36 IT'S A NEVER-ENDING NEED & PROCESS TO REACH OUT IN THE BEST WAY, FINDING FRIENDS;

37 ANY NOTABLE SUCCESS A BLENDING... IF NOT IMMEDIATE, THEN RESTING UPON MANY FOUNDATIONS PREVIOUSLY SET;

38 WITHOUT BUREAUCRACIES OR LEADERSHIP, WITHOUT HARMONY, WITHOUT THE TEAM---INFERIOR SONGS ERUPT GARNERING BUT FEW WINNING GAMES;

39 PROTECTED FROM MY OWN ARROGANCE, THINKING I'M SO CLEVER AND GREAT, SO MUCH SMARTER THAN YOU... IS JUST A LIE!

40 YET ALSO NOT COOKING BY COMMITTEE WHEN I MIGHT GIVE THE STEW MY OWN DISTINCTIVE FLAVOR;

41 UNAFRAID TO RUN AHEAD OF THE PACK FOLLOWING A PATH THAT ONLY I CAN SEE, BUT ALSO NOT CASUALLY LEAVING BEHIND MY FAMILY:

42 ---MUTUALLY SUPPORTIVE WHERE HELPFUL, TOGETHER ACHIEVING MUCH MORE THAN ONLY LITTLE OLD ME...

. . . .

When I'm Lonely and Afraid:

43 IN THE SCARY, DEAD-BLACK OF MIDNIGHT, WHEN MY SOUL IS SHAKEN & TERRIFIED, I REACH DOWN DEEP INSIDE FOR LIGHT:

44 FINDING THERE MY BRIGHT CRYSTAL CATHEDRAL SHINING, GLOWING, SCINTILLATING, DELIGHTING, AND EXERCISING MY IMAGINATION;

45 NOT CALLING-UP FORMLESS, HORRIBLE DEMONS, BUT APPLAUSE FROM THE LORD INVIGORATING MY SPIRIT;

46 CHEERING ME ON TO GREATER HEIGHTS WHERE, PERHAPS---EVEN THOUGH NO OTHER HUMANS MAY AGREE---THE ALMIGHTY SAYS I'VE GOT WHAT IT TAKES!

47 FINDING MY AIM, TAKING MY NEXT STEP, I'M DISTRACTED FROM AWFUL SHADOWS---FINDING EXCELLENT, PRODUCTIVE ESCAPE!

48 NOT TO BASELESS FANTASTICAL DREAMS BUT FEET FIRMLY SET ON REAL POTENTIAL, ANCHORED-INTO A TANGIBLE REALITY:

49 PROTECTED IN MY TRANSPARENT CRYSTAL CATHEDRAL BRAINSTORMING EXTREME POSSIBILITIES... EVALUATING, PRIORITIZING, AND PLANNING;

50 SECURE IN GOD-GIVEN PERSONAL ABILITIES NO MATTER WHETHER OTHERS SAY "YEA" OR "NAY" OF MY EARTHLY STATE, BE IT HIGH OR LOW;

51 KEEPING BUILDING & EXPANDING UPWARD IF ONLY IN MY OWN MIND: SAFE AND FREE!

. . . .

I, Me, We:

⁵² WHEN I LOOK AT YOU I SEE MYSELF LOOKING BACK AT ME:

⁵³ THERE BEHIND THOSE CURIOUS EYES A VERY REAL PIECE OF ME RESIDES;

⁵⁴ SEPARATED BY SPACE AND TIME CONNECTED DIRECTLY IN THE SPIRIT;

⁵⁵ IF I HURT YOU IT BRINGS HARM TO ME... WHILE HELPING YOU MAKES ME HAPPY:

⁵⁶ NOT JUST ENLIGHTENED SELF-INTEREST BUT GENUINE SYMPATHY, EMPATHY, & LOVE;

⁵⁷ INSPIRING AND CONSTRAINING MY ACTIONS TURNING LIFE FROM CONFLICT INTO FUN, MY LONELY STRUGGLING SUPPLEMENTED BY SYNERGIZING:

⁵⁸ DOING FOR YOU IN HUMBLE GRATITUDE FOR WHAT YOU'VE ALREADY DONE FOR ME, IN TURN IN THANKS FOR WHAT I'VE ACCOMPLISHED SUPPORTING, HONORING, AND NURTURING YOU;

⁵⁹ ALL POSSIBLE, REASONABLE, AND PRODUCTIVE---WHEN YOU AND I BECOME "WE."

. . . .

Light from the Lord:

-Verse 1-
[60] BRING IT UP IN ME, DEAR LORD, THAT GOLDEN, GLOWING LIGHT;

[61] GROW IT UP FROM LITTLE SPARKS, FAN IT INTO A MIGHTY FIRE, AND DRIVE AWAY THE NIGHT.

-Chorus-
[62] I AM YOUR CREATION BEAUTIFUL AND BRIGHT;

[63] FILLED WITH YOUR SPIRIT BURSTING TO GET OUT;

[64] NOT JUST EMOTIONS BUT TANGIBLE DELIGHTS;

[65] PUTTING WHERE WAS NOTHING---SOMETHING VERY NICE.

-Verse 2-
[66] WALKING ON THE GOLDEN PATH, LINKING HANDS WITH FRIENDS, IT MAKES ME FEEL VERY GLAD;

[67] DRAWING STRENGTH FROM ALL, PRIVILEGED TO LIVE.

-Chorus-
[68] I AM YOUR CREATION BEAUTIFUL AND BRIGHT;

[69] FILLED WITH YOUR SPIRIT BURSTING TO GET OUT;

[70] NOT JUST EMOTIONS BUT TANGIBLE DELIGHTS;

[71] PUTTING WHERE WAS NOTHING---SOMETHING VERY NICE.

-Verse 3-
[72] SURE THERE'S TOUGH TIMES WHEN I DOUBT AND FEAR;

[73] BUT I'VE YOUR LIGHT TO GUIDE ME, TO SHOW ME THE BIG PICTURE, AND DRIVE AWAY MY TEARS.

-Chorus-
[74] I AM YOUR CREATION BEAUTIFUL AND BRIGHT;

[75] FILLED WITH YOUR SPIRIT BURSTING TO GET OUT;

[76] NOT JUST EMOTIONS BUT TANGIBLE DELIGHTS;

[77] PUTTING WHERE WAS NOTHING---SOMETHING VERY NICE.

-Verse 4-
[78] WARM ME FROM WITHIN, DEAR LORD, THAT PLACE ONLY I CAN FIND;

[79] WHERE I MEET ALL IN YOUR PRESENCE, BASKING IN DIVINE POWER, AT YOUR VERY HEART.

-Chorus-
[80] I AM YOUR CREATION BEAUTIFUL AND BRIGHT;

[81] FILLED WITH YOUR SPIRIT BURSTING TO GET OUT;

[82] NOT JUST EMOTIONS BUT TANGIBLE DELIGHTS;

[83] PUTTING WHERE WAS NOTHING---SOMETHING VERY NICE.

. . . .

When the End is Near:

84 I'VE GIVEN IT A GOOD TRY, NO REASON TO BE SAD OR CRY;

85 EXPERIENCED LOTS OF POWERFUL THINGS, SEEN MY SPIRIT SOAR AND FELT IT BLEED;

86 HELD NEWLY-HATCHED SNAKES IN MY HANDS, AVOIDED CONFLICTS OR TAKEN A STAND;

87 BEEN TO THE TOPS OF MOUNTAINS, SAILED THE SEA... TOSSED BY A HURRICANE OR BALMY BREEZE:

88 DOING BATTLE WITH MOTHER NATURE, MOST TIMES DEFEATED BY HER CRUELTY;

89 YET OCCASIONALLY SHE'S TAKEN PITY, SMILED ON ME, AND LET ME SUCCEED;

90 GRUDGINGLY GIVING UP SOME PRECIOUS SECRET, ALLOWING ME NEW INSIGHT... A REVELATION THAT'S AMAZINGLY EXHILARATING, THE GREATEST FUN OF ALL:

91 WHERE BEFORE THERE WAS NOTHING YOU'VE MADE A WONDERFUL FANTASY REAL;

92 SO EVEN THOUGH PAINS & DISTRESS MAY INCREASE---WHILE VULTURES CIRCLE FOR THEIR GORY FEAST---I'LL HAVE TO PROCLAIM IT'S BEEN QUITE A RIDE:

93 ALL IN ALL, WORTH PUTTING UP WITH THE NEGATIVES... AS WITH MY LAST, TORTURED, GASPING BREATH I CROAK-OUT WORDS THAT DEFEAT DEATH:

94 LOOKING NOW NOT BACKWARD BUT FORWARD, CONQUERING UNCERTAINTY AND TERMINAL FEAR...

95 ---CLUTCHING MY MEMORIES TIGHT INTO MY SOUL I SAY: *"IT'S BEEN INTERESTING TO BE HERE, BUT I'M GLAD TO BE GOING HOME."*

Lyle 30:1-420

DEBATES & DISCUSSION

Beginning of the Trial

¹ In response to Lyle's dangerous request to be used as God saw fit, the Lord chose to take Lyle in the spirit---away from everything else---to the very top of a secluded, towering, wind-blown mountain;

² Completely separated from the urgencies and priorities of everyday matters, high above the hectic struggles of our day-to-day human grind... Lyle found himself set down upon the highest peak of an isolated chain of mountains... in rarified, thin air:

³ Where Lyle's labored breaths made a fog in front of his face; an icy blast causing him to clench his arms about his upper torso... shivering and gasping, there at the top of one of earth's highest points---right on the edge of a sheer cliff:

⁴ Just one misstep or stumble surely causing him to free-fall quickly thousands of feet downward... to vanish into mists far below covering hard boulders and certain death;

⁵ So high up that he actually looked *down* upon some clouds floating through the chain of peaks... a chain of mountains that stretched out in all directions to a far horizon; massive giants pushing bald, hard, stony heads above the weather's turmoil and confusion;

⁶ The peaks standing there as imperial stoic witnesses to the planet's fragility, staring up into the darkness of outer space---as silent testimony to the thinness of earth's precious atmosphere;

⁷ No animals, plants, or people present on that peak except for one lonely, gnarled, leafless tree... its naked branches thrown-out defiantly, scraping the dark sky hovering so close above:

⁸ The twisted branches shuddering in gusts of icy wind; the tree's thick roots clutched-down into cracks in the rock; valiantly struggling to hang on, not be blown off the small rocky peak... somehow to *survive*!

⁹ **Lyle** (*whispering in fear as he shuddered, his arms clenched tight about his chest, stunned at being transported across the world to the mountain top---yet knowing, somehow, that it was the work of God*): "Why have you brought me here, Lord?"

¹⁰ **The Lord** (*deep & resonant voice booming out of an instantly-appeared, golden, suspended, and pulsating light*): "I HAVE CHOSEN TO PUT YOU TO THE TEST."

¹¹ **Lyle** (*bowing his head, closing his eyes, weakly replying*): "Yes, Lord... what must I do?"

¹² **The Lord** (*voice echoing back from the surrounding, sunken rocky canyons far below*): "YOU MUST DEFEND YOUR UNDERSTANDING OF ME. STAND FIRM IN YOUR BELIEFS. BUT DO NOT MISTAKE YOUR OWN CERTITUDE FOR TRUTH."

¹³ **Lyle** (*cautiously raising his head, blinking*): "Yes, Lord---but how will I know the difference?"

¹⁴ **The Lord** (*a hint of amusement in his powerful voice*): "THAT WHICH ENDURES THE FIRE OF RIGOROUS, ANTAGONISTIC EXAMINATION MAY HAVE VALIDITY. ONLY IN THIS MANNER CAN YOU TRULY APPROACH MY THRONE. DO YOUR BEST TO THINK AND SPEAK HONESTLY."

¹⁵ **Lyle** (*scared but resolute*): "As you will, Lord... and what, then, is it... that I should face?"

¹⁶ **The Lord** (*as the shimmering glow expands to surround and briefly warm the shivering Lyle*): "YOU ARE ON TRIAL FOR YOUR LIFE. PASS THE TEST AND YOU WILL BE GIVEN THE REWARD OF ADVANCING TO FACE YET MORE-DIFFICULT CHALLENGES. FAIL AND YOU WILL BE UTTERLY CRUSHED AND DESTROYED, TOSSED OFF THIS HIGH PEAK TO FALL DOWN THE CLIFF, NEVER TO BE SEEN OR HEARD FROM AGAIN. THESE ARE THE STAKES UPON WHICH YOU DEFEND YOUR CONCEPTION OF MY WILL."

¹⁷ **Lyle** (*breathing easier, starting to get somewhat oriented*): "Yes, Lord... but I am not worthy to defend you. I am often confused, uncertain... I make many mistakes. My faith is weak... not even what I would want it to be, let alone enough to inspire others. Why should you choose me to be here when surely many of your other disciples could do better?"

¹⁸ **The Lord** (*voice moving away as the golden light contracts then slowly fades---speaking with a hint of amusement*): "CONSIDER WHY YOU SO READILY QUESTION THE LORD YOUR GOD, LYLE. EMBRACE PURIFICATION BY FIRE. A PANEL OF FIVE WILL JUDGE YOU. THEY ARE A ***CRITIC***, A ***FANATIC***, A ***SEEKER***, A ***BYSTANDER***, AND A ***LAWYER***. THE LAWYER WILL CHAIR YOUR

PANEL. THEIR COLLECTIVE DECISION AS TO YOUR FATE WILL BE FINAL. ABOVE ALL, IN MOUNTING YOUR DEFENSE TO THEIR ACCUSATIONS, DO NOT FAIL TO QUESTION YOUR OWN ASSUMPTIONS."

19 And so the golden light vanished, leaving Lyle standing alone on trembling legs, having heard no direct answer to his last question save a command for self-examination. He was still greatly puzzled and scared...

20 ---as icy wind whistled around him, seemingly cutting him to the bone, Lyle wavered there on the edge of the jagged precipice... looking out across the foreboding expanse, standing precariously on the cold rock;

21 With hardly the space of a small room to move about there on the flat top of the peak. The skeletal tree was at his back. And then he heard another voice---much weaker but shriller than the Lord's voice had been---behind him shouting-out: *"THE TRIAL WILL BEGIN!"*

22 Whirling-about, Lyle saw materializing a long white-marbled table... with five mysterious figures imperiously-sitting in lofty silence behind its flat surface:

23 They were enthroned, as it were, upon high-backed clear crystalline chairs, each person wearing black robes, and each of their faces concealed by jeweled masks:

24 All in a line---from left to right, facing Lyle behind the marble table---they sat motionless, stern, and implacable... the masks hiding the people's features and identities behind **RUBY-RED, DIAMOND-REFLECTIVE, EMERALD-GREEN, SAPPHIRE BLUE,** AND **TOPAZ YELLOW.** The main speaker at the far right of the table (*speaking from behind his yellow mask*) abruptly commanded: "APPROACH THE BENCH!"

25 Black eyepieces set-into their masks obscured even their eyes;

26 Lyle felt a shiver of fear go through his spine at the cold, hostile command from the totally impersonally-concealed Judge; he hesitantly moved forward, to stand facing them.

27 **Lawyer** (*from behind the yellow-jeweled mask, speaking now in a normal but very stern voice*): "How do you plead?"

28 **Lyle** (*softly but defiantly*): "I am innocent of deception."

²⁹ **Lawyer** (*waving black-robed arms upward, yellow-gloved hands out-stretched*): "Under the Authority of Almighty God, we shall see!"

³⁰ Around all of them sprang-up an all-encompassing transparent globe that cut-off the wind. The shrill "whine" faded. The icy blast lessened... then stopped.

³¹ The oxygen levels were restored to an ocean-level normal. Welcomed warmth snuggled them now instead of the previous freezing cold. A curious quiet surrounded them. Lyle forced himself to calm down...

³² ---taking a moment to catch his breath, gather his wits, and steel himself... resolved to face whatever challenge the Lord might require of him.

³³ **Lyle:** (*speaking with quiet determination*): "I am ready."

. . . .

Interrogation by the Critic

34 Outside the transparent shield, high clouds began to obscure the sun; gloom descending to shadow the mountaintop-proceedings in a dull, gray blanket;

35 Then bursts of rocky hail began bouncing off the protective sphere... making a strange "*rat-a-tat-a-tat*" sound, jarring and frightening;

36 All of this happening as the Critic imperiously rose from his seat, his arms held straight down at his sides, his red ruby-mask hiding his face, his black robes hanging rigidly...

37 **Critic** (*now speaking softly, such that Lyle could barely hear him*): "As I understand about your 'new' religion, Lyle... you claim neither direct inspiration from God, nor any miracles to prove that God supports what you are saying... nor established personal authority of any kind at all! Is that correct? ---and if so, then why should we believe anything at all that you are saying concerning this supposed new way to approach religion and spirituality?"

38 **Lyle** (*pausing to gather his thoughts... then speaking clearly and forcibly*): "I claim the ultimate authority! Even tricksters can seem to work miracles. Anyone at all can claim God spoke to him or her in some sort of trance or vision. I, however, ask you *not* to trust anyone, let alone me, to set your path to God! You should choose to believe what I say only if you find it in your own life to actually be *reasonable*, *useful*, *respectful*, *beautiful*, and *honorable*... what I call 'RURBAH'! I put to the forefront, then, the Ultimate Test of *any* religion or system of belief: your own careful evaluation and conscious decision to accept rather than reject. This standard goes far beyond what belief-system you inherited at your birth, societal dominance, or local tradition! I demand or try to force upon you... nothing! I hold over you neither exclusive claim to God's mind, God's divine power, or any supposed personal prestige I might possess! I put it all in *your* own hands, to freely accept or reject based upon your own clear thinking. If you put the entire concept of my ideas---or pieces thereof---to the test and find that it makes sense, has good consequences, does not hurt people, inspires you, and makes you proud of what you do... then accept either that part of what I claim, or the whole thing, as you wish! If not---if it fails your own personal variation on 'RURBAH'---then throw out what remains, or the entire thing if that's the case... into the trash with it!"

39 **Critic** (*leaning forward, slowly laying his red-gloved hands flat upon the white marble of the table*): "So then---cutting through your clever rhetoric---I take it that you agree that this so-called 'Creative-Theology®'

has no basis in tradition nor in established authority... and neither is it authorized by the Almighty??"

⁴⁰ **Lyle** (*moving forward two steps to stand directly across the marble table from the ruby-masked Critic*): "By no means! All throughout the history of self-and-God-aware humans, the best religious-spiritual Holy Writings agree with what I say! Look closely at the teachings from history's religious giants, those who founded the world's great religions. Do they not all agree that we each have a personal responsibility to use our particular talents to glorify and honor our God? Is not faith made evident by action? Vague belief which does not motivate us to improve our lives is worth nothing! Are we not taught that God will 'spit from His mouth' those who are 'lukewarm'? And is not a transcendent, deep joy the desired state of enlightened spiritually-minded beings---rather than abased self-ridicule and suffering? Two things are sanctified and affirmed in the best of our historical religious strivings, which are also at the heart of Creative-Theology®: 1) empowering the best in ourselves and others by attempting to do marvelous things; and 2) deriving from that effort deep satisfaction and joy!"

⁴¹ **Critic** (*his red mask turning away from Lyle to the side---refusing to meet Lyle's intense stare*): "Assuming for the moment that some of what you teach does agree with principles from established Sacred Texts... what do you offer that is new? 'Looking to a spirit world', or walking some 'Golden Path', or seeing God in all aspects of the universe, or having God applaud our good efforts and achievements, or recognizing a spiritual connection between all humans---even perhaps between all living creatures---those concepts were all first articulated thousands of years ago! And even if you do somehow claim a minor different twist on how technically to have the best religion or spirituality... why is there any need for such since many established religions and their offshoots, plus minor religions & spiritual-disciplines, already existing in the world---*why* do we need to have yet *another* slightly different flavor of what already exists?"

⁴² **Lyle** (*crossing his arms resolutely, refusing to back down from the Critic*): "Yes, you make a good point, Critic. It is true that most of the elements of 'Creative-Theology®' aren't novel ideas... but that in itself simply demonstrates that intelligent, honest people looking to God often come to the same valid conclusions! But even though at the heart of most of the established religions and spiritual pursuits is the potential for a great up-swelling of the best type of tribute to God, *God's spark of Creativity that He has put in each of us* is often beat-down and obliterated! The very religious Leaders and structures that you would think should be helping people use their talents to do great things for God instead swamp their 'flocks' with overpowering negatives! The result is humans stupidly

insisting on inserting into their religions and spirituality that which pollutes their attempts at Godliness! So in place of a divine sympathy and compassion, often what results is intolerance and hate! Similarly, in place of exultation and advancement... often what we see is domination and increased restrictions! In place of careful and continual exploration and learning... often we get exactly the opposite: rigid answers, tunnel-vision, and retreat! In place of useful service... what we often see is rote repetition and empty ritual! In place of respectful sharing... we often, sadly, receive again the exact opposite: exclusion, control, or coercion by sword or gun! In place of synergistic fellowship and mutual appreciation... often the contrary occurs: division and hate! Creative-Theology® deliberately cuts out all of those negatives, freeing the human soul to soar with God instead of cowering twisted and sour! Plus, Creative-Theology® sees the *best worship* to God not as repetitious traditional ritual, but in the very act of exercising God-given Creativity! *This* is the main thing to be showcased and applauded in regular group religious gatherings---not just talking about the underlying Principles, but spending our 'church' time mostly working actively to actually *do* what we are 'preaching'!"

43 **Critic** (*shaking his masked head back and forth in distain and rejection*): "Hah! You spout vague generalities that mean nothing! This 'Book of Lyle' you claim to be in the process of writing is long on fancy words but lacks specifics. Anyone can claim that they can 'free the soul' while in reality achieving little or nothing more than does any existing, established, traditional religious group---indeed, so has proclaimed every other charlatan throughout history! Your emphasis on actually doing the teachings may be laudable, but many religious orders have come into being with that very goal as their reason for existing! Again, you have nothing new to offer us!"

44 **Lyle** (*moving back a step and turning thoughtfully to the side*): "Yes, I agree, Critic. To assume I have some new 'revelation' would be in error! I, in fact, do over-emphasize the 'newness'. Thank you for correcting me. But even though the pieces are certainly out there in the religious world, already in existence, Creative-Theology® brings it all together in one powerful package---with a distinct and easily understandable name and AIM. As to my dealing from 'vague generalities', I invite you to consider the fact that the 'details' in religion often have the undesired consequence of producing death... while flexible Principles often give life!"

45 **Critic** (*for the first time sounding unsure of himself*): "What? Your words don't make sense! Now you speak not just in generalities, but in nonsensical riddles!"

46 **Lyle** (*pointing a finger directly at the Critic's glowing-red mask*): "We humans just by our curious nature want 'the' answer to every question!

Is that not so? It is also part of our survival instinct. Uncertainty is dangerous. Certainty is soothing. We find a great comfort in knowing what's before us. So even though established religions and many spiritual disciplines lay out powerful, positive Principles... we believers then often insist on restricting those Principles by trying to pre-define their application in every situation---whether for ourselves or as an excuse to gain power by imposing our beliefs on others! This is an exercise in disrespect, both for the other people and for the Principles themselves. In essence, by becoming some 'guru', I'd be saying that 'I' can understand all situations and dictate for you how you should best run your own life! Certainly it is important to figure out how to implement Principles within a helpful framework. God willing, I do in fact hope to write yet another book after 'The Book of Lyle', one that will suggest how people might implement Creative-Theology® either as a religion unto itself, or within already-established traditions, or as a personal philosophy. Its title will be: 'Creative-Theology® '. However, the point of that book will not be to take control of other people's lives... but rather to take necessary *personal* responsibility for conducting our own affairs in the Godliest manner possible; and to know *how best to motivate and support people* working together to be more than they can be individually. To that end, it is by far best to stay on the level of understanding fundamental, flexible Principles---while allowing each person to determine the most appropriate application of such in their own particular lives and circumstances."

47 **Critic** (*slowly lowering himself back into his seat*): "Laying aside the case you have just made for religious chaos... even if what you are saying were true, Lyle, would not the implementation of this 'different' mode of religion likely cause more friction, conflict, fighting, and harm than overall good?"

48 **Lyle** (*moving thoughtfully back another step himself*): "In some cases, yes. And in those circumstances I'd *not* want people to try to force this new mindset on those who don't wish it, on those who are happy with their present beliefs and practices, or whose faith is inexorably tied to their tradition. But that would not stop those people who want a better way---those whom I label the 'unsatisfied seekers'---to quietly separate and proceed onward; nor for people to practice Creative-Theology® in their own individual lives and minds... even while continuing within their traditional religious structures, while being careful to not cause any problems or frictions. Also, within an established traditional religious group the appointed Leaders would gain great insight into how to *prevent* conflict and fighting in their work groups! 'People-Process' is often *absent* from whatever religious leaders get by way of training, if anything! This 'Godly Quality Management' is a key part of what I'm teaching! And I will explain all this in detail in my book called 'Creative-Theology®'!"

⁴⁹ **Critic** (*folding his arms across his chest and tilting his masked face to the side*): "Your words have a slick veneer of intelligence and compassion, Lyle. But like so many other so-called 'gurus' before you---I suspect you are in it just for the fame, the money, or the power! Is that not true?"

⁵⁰ **Lyle** (*folding his own arms across his chest, standing tall and defiant before the panel of seated judges*): "No, Sir, you are wrong! First of all, I did not claim to be some 'guru'! I said 'if' I were to do so I'd be wrong! I'm not looking to gain power over other people! Also, this is not my only endeavor in life. If it fails, I have many other pursuits to well-occupy whatever time I have remaining in this world. And as to getting rich from this, hah! I only take money for delivering clear value, as when someone purchases one of my books for a nominal fee. Actually, that would be a new experience for me to profit financially from my efforts! To-date I've had to spend far more money out of my own pockets---gleaned from my modest paychecks for my 'regular' work---than the pittance I've received back for my religious works and efforts. Also, since I'm explicitly rejecting any claim to some special status, any 'power' I might obtain will simply be to empower *others*! Whether you choose to believe it or not, my dear Critic, my main motivation---as far as I can understand myself---is truly in pleasing my Lord by exercising His talents as He has seen fit to put them within me! I do think I have a particular talent that's being expressed writing this book! I do feel a certain compulsion outside of myself to continue this project... whether or not it brings me *any* fame, money, or power! Also, I actually *welcome* your criticisms to help me bring my ideas into better focus. You are truly helping me test both my conclusions and assumptions... to recognize and correct my own mistakes... and thus to improve my thinking! *Thank* you, Critic!"

⁵¹ There was a moment of silence when Lyle finished speaking. Suddenly, a renewed pounding of hail upon the overhead shield echoed loudly within the enclosed, transparent structure.

⁵² **Lawyer** (*speaking shrilly from the end of the marble slab*): "ANY MORE QUESTIONS, CRITIC?"

⁵³ **Critic** (*looking away from Lyle, his head tilted dismissively upwards toward the pounding hail*): "I've heard enough."

. . . .

Interrogation by the Fanatic

⁵⁴ **Lawyer**: "Then the next judge may proceed."

⁵⁵ Abruptly, the hail ceased, the existing gloom deepened dramatically, and the weak light in the dome almost vanished---Lyle looking up in alarm at the sky...!

⁵⁶ ---as thick black high clouds covered everything and sheets of rain slammed down, startling Lyle; flashes of lightning abruptly & intermittently lighting the dark peak, alternating white/black!

⁵⁷ Delayed thunder BOOMING throughout... the marble tabletop now glowing with a dim white light from within its own structure... highlighting the five black-robed figures seated behind-and-above it;

⁵⁸ Each mask of the judges glowing in the darkness with its own particular color: pulsating *red*, mirrored-*white*, shimmering-*green*, steady-*blue*, and pervasively-spreading *yellow*;

⁵⁹ As an ominous GROANING and CRACKING broke the silence ... the twisted tree at the back of the seated figures suddenly shuddering, jerking, its rope-like roots doubling then tripling in size, JACKHAMMERING themselves down deeper into the cracks in the surrounding rocks...

⁶⁰ ---SPLITTING the rocks further with powerful blows as the writhing roots fitfully spread outward... then settled back, the ancient plant seemingly satisfied, resting...

⁶¹ ---grotesquely-giant roots now covering the rocks behind the panel.

⁶² **Fanatic** (*snappily jerking to his feet, leaning forward, and drawing out a long sharp dagger from beneath his robes... then throwing it with a clatter down upon the stone tabletop*): "LYLE, YOU ARE A BLASPHEMER AND LIAR! AT BEST, YOU ARE A DELUDED FOOL! AT WORSE YOU ARE AN AGENT OF SATAN! YOU MUST REPENT OF YOUR LIES AND ACCEPT THE TRUTH, OR GOD WILL DESTROY YOU---IF HE WILLS, *BY MY VERY OWN HAND*!!"

⁶³ **Lyle** (*narrowing his eyes, framing his answer carefully*): "Please consider, Fanatic, that 'truth' may not be only what you happen to understand at this moment. Could it, perhaps, be God's will that I help *you* in some way---whether great or small, profound or trivial---to deepen, widen, expand, make more substantial, or strengthen *your* faith. I do not think that Creative-Theology® is at its heart in opposition to your holy

writings, traditions, or doctrines. If you should choose to look carefully at Creative-Theology®, perhaps you may find that it is merely a sermon of mine discussing how to do even better at applying your own most cherished principles? As such, might it provide an additional method of implementing your own most important goals, which I assume to be: 1) moving ever closer to God, 2) while helping others do the same, and 3) fully honoring the Lord by using all your talents and abilities to accomplish good things? Last, but surely not least, please consider that God could certainly strike me down dead at this very moment if He wished... yet for His own reasons He allows me to be alive and conversing with yourself and these others. Do you presume to usurp God's authority by prematurely taking upon yourself final Judgment when He has deliberately given people the freedom to make their own decisions, regardless if they are right or wrong?"

64 **Fanatic** (*pounding his white-gloved fists down onto the table, the dim light flashing impressively from the faceted surfaces of his mirrored mask*): "HOW DARE YOU SPEAK TO ME WITH SUCH INSOLENCE?! IT IS CLEAR TO ALL AT THIS TABLE THAT YOU, LYLE, ARE A DOG IN LEAGUE WITH THE DEVIL! YES, YOU SPEAK WITH SOFT AND BEGUILING WORDS, AS BEFITS AN AGENT OF THE MOST-CLEVER, DELUDING SATAN! BUT BY YOUR VERY REFUSAL TO NAME, LET ALONE EVEN ACKNOWLEDGE, THE TRUE LEADER FROM GOD, OR THE TRUE HOLY WRITINGS, YOU CONDEMN YOURSELF! I HAVE NO NEED FOR A DEVILISH CREATURE SUCH AS YOU TO LECTURE ME ON MY OWN HOLINESS! GOD HAS GIVEN TO ME THE TRUTH AND THE DIVINE AUTHORITY TO PROCLAIM IT! OF THAT THERE IS NO DOUBT! FURTHERMORE, IF HE CHOOSES TO USE ME TO BE HIS MEANS OF EXTERMINATING EVIL LOWLY SCUM SUCH AS YOU---NOT BESMERKING HIS OWN HOLINESS TO DEAL WITH YOU DIRECTLY---THEN THAT IS THE LORD'S JUST AND DIVINE RIGHT THAT YOU DIE AT MY HANDS!!"

65 **Lyle** (*involuntarily cringing backwards as another lightning-strike briefly lit the dark scene in blazing white, reflected brightly off the Fanatic's diamond mask*): "Sir, I am *not* a subhuman! Look at me! I am a thoughtful, reasoning person. I *admit* I do not know all of the truth! I admit I am not perfect in applying that which I do know. Furthermore, I *am* willing to learn from *you*! I have no doubt that after carefully considering our encounter here I will gain fresh insights into righteousness and holiness! I am happy for you to help me understand ever-better... even for you to correct my mistakes! Look at me! Look hard at me! Look past your preconceptions and prejudices! If you do so, you will see before you not just another Seeker similar to you---trying in his own confused way to move closer to Divinity---but you yourself! I *am* you! *You* are *me*! We are *together*! I invite your help... and perhaps I might even have a small

insight here or there that could help *you* in your own journey to move yet-closer to God! I might even help you to better understand your own Holy Writings, to honor your Leader more fully, and to please God even better than you do now---if not in substance, then perhaps in application!"

⁶⁶ **Fanatic** (*laughing quietly as he leisurely reached out to pick up the dagger from off the tabletop, then hold it point-out, aimed straight at Lyle*): "You will help *me*?? But you have nothing I need! I have everything I need already. I have a full understanding of the Holy Writings, given to me directly from God Himself! I am *not* a 'learner'! I am a *teacher*! You, however, are a confused bumbler---while I am The Recognized *Authority*! Yes, I agree that you could certainly learn a lot from me if you would rid yourself of your Evil! Of course you'd have to sit down at my feet, shut your deceitful mouth, and open your mind fully to my Wisdom. Only by listening respectfully to my sermons could you truly 'come to God'! And 'coming to God' is not a matter of degrees, you idiot! It is a matter of simply seeing and accepting God's Truth... or rejecting it, as do you! But by your *own* admission you *refuse* to see the Truth and so must suffer the consequences!"

⁶⁷ **Lyle** (*hunching over, feeling lost in the continuing darkness, beaten-down by the pounding torrents of rain smashing into the top of the globe, cowed by the thunder booming all around the peak, now speaking loudly to try and be heard over the escalating roar*): "BESIDE MY NOT SPECIFICALLY AND EXCLUSIVELY ENDORSING SOME SPECIFIC ESTABLISHED RELIGION OR HISTORICAL SPIRITUAL LEADER OVER ALL THE REST, OR REPEATING EXACTLY WHAT'S ALREADY VERY WELL WRITTEN IN ACCEPTED HOLY BOOKS... WHAT IS IT THAT YOU FIND SO OBJECTIONABLE IN MY WRITINGS?"

⁶⁸ **FANATIC** (*obsessively jamming the dagger down repeatedly into the marble tabletop, chipping out little chunks of white-glowing stone as he yelled back at Lyle*): "I WILL INSTRUCT YOU ON THE ERROR OF YOUR WAYS, LYLE! YOUR 'Creative-Theology®' IS JUST A LOT OF PSYCHO-BABBLE AND HUMAN-CENTERED PHILOSOPHY---A PERVERSE ACCOMMODATION TO EVIL THAT REFUSES TO TAKE A FIRM STAND DENOUNCING SIN! IT AVOIDS TRUTH BY GIVING ONLY FUZZY, EASY DICTATES THAT INDIVIDUALS CAN MAKE INTO ANY SELF-SERVING FORM THAT THEY WISH. IT CUTS-OUT ALL THE HARD THINGS GOD DEMANDS FROM US: SACRIFICE, SELF-DENIAL, THE JOY OF PAIN, EXACTING HOLY RITUALS, SUBMISSION TO AUTHORITY, AND ESPECIALLY THE FIRM CONDEMNATION OF SIN! THE TRUTH THAT TRULY COMES FROM GOD FIGHTS AGAINST SIN WITHOUT QUARTER, BATTLING EVIL! YOU FAVOR THE EASY THINGS WHILE CONVENIENTLY FORGETTING

WHAT'S HARD IN TRULY-FOLLOWING OUR ALMIGHTY, DEMANDING, AND UNFORGIVINGLY-EXACT GOD!"

[69] **Lyle** (*now feeling emotionally battered-down by the continuing sheets of rain mixed with flashing lightning, but still managing to speak firmly and loudly*): "THOSE ARE POWERFUL ACCUSATIONS! SOME OF THAT MAY BE TRUE... HOWEVER, I BELIEVE YOU ARE MISSING A HIGHER REALITY THAT PUTS WHAT I'M SAYING INTO COMPLETE PERSPECTIVE. I, IN ESSENCE, AGREE WITH YOUR POINTS---BUT ON A HIGHER PLANE FROM THAT WHICH YOU'RE DESCRIBING HERE TO THE PANEL: NAMELY, THAT THERE'S A MORE DIFFICULT CHALLENGE GOD HAS GIVEN TO US THAN MERELY DOING A LIST OF GOOD THINGS AND AVOIDING A LIST OF BAD THINGS. I MENTIONED ALREADY TO YOU THAT Creative-Theology® CAN BE DISCERNED AT THE HEART OF ALL THE GREAT HISTORICAL RELIGIOUS LEADERS' TEACHINGS: SUCH AS IN THEIR URGING OF THEIR FOLLOWERS TO USE THEIR GOD-GIVEN TALENTS AND ABILITIES TO HONOR AND GLORIFY THE LORD. HERE, I HOLD-UP TO ALL OF YOU WHO ARE JUDGING MY WRITINGS THE GREATEST CHALLENGE OF ALL: TO *FULLY EXPRESS THE CREATIVITY OF GOD*! THIS IS THE BEST, HIGHEST SERVICE AND WORSHIP WE CAN GIVE TO GOD. AS ANY PARENT WISHES FOR THEIR CHILD TO FULLY DEVELOP, TO NOT BE STUNTED OR HELD BACK IN INTELLECTUAL OR PHYSICAL GROWTH, BUT TO ATTAIN THEIR HIGHEST POTENTIAL---SO ALSO DOES GOD WANT AND EXPECT THE SAME OF US! AND THIS IS BEST ACHIEVED NOT BY WALLING A PERSON INTO A CLOSED ROOM, BUT BY GIVING THEM THE SPACE, FREEDOM, AND SUPPORT TO EXPLORE, TEST, AND DEVELOP THEIR OWN PARTICULAR MIX OF TALENTS AND ABILITIES. SURE THEY MAY MAKE MISTAKES. SURE THE LOVING PARENT DOESN'T WANT THEM TO GO DOWN EVIL OR DESTRUCTIVE PATHWAYS, STRONGLY ADVISING AND TEACHING THE CHILD TO AVOID SUCH. BUT WHEN THAT CHILD BECOMES A FULL-THINKING ADULT, AND IS MATURE ENOUGH TO MAKE HIS/HER OWN DECISIONS, THE LOVING PARENT STEPS BACK AND ALLOWS THEM TO GO FORWARD ON THEIR OWN. YES, IT PAINS THE FATHER OR MOTHER WHEN THEIR DAUGHTER OR SON DOES BAD THINGS TO HIM/HERSELF, OTHERS, NATURE, AND TO THEM AS THE LOVING PARENTS. BUT THE TRUE AND BEST LEARNING DOES NOT COME FROM LECTURES AND LAWS---NO MATTER HOW 'AUTHORITATIVELY' ARTICULATED---BUT FROM THE CHILDREN DISCOVERING DIRECTLY WHAT IS GOOD VERSUS BAD. THE SMART KID, OF COURSE, IS EVER-OBSERVING AND LEARNING, GIVING STRONG WEIGHT TO WHAT HIS/HER PARENTS SAY, AND TO WHAT HE/SHE CAN DISCERN SECONDHAND. BUT BY GRANTING THE CHILD THAT VERY FREEDOM TO MAKE HIS/HER OWN

DECISIONS, IT ENGENDERS A DEEP APPRECIATION AND LOVE IN THE CHILD FOR THE PARENTS, SUCH THAT THE KIDS MAY EVEN WANT TO DO GOOD THINGS OUT OF A SENSE OF MAKING HIS/HER PARENTS PROUD. FURTHERMORE, ANY LIST OF 'DON'TS' IS ALWAYS INCOMPLETE, LIMITED, AND IMPRECISE. FOR EXAMPLE, WHAT FOR ME MIGHT BE A TERRIBLE PERSONAL INSULT TO GOD FOR YOU MIGHT BE OF NO MATTER WHATSOEVER! LIKEWISE, ANY LIST OF 'DO'S' IS ALSO ALWAYS INCOMPLETE, LIMITED, AND IMPRECISE. WHAT COVERS ALL SITUATIONS, HOWEVER, IS A SET OF *COMPREHENSIVE AND OVERLAPPING PRINCIPLES*, BY WHICH YOU OR I CAN CONSIDER EVERY PARTICULAR SITUATION THAT COMES UP AGAINST US... EVEN THINGS THAT ARE TOTALLY NEW, NOT EVEN THOUGHT OF OR TALKED ABOUT IN OUR CHOSEN HOLY SCRIPTURES OR BY OUR FOUNDING RELIGIOUS LEADER(S). AND THE VERY BEST MOTIVATOR IS NOT THE PAIN OF TOUCHING INDISCRIMINATELY-LIT AND DESTRUCTIVE BLAZES, BUT THE ENDLESS PROSPECTS OF WARMTH, SMELTING, COOKING, ENERGY, AND BEAUTIFUL CREATION BY CAREFULLY-APPLIED, EXQUISITELY-CONTROLLED FIRE.   IN OTHER WORDS, IT'S FAR MORE CHALLENGING AND EFFECTIVE TO BE 'FOR' THE PARTICULAR ELEMENTS AND CONDITIONS THAT BUILD, EDIFY, GROW, AND INSPIRE A PERSON THAN TO BE 'AGAINST' THE THINGS THAT TEAR-DOWN, DISHEARTEN, SHRINK, AND DEADEN THE SPIRIT! BY EXPANDING THE NOBLE, THE HEARTENING, AND THE BEST ASPECTS OF OUR GODLY & HUMAN NATURE---SINCE THERE IS LIMITED TIME, SPACE, AND POSSIBILITY IN EACH OF OUR INDIVIDUAL EXISTENCES---WE CAN *PUSH OUT* THOSE NEGATIVE ELEMENTS THAT HOLD US BACK AND LIMIT OR POTENTIAL. THIS IS THE MOST-EFFECTIVE TEACHING, THE HIGHEST CHALLENGE TO US... AND THE MOST JOYFUL ROUTE TO STANDING HAPPILY IN THE PRESENCE OF OUR PROUD FATHER, THE ALMIGHTY GOD. THE ROUTE, HOWEVER, OF PUTTING SIN FIRST AND FOREMOST IS TO DEADEN THE SPIRIT OF EVERYONE SINCE HUMAN PERFECTION IS IMPOSSIBLE!"

[70] **Fanatic** (*dramatically feeling with a gloved finger at the sharp edge of his dagger before slowly concealing the knife back beneath his black robe; then, leaning forward, he spoke more quietly and ominously in a lull of the thundering lightning and rain*): "I do compliment you Lyle... you indeed are a great Deceiver. You place Ultimate Authority in the hands of each little person. What a deceptive and dangerous lie! It is only through the Holy Writings and total allegiance to God's Anointed Messenger that a person can know how to conduct his or her life. And should there be any doubt or confusion as to what something in the Holy Writings means, they need only ask me, a certified spokesman for God---

an acknowledge 'authority'---who speaks directly from God! I am happy to immediately give them the specific answer they need, which they only have to accept and do! There is no other path to Salvation, certainly not in your silly little 'Creative-Theology®' scribbles!"

71 **Lyle** (*straightening up and nodding grimly*): "Very clearly stated, Fanatic. I must respectfully disagree with your narrow notions of 'salvation'. I return your 'compliment', though, in acknowledging and even admiring your dedication and zeal for God. But I fear your zeal is sadly misguided... to ultimately produce the exact *opposite* of that which you so fervently seek."

72 **Fanatic** (*laughing shrilly as he settles slowly back into his seat*): "Yes... we *do* 'disagree'... indeed! I know the Truth and you dishonor and attempt to dismiss that Truth by mislabeling it as merely my 'opinion'. And whatever it is that you like in life---whatever agrees with your little human desires and prejudices---you conveniently sanction *it* as being the truth... Well, for your tiny little selfish ears let me make the Truth plain: *I* am saved. And *you*---you ignorant fool spouting stupid subversive nonsense---you are forever, completely, and horribly *damned*!"

73 **Lawyer** (*loudly slapping his yellow-gloved hand down upon the marble surface of the table*): "Any further interrogation of the accused, Fanatic?"

74 There was a disdainful silence...

75 **Lawyer**: "Then let us move on to the next Judge!"
. . . .

Interrogation by the Seeker

76 High overhead, the clouds suddenly parted and sunlight came streaming down. One brilliant shaft lit up the globe, dispelling the darkness in a soft yellow glow. The welcomed light warmed Lyle's cold bones and relaxed his clammy fear;

77 The pounding torrents of rain lessening, receding to a patter, then were gone as the dark clouds overhead continued to break up and drift away... exposing the vast range of mountaintops in all their lofty glory. Lyle was struck again by the isolation of himself and his jury, perched precariously there in a rarified-exclusive retreat high up in the sky.

78 As if responding to the mellower environment, the tree behind the jury suddenly sprouted *leaves*... tiny buds widening, pushing-out large green panels that quickly covered the bare, skeletal branches...

79 ---as the newly-massive roots *shrank*, returning back to their previous size, the fresh fractures in the rocks melding back together, the surface of the peak softening and smoothing.

80 **Seeker** (*standing up, emerald-green mask shimmering as the face behind it spoke in a soft, high, female voice*): "Some of what you say is interesting to me, Dr. Lyle. I'd like to pursue those aspects further, yet I don't wish to renounce beliefs I already hold to be true. How would you suggest I proceed with your interrogation?"

81 **Lyle** (*happy to have the opportunity to now present his views to a seemingly-sympathetic, interested person*): "Seeker, I suggest that you proceed carefully, thoughtfully, and with concern... not only as to your own overall well-being, but also for those around you. But be aware that to accept some or all of what I teach... you need *not* cut-off ties with your existing religious framework, beliefs, or friends! Also, you don't need to be offensive to those who might consider what you may learn from me to be different, dangerous, or wrong. However, do consider what of Creative-Theology® might easily and helpfully fit into your existing religious framework! For instance, are 'small-group' work-or-study teams allowed by your existing religious leadership? If so, you might be able to suggest or even facilitate exploring the interests and talents of your team: not just in doing repetitive or ordinary tasks, but attempting things that are novel and creative! Such a small shift in focus might make boring or low-productive work into something that's tremendously fun, stretches the abilities of your people, allows everyone to grow, produces the best learning experience, and results in tangible achievements supported and applauded by your leadership!"

⁸² **Seeker** (*nodding thoughtfully*): "Yes, I see what you are saying. But it's not always that easy... What if those in charge of my congregation would not allow me, a woman, to take a lead role even on an 'unofficial' team? Or what if their concept of 'church work' is very limited, where any innovation at all is regard automatically as being wrong? Or what if the members around me don't desire anything unusual or creative? Or what if they are coming to church mainly to engage in 'status-quo' rituals?"

⁸³ **Lyle** (*smiling sadly*): "Those, unfortunately, are common situations. Even in our seemingly enlightened age, many people find comfort religiously in plodding through meaningless ritual, hearing empty rhetoric, and adhering to unproductive doctrines. Furthermore, many people to feel 'right' and 'blessed' in their traditions endorse blatant discrimination and dominance---especially of males over females. Many with sincerely-held religious beliefs suspend consideration of what's best under different situations for the demands of rote obedience to their traditions. In those situations one might consider quietly and respectfully finding another place to better-exercise your own spirituality. Sometimes it is even possible to discover this better place while still maintaining whatever connection desired with the more-restrictive, yet still-cherished traditional environment. Or, if a person simply feels trapped in that tradition and unable to depart, then he/she can still find complete and total freedom within the privacy of his/her own mind to practice Godly Creativity."

⁸⁴ **Seeker** (*crossing her arms as she sits back down*): "How so?"

⁸⁵ **Lyle** (*walking over to the edge of the surrounding globe and pointing out to the many peaks of the surrounding-receding majestic mountain range, now brilliantly-lit by the sinking sun*): "God's wonderful Creation that we see all around us can inspire many things: philosophical speculation, debates about morality, wise applications addressing immediate problems with which we continually struggle, powerful poems, magnificent songs, amazing paintings, engineering marvels, or other creative pursuits... all replete with inspiration, energy, and motivation! And the truly wonderful thing about all of this Godly Creativity is that it need not require any paper, computers, materials, or expensive and difficult adventures. It can all be accessed and fully utilized within your own God-given imagination! Even when trapped in the most terrible, restrictive, and soul-deadening environment we can still be completely free inside of our own heads! It is a part of the 'Golden Path' that is always available to us---there ready to be immediately grasped: pulling us up out of even the most horrible, oppressive situations. No one can deny this to you as long as you keep it private! All it takes is awareness, intent, and practice."

⁸⁶ **Seeker** (*relaxing her tensed, crossed arms and now leaning backwards in her clear, crystalline chair*): "Sounds wonderful! But surely it can't be that simple. How does anything get accomplished if..."

⁸⁷ **Fanatic** (*abruptly jumping up from his chair, knocking it over backwards*): "NO IT IS *NOT* WONDERFUL! IT IS SUBVERSION! YOU AS A TRUE BELIEVER---AND ESPECIALLY AS A STUPID *WOMAN*---MUST LISTEN INTENTLY WITH YOUR ENTIRE MIND TO YOUR RELIGIOUS INSTRUCTION! HOW *DARE* YOU THINK YOU HAVE THE RIGHT TO DAYDREAM DURING SERMONS AND THINK FOR YOURSELF! THE PATH TO GOD IS THROUGH DUTIFUL OBEDIENCE, NOT FANTASIES! AND YOUR DUTY AS A GODLY FEMALE IS SIMPLE AND CLEAR: TO FULLY *SUBMIT* TO YOUR MALE RELIGIOUS LEADERS AND HUSBAND! YOUR FEEBLE ATTEMPTS AT INDEPENDENT THOUGHT AND ACTION RISKS THE SALVATION OF YOUR ETERNAL SOUL! IT IS A HERESY OF THE..."

⁸⁸ **Lawyer** (*also rising up from his chair*): "CEASE YOUR INTERRUPTION, FANATIC! You've had your time. I allowed none to interrupt you! A time for your final conclusions and verdict will come shortly. Under the authority bestowed upon me by Almighty God to chair this panel, this proceeding will be done *decently and orderly*! SIT YOURSELF BACK DOWN, SIR!"

⁸⁹ **Fanatic** (*angrily balling his glittering fists and raising them above his head, but sullenly quieting*): "But when blasphemous untruths are spouted...!"

⁹⁰ **Lawyer** (*striding around the end of the table to stand beside Lyle, squarely in front of the Fanatic*): "I *SAID* TO SIT BACK DOWN, SIR---AND BE *QUIET*!"

⁹¹ **Fanatic** (*angrily turning away to right his chair and pull it back to the table, muttering beneath his breath as he clutched his robes to his sides and settled back down...*): "God's Truth will win..."

⁹² **Lawyer** (*now moving back around the marble table to again take his own seat*): "Continue, Seeker."

⁹³ **Seeker** (*shakily nodding over at the Lawyer*): "Uh... I thank you, Lawyer... uh, now what were we talking about...? Oh, yes. Dr. Lyle, I... *agree*... with the Critic that what you want to offer is very nebulous and general. So just how would a person actually try to implement what you are teaching other than exercising one's imagination or interacting with others on some sort of team?"

94 **Lyle** (*taking a deep breath to also steady himself before proceeding, somewhat taken-aback by the Fanatic's violent interruption and the Lawyer's intervention*): "This is... the key point... of it all, Seeker. You raise a very integral question. Creative-Theology® is imminently *practical*, replete with tangible results. It's not just some theoretical notion composed of vague generalities. In Creative-Theology® our greatest worship to God is not sitting passively or participating in some 'worship' service or even discussing things in some small group... rather it is actually *exercising* our God-given talents, abilities, and resources attempting to do things that are reasonable, useful, respectful, beautiful, and honorable. The point is to deliberately 'institutionalize' effective Processes that work smoothly together in the overall System to advance spiritual Quality! Doing such requires careful *thought*---perhaps brainstorming on one's own or with others; or study of books on the subject; or bringing in outside consultants; or observing how others deal with that situation---then *evaluating* with clear criteria the possibilities for action. From this comes *prioritization*, then *planning* of detailed actions; then actually *doing* things, *studying* what happened, and continually improving! It is *customer-driven* meaning that what we do has real, measurable value to other people! It is *dynamic*, meaning we're all the time looking to build upon what came before to go ever further, higher, and better! It is *synergistic*, meaning---if it is our desire---we can work with others to do better than we could on our own! It is *creative*, in that where before there was a boring, uninteresting, empty blank space we put instead something that is fresh, exciting, and amazing! It is *process-driven*, meaning not chaotic or spur-of-the-moment. It looks to honor God best by *actually doing* what he most wants from us... not just by reading, listening, saying, praying, or singing the same words over and over! In fact, congregational regular meetings of Creative-Theologists are *Celebrations* of creative efforts by the members, not rote rituals dutifully and boringly or even emotionally plodded-through. It is *empowering*, meaning that power is not limited to a favored few. Rather, everyone is given the means plus the support required to use their different talents together. It is *bottom-up* fueled, not just top-down driven... in that the designated Leaders are first and foremost trained, certified *Facilitators* who see as their number one duty to help their people together exercise their God-given talents attempting to do great things to the glory of God! Leadership accomplishes this by creating within the structure of the organization carefully-controlled *creative-spaces* within which, in turn, each person is encouraged and able to exercise their talents! Also, Enlightened Leadership provides effective *training* to all who participate in their different roles! Indeed, the Facilitative Leadership *takes out of the way roadblocks* while *supplying needed resources*. And finally, Godly-wise Leadership maintains a broad perspective (*Vision*) by managing the dynamic *system* such that the creative processes can be channeled for the good of the entire congregation."

⁹⁵ **Seeker** (*nodding vigorously*): "Yes, yes! I see! Your Creative-Theology® really is very different from the way most established religions conduct their business! All the religions I'm aware of have top-down leadership whose main job seems to be to 'defend the Truth' rather than help people use their talents! I see now from what you say that they are more interested in controlling people to think *their* way rather than *empowering* them to do great things for God! They want to keep things safely the same rather than try potentially-dangerous advances. They tend to look backwards instead of forward. However, as much as I agree with your analysis there, Dr. Lyle... I see a big problem! Most of the people I know *aren't* creative! In fact, *I'm* not a creative person! I can't write poems, paint pictures, compose new songs, or invent new things! What you are describing sounds wonderful for a few highly-talented people. Perhaps the rest of us are better off just staying in our more traditional, non-demanding religious settings... keeping our mouths shut and following the lead of those more talented than we..."

⁹⁶ **Lyle** (*moving forward to plant the palms of his hands firmly down onto the marble tabletop and look straight into the black eye-covers set into the Seeker's emerald-green stony mask*): "I must respectfully disagree with you, my dear Seeker. If you are a living, breathing human---then you most certainly *do* possess a variety of talents! And when you see an empty space and use your God-given talents to put something there that is reasonable, useful, respectful, beautiful, and honorable... you are being *very* Godly-creative! Just because your religious leaders don't know how or aren't interested in nurturing, facilitating, and growing those talents does not mean that each of their members would not be energized, enthused, inspired, and edified if your leaders would *learn* to do so! And it's also quite true that creation need not be limited to artistic endeavors. Thus 'creativity' is not just something that a few genius artists do, but something that is open to everybody! A mother bringing up children into God-and-fellowman-respecting maturity is accomplishing powerful creation. A small group of like-minded folks putting together an effective program to feed local homeless people while teaching them mindful-Godliness is doing excellent creation. A book club exploring new religious writings for enhancing their own mental understanding is doing strong creation. A gardener planting seeds around town in empty lots to bring up fields of flowers to cover trash heaps is doing excellent creation. Working hard at one's job taking every opportunity to behave reasonably, be helpful to others, avoid hurting others, being proud of his or her work, making things a bit more attractive---is also demonstrating Godly Creativity. In all areas of human endeavor when empty spaces are filled with things that conform to the Five Pillars of Creative-Theology®, 'RURBAH', they honor God in the best possible way: giving Him the best worship that He most desires from us His children!"

⁹⁷ **Seeker** (*pushing her green-gloved hands forward on the table to almost touch Lyle's outstretched hands*): "That is inspiring, Dr. Lyle! But then are you saying we don't need the traditional weekly congregational gatherings to worship God properly? Is your Creative-Theology® just another way of saying that we should just live good, productive lives?"

⁹⁸ **Lyle** (*looking over pointedly at the angrily-fidgeting Fanatic*): "No, Seeker. I am not saying we should do away with our regular worship services. Local Creative-Theology® groups definitely need to regularly congregate... but *not* simply to repeat the same words, the same rituals, honoring the same traditions over and over. I understand that to do so *is* the main point of many formal religions: to provide a known and comfortable place for religious tradition to 'soothe our souls'. Thus many people are quite bonded to their religious repetitions and quite offended at even minor changes thereto, thinking that some 'heresy' has occurred. But, to be quite frank, many of those so-called 'worship' services are often very boring and unproductive... something often done more out of a sense of duty than shared joy; or even done out of fear rather than edification! But if it is so painful to us, then how do you think the Eternal Lord feels seeing us using up most of our precious 'religious' together-time to just sit on pews getting lectured on what we already know? Sure, we need to come together regularly to truly encourage each other, learn more and better, and synergize our particular talents with those who will supplement us where we are weak! Even for those with dynamic, exciting services---what is really accomplished? If that's the extent of it all, to come together and be 'jacked-up', how is it any different from attending a good musical concert? Other than good feelings, what has resulted from the meeting? But we *don't* need to come together religiously mainly to either be bored or conversely have our emotions superficially and shallowly heightened! Sure, I enjoy an entertaining concert or performance as much as the next person. But the highest form of inspiration is when we celebrate our *own* efforts *collectively* aimed at productive endpoints. And please note here that I am talking about my individual *efforts*---in collaboration with your efforts---whether or not those attempts result in any successes! In short, Seeker, we need more gatherings that showcase the applied talents that God has given to you and me! We need gatherings that acknowledge, promote, and *celebrate* Godly Creativity! And that is not just '*look at me, look at me*' but 'LOOK AT *US*'! IT'S WHEN WE VALUE EACH OTHER SO HIGHLY THAT 'PERFORMING' BECOMES 'PARTICIPATING'! OUR HIGHEST PLEASURE ISN'T JUST OTHER PEOPLE CLAPPING FOR US BUT HELPING OTHER PEOPLE WITH US USE OUR GOD-GIVEN TALENTS TOGETHER---CELEBRATING AND EXERCISING OUR HOLY CONNECTION TO EACH OTHER! So, for example, in Creative-Theological gatherings, people might do the following: 1) give interesting reports on what they or small groups of the

members are doing, showing results where things have succeeded; 2) detail the progress they are making; 3) demonstrate their art and other wonderful creations; 4) sing and perform together new compositions; 5) bring in featured speakers with fresh ideas to deepen and broaden our faith in God; 6) inspire each other with 'value-added' revelations that continually go deeper, wider, higher, more-complex, and more-substantial; and 7) ANYTHING ELSE THAT WE CAN DO NOT JUST AS OBSERVERS BUT AS PARTICPANTS---actually spending our 'church' time DOING THINGS THAT HAVE REAL POSITIVE IMPACT ON REAL PEOPLE! For instance, a 'worship service' could be praying, chanting, singing, and reading verses *DURING* BUILDING A HOME FOR DERSERVING HOMELESS PEOPLE, OR VOLUNTEERING THE CHURCH MEMBERS AT A SOUP KITCHEN HELPING FEED NEEDY PEOPLE, OR GOING FOR A HIKE THROUGH A PARK PICKING UP TRASH, etcetera, etcetera, etcetera---limited only by the imagination of bottom-up creativity! So services *change* from being mainly viewed performances to being *mutual participations*: where the congregation together sings songs, speak poems, joins in productions composed by those particular members blessed with overtly-artistic talents, and works on collective tasks! And, yes, traditional elements can also be part of the mix: where members lead prayers, give talks, and perform solemn ceremonies... just not the same format all the time! Also, everything need not be new. There is, indeed, some value to repetition, tradition, and ritual. Also, periodic gatherings would certainly not be uncontrolled chaos! While not being ritualistic repetition, gatherings would be very carefully constructed by leadership to meet clear AIMs! 'Purpose' would *not* be coopted by procedure! Everything would still be done 'decently and orderly'---but always with clear purpose kept at the forefront: *doing* rather than mainly just talking or singing! So Enlightened Leaders would keep Purpose to the forefront, ever evaluating and improving on meeting agreed-on clear AIMs! Talking is necessary. That is, indeed, our main mode of communication. But the greatest joy, satisfaction, and benefit are always in the *doing* rather than just passive listening or talking! AND THAT 'DOING' IS MOST ENJOYABLY DONE AS A GROUP ENDEAVER WHERE WE JOIN TOGETHER TO SUPPLEMENT AND COMPLEMENT THE EFFORTS OF EACH OTHER! And I'm not speaking of 'make-work' activities imposed from above that do little to exercise your particular talents. I'm also not speaking of trivial pursuits that have no real impact. I *am* speaking of MOBILIZING THE FULL POTENTIAL OF EVERYONE IN THE CONGREGATION FOR TOGETHER EXERCISING IN THE BEST WAY POSSIBLE OUR GOD-GIVEN TALENTS AND ABILITIES ATTEMPTING TO DO WONDERFUL AND AMAZING THINGS! And it would be done in ways to make best use of 'conservatives' or 'liberals'... or 'introverts' or 'extraverts'... where those best-suited to particular types of jobs would be encouraged to enjoy work in those areas... and where differing Values could still be honored for each person's preference! Individuals would be utilized where and how they are most effective, contributing to an overall greater combined effort! Yes, Seeker, this is a difficult, complicated, and even dangerous undertaking on the part of your religious Leadership! They in reality change from 'defend the Truth' being their main job description to: 'help people together best exercise their God-given talents to the glory of God!' This is a great challenge! They have to be experimenters and continual learners! It takes a great deal of humility and work to go beyond that which is usual in religious gatherings: i.e. that which is 'comfortably' safe, easy, and simple! And please understand, my dear Seeker that the Five Pillars of Creative-Theology® go far beyond simply being a good person living a productive life. After all, half of the term 'Creative-Theology®' is 'theology' which means the 'study of God'! It's not just what's called 'secular humanism' where people celebrate the positive aspects of humanity. It is a *'Godly* Creativity': creativity given to us as an amazing Gift by the Great Creator Himself! As an aside, dear Seeker, also please note that I use the traditional gender of male for what we conceive as 'God', as a convenience noting that God surely is not merely some superhuman with fleshly gonads! In religious writings across history 'God' has been referred to in both 'Father' and 'Mother' contexts! Thus you as a female should not feel suppressed by the notion of God as our Father! But back to the idea of RURBAH, the Five Pillars help us to build up our spiritual-physical Crystal Cathedrals that are not dependent on any 'acclaimed' results at all! 'Creative-Theology®' places our desire, motivation, and self-esteem fully into the loving hands of the Almighty God, while maintaining complete accountability and connection to all the rest of creation. It forces us to look beyond our own narrow self-interests, or selfish motivations in helping others, to the tremendous power of *synergy* in building and *joining* our personal Crystal Cathedrals with theirs! So instead of dutiful plodding, we can instead have rapturous sprinting! In addition, Creative-Theology® helps appointed Leadership to learn how to put into place good mechanisms in a viable system for helping their people accomplish those ends! That's because all of this doesn't happen automatically, easily, or overnight. It takes a lot of study and practice by individuals and Leadership to understand and use critical Quality Principles plus excellent Quality Techniques, Methods, and Tools. It takes real discipline and Vision to do thoughtful planning, careful experimentation, in-depth evaluation, and continual improve-ment! Plus there is mastering the 'people-process' necessary to learn how to best work with other people and help small groups to do the same. This 'facilitation' involves giving up personal power to get even more collective power! It requires appointed Leadership to acquire a strong, practical humility! It fosters a keen appreciation for time-management. Also, there's never a point reached when we 'know it all' and can just settle back into a comfortable routine. In Creative-Theology® we're always learning more, having fresh aspirations, and growing ever-closer to each other and to God in exercising our God-given talents. WE MOVE BEYOND BEING JUST SMART ANIMALS STRIVING TO SURVIVE AND BE HAPPY... TO BEING CREATIVE-THEOLOGISTS JOINING WITH EACH OTHER AND WITH GOD IN A HOLY CONNECTIVITY---not just to survive but to *thrive!*"

99 **Seeker** (*nodding thoughtfully*): "Yes... I see what you are saying, Dr. Lyle... it's amazing! I myself have always felt that my full talents were not recognized, utilized, or even wanted by my religious leaders. What you say about truly valuing each other is inspiring! *And it's not just my religious Leaders helping me develop and use my God-given talents, but me helping my church family myself---as they all in turn help me!* This 'Holy Connectivity' is an amazing concept to take from theory to action! Now I see what you are doing! Your books actually tell me the particulars as to HOW my church leaders---or myself alone if need be--can do this! I'm... very excited by what you are saying, Dr. Lyle! Sign me up! I'll be your first convert to Creative-Theology®!"

100 **Lyle** (*looking directly at each of the masked faces in turn before carefully replying*): "Thank you for your kind support, Seeker. But you need not 'convert' to Creative-Theology®. You need only grasp that which is easily within your own reach. Yes, if we had more religious leaders who understood and used Creative-Theology® principles and mechanisms, then it would be much easier for members of congregations to find and join together on the Golden Path. But you can be a Creative-Theologist without having to give up your present religious identity. *As you so astutely recognized, it's not just about the Leadership 'catching on' to Godly Quality Management! If they lack the imagination or desire to move beyond their traditions, you can do it on your own!* Sure, you probably won't have the same impact that those officially in charge of your group would have, but you can still have a big positive impact on your own! So you can maintain your religious-spiritual heritage---along with its traditions, rituals, and doctrines---while *also* being a Creative-Theologist! Yes, it may be difficult to do this without being offensive to those who see religion as painful conformance to a rigid set of restrictive dictates, but it *is* possible. The bottom line here is that nobody can force you to do anything you don't want to do! Yes, there may be consequences, sometimes severe, to refusing to let others take control of your life---but your fate is firmly and always in your own hands. The Almighty God has given each of us free will deliberately, for a purpose! Within our taking full responsibility for our own lives there is a tremendous burst of eye-opening revelation: releasing an explosion of pent-up Godly Creativity! Seeker, *don't let other people kill your joy of Godly Creativity*! They do not have that power. Do not cede to them your God-given freedom to excel and grow in the best, most-exciting, and most-productive types of Godliness."

[101] **Seeker** (*her voice choked-up with emotion*): "Thank you, Dr. Lyle. I believe you have opened my eyes..."

[102] **LAWYER** (*rising up from his seat and gesturing at the next, blue-masked figure*): "Ok, then. Let's move on. It's your turn, Bystander."

. . . .

Interrogation by the Bystander

[103] Wispy high clouds now moved over the horizon, obscuring the direct light, softening the heat of the sun... until everything suddenly become cool and dreamy;

[104] The Bystander's sapphire-mask shining with a pale blue light...

[105] ---as if he or she were the moon on a bright night.

[106] The tree behind the Judges kept its canopy of green but now *dangling fruits* of every kind sprouted from the branches, hanging ripe and ready to be eaten: a cornucopia of oranges, apples, walnuts, dates, pears, mangos, apricots, and every other sort of fruit...

[107] ---a feast of plenty, crowning the rocky peak with productive life.

[108] **Bystander** (*remaining seated, speaking in a high weak, wavering voice*): "Uh, ok... well... I'm not quite sure why I'm here... I don't really know much about this stuff... and I don't have any questions to ask Mr. Lyle..."

[109] **Lyle** (*smiling in a friendly way, putting his hands down to his sides*): "Then perhaps, if you don't mind, I can ask *you* some questions?"

[110] **Bystander** (*shrugging nervously*): "Uh... I guess so... but why?"

[111] **Lyle**: "Because I'm interested in what *you* have to say---I wish to learn from *you*."

[112] **Bystander**: "From *me*?? But *you're* the teacher, not me! Nobody pays me much attention or cares what I say. I'm just not very important..."

[113] **Lyle**: "Yes, that's sad, isn't it? Just because you're not some big expert in religious doctrines, holy writings, hallowed traditions, and power-structures---does *not* mean that you are *dead*, does it?"

[114] **Bystander**: "Dead? Nope. I'm alive, alright. But... so what?"

[115] **Lyle**: "You are aware of yourself. You are aware of the concept of God. You deal with lots of problems and challenges in your life. There are things you'd like to do, if only you could. You are smart. You have a good brain. You have ideas. You have talents. And---I suspect---you also have youth, strength, and enthusiasm! In short, you have tremendous potential! You, in fact, would make a wonderful Creative-Theologist!"

¹¹⁶ **Bystander**: "Huh? Well... ok... I guess I am young, like you say. And... I never had anybody say things like that to me before. But... I don't know how I should answer you..."

¹¹⁷ **Lyle**: "Well, first of all, why not stand up?"

¹¹⁸ **Bystander** (*slumping down lower in his/her seat*): "Uh... I guess I could... but why?"

¹¹⁹ **Lyle** (*stepping forward to then sit down on the edge of the marble tabletop, one hand flat on its surface, now looking sideways at the Bystander*): "Because then I suspect that we will take on the positional orientation of equals. That's important because *I* am *you*! And you are me. Yes, I'm a bit older. I have a bit more experience. But my time is running down. I'm getting slower and weaker. You still have tremendous potential. You have powerful talents waiting to be nurtured, grown, and vitalized for God! And while I'm winding down, you are coming up! So it's a great privilege for me to talk with you and encourage you to take the Golden Path!"

¹²⁰ **Bystander** (*standing up slowly, revealing him/herself to be only half the height of the other judges: clearly a child*): "Uh, ok. Well, I guess we're at the same height now! That was cool of you to do, Mr. Lyle. No one else before in my religion ever talked to me like I was all that important. But what is this 'Golden Path' you talk about? I guess I sort of believe in God, maybe, but it's not like I'm really convinced, you know?"

¹²¹ **Lyle** (*smiling*): "Well it does appear you have some questions to ask, now that you know someone's going to take you seriously. And sure, I know exactly what you are saying. You've probably been taken to your particular place of worship by your parents and just expected to believe what's happening. But all you mostly do is sit around and hear lectures. Even when occasionally the service is sort of fun, it's still imposed on you. You have no say at all in what's happening. No one asks you what might be interesting or fun to do. And yet they expect you to get all excited and convinced it's true when you have no real choice in the matter at all... at least not at this present stage of your life. Has anyone *ever* asked you 'What do *you* want?'"

¹²² **Bystander** (*nodding*): "Hah! That's funny, Mr. Lyle. No one cares what I want! My parents never even asked me that---and sure not the leaders at my church! But... maybe... it would be nice if someone would... so how would your 'Golden Path' be anything different?"

[123] **Lyle**: "If the adults around you were all Creative-Theologists, things would be very different indeed. You would be part of appropriate small groups that didn't just sit around getting lectured at or following someone else's orders---but would focus on your *own* interests and talents! The other people would help you do things that *you* figure are fun, that you see are very important, and that stretched and grew your own talents! You'd be learning new and exciting things all the time doing things that are very much appreciated by the people who you are really helping. And those 'customers' would tell you 'thanks' and really mean it!"

[124] **Bystander**: "Really? Wow! That sounds kind of cool. But... how could something like that really happen? Isn't that, like, some sort of dream or something?"

[125] **Lyle**: "Yes, Bystander. It is indeed a dream. But dreams are only possibilities waiting to happen. In an ocean filled with drowning adults, *you* could teach *them* how to swim!"

[126] **Bystander**: "No way...!!"

[127] **Lyle**: "Way! Yes, it is true! To do so within an existing traditional religion is difficult but possible. As long as you don't do something that offends your church Leaders or overtly goes against your traditions, doctrines, and rituals---then you have a lot of freedom to not only do exciting things on your own, but actually to take the lead in them!"

[128] **Bystander** (*sounding intrigued but puzzled*): "How?"

[129] **Lyle**: "As long as you are not seen as a 'trouble-maker' most religious groups actually like for young people to stand up and be counted. The traditional religious leaders enjoy having their youth step forward and be 'leaders' in their own circles. For instance, you could organize a youth group if you don't have one already. Even if there already is a youth group you could become one of its movers! You could help them figure out what's really interesting, what would be fun projects to do... not just going-through-the-motions doing regular traditional boring things! You'd probably need to get some of the adults, preferably parents, involved. Along with your supporting adults you'd have to present your plans to the Leadership and get their ok. Some of the things you'd like to do they'd probably turn down. But at least a few of your ideas would 'fly'. You could be the person who by your example and that of your friends really demonstrates to your religious group what it means to be a Creative-Theologist---all without ever having to say those words or offend them in any way!"

[130] **Bystander** (*speaking in hushed tones*): "*I* could be a leader...?!"

¹³¹ **Lyle**: "Yes! The best kind of all! And if you were to do a bit of studying---learning good 'people-techniques' and how to use some simple 'Quality Tools'---you could become a 'facilitative' leader!"

¹³² **Bystander**: "What's that?"

¹³³ **Lyle**: "It's not someone who orders other people around. It's a person who helps other people get what they really would like, if only the roadblocks were taken away and necessary support was there for moving forward!"

¹³⁴ **Bystander**: "But why should I bother with getting them what they want?"

¹³⁵ **Lyle**: "Because if you were in a group of like-minded people, and you helped them set objectives that you are most interested in, then they would help you get what *you* want---in other words, getting more for yourself than if you'd just tried to get your 'own thing'!"

¹³⁶ **Bystander**: "No way!"

¹³⁷ **Lyle**: "Way! Believe it, Bystander. It really works. Everybody wins. You win. Your friends win. The adults win. Your religion wins. Society wins. Nature wins. God wins. We all win! That's what's so much fun about Creative-Theology®! If properly implemented, everybody wins! So it's no longer a matter of beating someone else to the prize, having them lose, so that you can pick up a few of the remaining scraps! It's not about us stealing someone else's pie so we can get fatter while they starve! It's about making *more* 'pies' so that everybody has more tasty treats than anyone had before! It's not about forcing or tricking other people to do things 'my way'. It's about giving them power to get directly involved, learn the best way themselves, get committed, and voluntarily join us on the Golden Path!"

¹³⁸ **Bystander** (*slowly sitting back down, bringing up his/her blue-gloved hands to his/her blue-glowing mask*): "Wow! I never heard anybody talk like you before! I just thought I had to go to church whether I wanted to or not. I didn't think it could be something fun! You really blow my mind!"

¹³⁹ **Lyle** (*standing back up and stepping back from the table*): "Thanks, Bystander. You are what Creative-Theology® is all about. But, sadly, often you are taken for granted or ignored in regular, traditional religious groups. Even worse, you are 'demonized' as someone who 'only wants to have fun' when religious leaders take pride in being boring. But, you see,

you do have a choice. Soon you'll be a bit older, no longer under the authority of your parents, and can choose to just turn away from religion and spirituality to live the life you want. You're going to get all involved and caught-up in maybe higher-education stuff, jobs, marriage, babies, bills, hobbies, evil temptations... all demanding your time, concern, and efforts! And next to all of that, 'religious stuff' can easily be pushed out of your life. After all---in the face of all those other demands---unless you have good reason to continue in your religious group, why waste the time? But truly Enlightened Godly Leaders can give you the best reasons of all to 'stick with it' by adopting Creative-Theology® principles and techniques! They don't even have to change their doctrines, rituals, or cherished beliefs! They just need to learn more and better how to have the *best* worship, the *best* fellowship, and the *best* service! They need to 'connect' with you and be 'relevant' to your life---just like the original Founders did in their generations! But following Tradition above all else simply stops them from connecting with you! After all, Tradition looks backward instead of forward! To amaze and interest you in their religion, your religious leaders need to go behind their revered traditions to the actual Principles of their Founder! If they are brave enough to do that, they can earn your respect and participation before you 'drop over dead'----all of your choices finished!"

140 **Bystander**: "Uh... now you're scaring me, Mr. Lyle..."

141 **Lyle**: "I'm just telling you how it really is. It goes that fast! You turn around a couple times and you're old like me. If your religious leaders want you to 'stick with it' *they've* got to 'get their act together', *now*! If they wait until you're old then you'll be set in your ways. You'll probably not be able to change your path even if you want to do so. Right now, though, you've got a chance to decide the whole rest of your life. You can rise above your parents and religious leaders and choose to be *better* than them! Maybe you don't believe much in God or religion or spirituality at this moment. But don't forget you're going to drop over dead... soon! And I don't say that to scare you into grudgingly giving some time to church so you'll not 'go to hell when you die'! I say it to you because YOU HAVE AN OPPORTUNITY TO USE YOUR TIME TO TRY AND DO AMAZING THINGS FOR GOD! So when you're about to die and you look back on your life, what do want to see? Do you want your life to be something you're tremendously proud of---having done that which made sense, helped people, didn't hurt people, was beautiful, and was honorable? Or at the last do you want to see that you just 'got by'... that you were just like everybody else, having attempted nothing all that special or significant? And when all is said and done, will the Almighty God of the Universe be proud of *you*? Not many people choose the Golden Path, my friend. For all too many people it is much too dangerous, difficult, and complicated! Why bother? But where they might have had glowing Crys-

tal Cathedrals... they chose instead to live in shabby little mud huts made out of dung!"

142 **Bystander**: "Dung??"

143 **Lyle**: "Cow-droppings."

144 **Bystander**: "Gross."

145 **Lyle**: "More than just a little gross, my friend... it's sad! They *wasted the full potential of their lives*! They mostly ignored their very own God-given talents, abilities, and capabilities. And I believe that where we'll end up after this life is finished depends on what we did with our God-given talents in this life. If we reject the Golden Path then we will wind up falling into a bottomless black pit. And even more important than having our own ultimate fate hang in the balance is our effect on those around us. Did you know that even though you are still young, many people are influenced by your example? How many younger kids look up to you? And if you are lazy, selfish, and sullen... will they be motivated to be like you? But think of how many people might otherwise be *inspired* by you, *energized* by you, and *excited* by you---to rise to their own highest potential, all because of *your* Facilitative Leadership?!"

146 **Bystander**: "So, you're saying I've got a *responsibility*..."

147 **Lyle**: "Yes, not just to your Almighty Heavenly Father, God... but *also* to your parents, your friends, your acquaintances, to society, to humanity, to nature, and most of all to yourself! It's the 'respect' part of the Five Pillars of Creative-Theology®: Reason, Utility, *Respect*, Beauty, and Honor! And just as it is the hardest of the Five Pillars... it is also the most rewarding and powerful!"

148 **Bystander** (*gulping*): "That's heavy."

149 **Lyle**: "Yes, heavy. But it's also *not* horrible! It's the 'heavy' of having a tremendously fun challenge of doing something wonderfully exciting and meaningful! It's like going on a sailing expedition around the world, or discovering a new continent, or riding a spaceship to another planet, or building the fastest car in the world, or starting up and running your own business, or building an amazing website where thousands of people come to learn and explore!"

150 **Bystander**: "But... like you said about 'respect' those are *hard* things, Mr. Lyle! I can't do stuff like that! I'm just a kid... a *regular* kid... not some genius..."

¹⁵¹ **Lyle**: "You *can* ATTEMPT great things---but probably not all by yourself, that's true. But that is one of the beauties of Creative-Theology®---where our Crystal Cathedrals get 'edified' to their highest peaks by a number of people helping each other! You don't have to do it all by yourself! Others will help you!"

¹⁵² **Bystander** (*now audibly moaning, shaking his head from side-to-side in denial*): "But that's even *harder*, Mr. Lyle! I got what you said about maybe some friends of mine and a couple parents talking and coming up with a fun project or two that the Leaders might let us do. Ok. Maybe that's not so hard. But... all that other stuff you said! Going to the moon? Starting my own business? Stuff like that is really complicated! There'd be tons of things I'd have to learn!"

¹⁵³ **Lyle**: "Why yes, of course! It's just as I told you before: the Golden Path that leads upwards *is* dangerous, difficult, and complicated! But Creative-Theology® allows, encourages, and supports you to learn more and more and more: going ever *deeper, higher, wider, more complex,* and *more substantial*! And it's not just memorizing stuff to take some stupid test, like in school---after which you immediately forget most of what you crammed into your brain! I'm talking about things that are really useful and important... that you can really *use* to do important things that *you* want to do! That sort of stuff YOU *WANT* TO DO---and then, by the 'doing', is *burned into your brain by working with it*!"

¹⁵⁴ **Bystander** (*shaking his head in denial*): "But... but... there's no one to teach me neat stuff like that! Sure, I can go to school and take some courses, I guess... but most of that stuff I just forget like you said! School stuff is mostly just a bunch of junk I'll never use! And the things that my religious leaders teach me are, like, mostly moral things or rules... not practical stuff you can actually use! Also, it's mostly boring, not interesting at all! It does sound kind of radical what you're saying, Mr. Lyle---but I got no way to get to where you're saying I should go! I suppose maybe if there was a bunch of these 'Creative-Theologist' types of adults around to 'facilitate' me, maybe... but there's not! I'm all by myself!"

¹⁵⁵ **Lyle** (*speaking softly but intensely*): "Teach yourself."

¹⁵⁶ **Bystander**: "Huh?"

¹⁵⁷ **Lyle** (*choosing now to suddenly speak loudly and jarringly*): "YOU DON'T HAVE TO WAIT AROUND FOR SOMEONE TO COME AND LEAD YOU BY THE HAND, BYSTANDER! YOU CAN MAKE YOUR OWN WAY! YOU CAN DETERMINE YOUR OWN DESTINY! YOU CAN TAKE YOUR OWN LIFE 'BY THE HORNS' AND WRESTLE IT TO THE GROUND! YOU CAN TAKE CHARGE *YOURSELF*! *YOU* CAN TEACH

YOURSELF! That is... if you know where you want to go---if you have an 'AIM'!"

¹⁵⁸ **Bystander** (*now sounding very confused, cringing backward from Lyle's fierce words*): "But... but *how*? How can I teach myself something I don't know? And what's this 'AIM' thing???"

¹⁵⁹ **Lyle** (*now speaking softly and kindly*): "What do you want out of this life you have, Bystander? What do you want to get? What do you want to do? When you add everything up and resolve it into one clear 'vector', where is that arrow pointing? WHAT DO YOU WANT? Figure that out for yourself and then *go* for it! Read a book on the subject you are interested in! Search on the internet for helpful information! You could read *my* books about motivation and facilitation! View some of my free short videos at my website where I give you important 'take-home' messages, at LylePublishing.com or Creative-Theology.org! Talk to people who are already expert at what you're interested in doing. Give it try. Experiment! Take one step forward towards a big goal! See what happens. Step back and think about your results, especially if it doesn't succeed! Look at failure as just a way of figuring out what *doesn't* work. You don't have to wait for someone to come teach you about interesting things! It doesn't matter that you are young. Many young people have amazed their parents and friends by getting really interested in something and forging ahead on their own! Fortunately, though, there are many good people eager to lend you a friendly helping hand, especially professionals. They are often quite flattered to know that a young person is seeking their help. Professionally, some will even offer paid apprenticeships to qualified young people. Of course I'm talking about always being careful and doing everything upfront and in the open with other people. Yes, some less-than-honest people might try to take advantage of your youth and enthusiasm. Be wise! But also don't be stopped by the limitations of your parents or religious leaders! You can *surpass* them... not by rebelling doing bad things, but by being *even better* than they are in many ways! Sure, seek their help and support. Don't needlessly offend them. But if they can't take you higher, then proceed on your own! Many people have achieved amazing things when they didn't have hardly any formal education in that area at all! They wanted to learn, so they taught themselves what they needed to know! Did you know that Abraham Lincoln became a president of the United States of America after being in congress after being a successful lawyer when he only had a few years of formal education? He *taught himself* by reading books and applying what he learned! And that was, like, a long time before there was any Internet or computers giving easy access to all the knowledge of the world! Now just like Mr. Lincoln you may not know your ultimate AIM right now! Your goals may change radically as you learn and accomplish more throughout your life! But you're not just drifting along, content

with whatever! Like President Lincoln you're USING YOUR GOD-GIVEN TALENTS IN GODLY WAYS ATTEMPTING GREAT THINGS!"

160 **Bystander**: "Oh... that's *really* a radical idea, Mr. Lyle! I never heard anyone talk like you before! But... but... I just wouldn't know how to even start...!"

161 **Lyle**: "Like I said, my young friend, if you wish you can start by reading *my* books! They give you lots of powerful ideas and ways to achieve your goals that you never thought of before! Just go to my website at http://www.LylePublishing.com or http://www.Creative-Theology.org to get access to my books! I go through the important Principles and give you the very best Quality Tools. Sure it's not some superficially-entertaining video-game. But it's practical and useful. Also, it is challenging. Do you have what it takes? I, at least, know that you *do* have what it takes. I have faith in you. I believe in you! And I'm willing to help you! Do you need someone to listen to you and give you helpful advice? I'm there for you! Just send me an e-mail to Dan-Lyle@LylePublishing.com with any questions, comments, or ideas you'd like feedback on! I'd be glad to hear from you... assuming that I manage to survive this interrogation that is... I *want* to help *you*, which is why I put out all the time and effort to write these books! And if you don't have a credit card or your folks won't buy you a hard copy or online copy of my various books, like I said---I have lots of free videos on my sites where I give you all sorts of free information on the 'take-home messages' from my books! Plus I'll even give you a free online copy of whatever book you're interested in if you can't pay the few dollars for one of them! Just e-mail me you're your request and I'll give you a link to download a free copy! My works are there to open your eyes to possibilities, point you to the higher path, and give you the tools you need to get there---if that's what you want to do! Sure, it would take a little work and time on your part, but everything worthwhile takes some effort! But what I'm telling you here is that you are NOT alone! I'm happy to help you in all good ways! Find your AIM and go for it using your God-given Gift that's already inside of you! So, you see, not only are those ready to give you a helping hand, even God is there with you!"

162 **Critic** (*tentatively raising his hand to interrupt*): "May I say something?"

163 **Lawyer**: "You may speak."

164 **Critic**: "My dear Panel Members---Lyle has just revealed his true colors, no different than any other controlling 'guru'. Here he is bothering some innocent young child who is quite content with the beliefs that his/her parents have given to him or her. And despite Lyle's lofty rheto-

ric of some 'new' approach to religion and spirituality, in the end he---like every other sly, deceptive 'guru'---insists that the child be 'converted' to his particular way of thinking or be forever damned! Also, he seeks to proselyte the child... to bring him or her into his direct influence! Lyle carefully rejects the label of being a 'cult-leader' but his actions speak otherwise! He claims a mandate from God to subvert the life of an innocent child!"

[165] **Bystander**: "Uh, like... I didn't quite get that idea from Mr. Lyle, Mr. Critic, Sir...uh..."

[166] **Lawyer** (*pointedly addressing the Bystander*): "Did I not hear Lyle tell you that if you don't find his 'Golden Path' then you are going to get cast into some 'bottomless black pit'?"

[167] **Bystander**: "Well, I guess he *did* say that..."

[168] **Critic** (*jumping into the middle of Bystander's response*): "---and did not Lyle just now say you're to go and study his writings? It sounds a lot like some second-hand, inferior version of your own Holy Scriptures, don't you think? And do you want to come under his influence in some weird cult? In your own 'church' you spoke of, isn't it a lot safer and more comfortable than going off with some strange person?"

[169] **Bystander**: "Well, come to think of it... I suppose..."

[170] **Lyle** (*sternly interrupting*): "Don't listen to the Critic, Bystander! He finds fault with anything. He wants to feel powerful by cutting you down. Sure, we have to be practical and realistic in everything---willing to see the negatives alongside the positives---but not to the point of killing your dreams, draining away your potential, or sucking the joy out of your spiritual life! If you let the Negatives rule your life you'll always be unhappy... and you'll never dare to try to achieve anything! And I AM NOT A CULT LEADER! I DON'T PREACH OR TEACH 'WEIRD' STUFF! I'M NOT TRYING TO TRICK YOU INTO DOING ANY SORT OF BAD THINGS! But the Critic *is* correct in that all religions, my young friend, did originally start out as so-called 'cults' that were denounced and vilified by the established traditional religious leadership! The Critic is *also* correct that I am teaching things that are not the 'traditional' way of doing things! But what I teach is 'different' because it is BETTER! And it all goes back to the Principles that your traditional church leaders claim to believe in! Plus, it also goes back to the actual techniques that the Founders of the great religious used! If you, my young friend, follow in the core teachings and examples of your Founder then you will on your own discover Creative-Theology® without any need of 'following' me at all! I ask you to cut through blind tradition, boring rituals, stifling

church structure, and set-in-concrete doctrines to thus allow yourself to be the TRUE FOLLOWER OF YOUR RELIGION'S FOUNDER!"

171 **Fanatic** (*slapping his gloved hand with a "bang" down onto the marble tabletop as he inserted himself loudly back into the argument*): "BYSTANDER, OPEN UP YOUR EYES! LYLE IS TRYING TO FOOL YOU! ARE YOU GOING TO LISTEN TO HIM OVER YOUR PARENTS AND YOUR TRUSTED RELIGIOUS LEADERS? ARE YOU GOING TO LET HIM LEAD YOU AWAY FROM THE INSTITUTIONS THAT PROTECT AND COMFORT YOU? Yes, Lyle's deceptive words are seductive, aren't they? But they also *scare* you, don't they? He wants to lead you on a 'journey' where you don't know what's going to happen... versus your beloved religion where you always know exactly what's going to happen! Lyle's philosophy is *dangerous*! Even *he* admits it's dangerous! Ah, but---my young friend--- you don't have to be scared of *me*... *I'm* your *real* friend! I *see* that you are confused and scared! But I'm not the one telling you to go off floundering on your own trying to do the impossible! Stay right where you are right now... comfortable and safe! And if you've got questions, just listen to *me*! I won't mislead or confuse you! I'll give you the straight, easy answers---direct from God! I won't give you some confusing 'maybe'... I'll tell you the straight-out 'yes' or 'no'! The Truth is *not* hard to know or to follow. So don't bother your head with Lyle's nonsense! Just believe what I tell you and you will be safe and..."

172 **Seeker** (*angrily interrupting the Fanatic*): "There's more to the world than just your hateful lectures and exclusionary rules, Fanatic! Bystander, look to your *heart*! If you give-in to the Fanatic your world will be narrow and mean! You can be your *own* person---just like Dr. Lyle says! The Fanatic wants to make you his slave! The Critic wants you to agree how 'smart' he supposedly is! And the Lawyer just wants you to keep your mouth shut and follow the rules, no matter whether they are good or bad! Dr. Lyle wants to help you get to where *you* want to go! He's the only one here who's really interested in *you*!"

173 **Lyle** (*nodding appreciatively in agreement*): "The Seeker is right about me, Bystander. The Lawyer looks to take power away from you and give it to 'authorities'. The Critic is only happy when he's cutting you down and keeping you pinned under his thumb. The Fanatic wants take outright control of your very soul! I'm here *not* to try to cut you down or control you, but to 'empower' you... to help you get the power you need to make your own good decisions and do the things that you find to be truly good for yourself! There's a huge difference between my approach and that of most of your religious leaders. I'm not putting you into a little tight box of my own making. I'm opening up the universe for you to..."

¹⁷⁴ **Critic** (*waving his arms in the air as he jumps up, interrupting Lyle in mid-sentence*): "Lyle's ideas are so full of holes you could get lost in them, Bystander! Stick to the 'tried and true'! Don't be bothered with Seeker's fanciful flights of imagination! The Fanatic's a bit over-excited, true, but he's got the right idea. Your parent's religion has survived the test of time! It's already been vetted by society! And it's there for you right now because it works! You don't need to look to some untested, strange philosophy like Lyle's! Just do what you are told! There's no need for you to have to think for yourself! Every thing's already been figured out by people far smarter than you! Just sit back, relax, and don't rock the boat..."

¹⁷⁵ **Bystander** (*putting his blue-gloved hands to the side of his masked head*): "SHUT UP! WILL YOU ALL PLEASE JUST SHUT UP! I'M REALLY CONFUSED! I DON'T KNOW WHY I'M HERE! I WANT TO GO HOME..."

¹⁷⁶ Lyle stood back, sadly watching the four Judges now arguing all at the same time, shouting at each other in one long noisy burst:

¹⁷⁷ ---a violent flood of simultaneously-incomprehensible angry voices loudly rumbling; as they all stood up and began not just yelling but actually *shoving* each other!

¹⁷⁸ **Lawyer** (*a BLAST of brilliant yellow light exploding from his mask---momentarily blinding & silencing everyone*): "ORDER! I WILL HAVE ORDER! ORDER IN THIS COURT! EVERYBODY SIT DOWN AND BE QUIET OR THERE WILL BE CONSEQUENCES!!"

¹⁷⁹ At that the other four subdued, quieted, and---still shaking their heads and mumbling angrily---sat back down in their respective crystalline chairs.

¹⁸⁰ **Lawyer** (*nodding in satisfaction as he also sat himself back down*): "So, Lyle... you're now down to the last and most exacting of your interrogators---ME!"

. . . .

Interrogation by the Lawyer

[181] The wispy high clouds abruptly were swept from the sky... as in their place roiling-black storm clouds gathered, darkening the protective globe;

[182] And a powerful, hurricane-force wind *slammed* into the globe, "*whining*" around them bringing bursts of rain that hammered into the shield like bullets; the transparent sphere swaying back and forth, stressed...

[183] Lyle gasped in amazement as every single one of the tree's beautiful fruits fell, smashed, rolled away on the hard rocks, and were instantly *rotted*;

[184] A sickenly-sweet smell of decay filled the containing globe... but quickly was absorbed by leaves turned brittle and brown that tumbled down to cover the rotted fruit with their own crumbling mass... the tree once again standing stark and barren:

[185] ---thrusting, as before, its gnarled branches up at a baleful, angry sky; now shorn of its glorious crown, its productive seed, and its vitality... the skeletal plant seemed *sad*.

[186] **Lawyer** (*speaking precisely and softly*): "Alright, then. Let us cut to the final, central issue. You touched on this with the Critic, but I want to nail it down. What Authority supports your teachings? I take it that you reject the long-established, accepted, existing Holy Writings?"

[187] **Lyle** (*turning to his right to face the Lawyer who was seated at the very end of the marble table; who in the darkness looked ominously like a ticking time-bomb ready to go off, his mask glowing a cautionary pulsating-YELLOW*): "No. I do *not* reject the established Holy Writings."

[188] **Lawyer**: "If you do not reject the Holy Writings, then by them you stand condemned. None of them sanction your writings. Most of them strictly forbid extensions of themselves. By their Authority---which you say you accept---your teachings are simply wrong. Is that not so?"

[189] **Lyle** (*slowly shaking his head from side to side in denial*): "It is true that I don't reject the Holy Writings, but at the same time neither does my authority stem from them."

[190] **Lawyer** (*slowly putting a hand up to support his lowered chin*): "So... you say you neither reject them nor accept them. This is a very weak argument! But if you do not use them for authority, then from where do you claim validity?"

¹⁹¹ **Lyle** (*abruptly speaking forcefully, trying to rock the Lawyer from his confident denial*): "MY AUTHORITY COMES FROM WITHIN THE STRUCTURE AND FUNCTION OF THE HUMAN MIND: THE RATIONAL FRAMEWORK WITHIN WHICH GOD HAS CHOSEN TO IMBED OUR SOULS, THE SAME ULTIMATE AUTHORITY THAT WE ALL USE TO RECOGNIZE AND BELIEVE THE ACCEPTED HOLY WRITINGS THEMSELVES!"

¹⁹² **Lawyer** (*lowering his hand off his chin and tipping up his head in apparent amusement*): "Yelling at me will do you no good, Lyle. Apparently I've touched a nerve. And I assure you, speaking in riddles will do you no good against a strong legal mind such as mine. Authority simply does not stem from each individual. There must be precedence and group agreement for any authority to exist. To devolve authority to each individual is a prescription for utter societal chaos and disaster. Your argument, Sir, is *mute*!"

¹⁹³ **Lyle** (*narrowing his eyes in defiance*): "No, my dear Lawyer. I respectfully disagree. The rules of society---whether they are enshrined as Holy Scriptures or as established Laws or Precedence---rest upon the willingness of each individual to see within those dictates a greater good. I simply choose to go to the source of any accepted Law's validity: the conscious agreement of each individual to abide by that traffic light at an intersection because it is *reasonable, useful, respectful, beautiful,* and *honorable*! All of those judgments rest upon the God-given ability of each person's mind to comprehend, evaluate, and accept not just some Institution as ultimate authority... but the actual Greater Good thereby engendered!"

¹⁹⁴ **Lawyer** (*thoughtfully touching his yellow-gloved fingers together in front of his mask*): "You are again wrong, Lyle. Most people do not need nor do they bother to go through any such a complicated thought process. In fact, they don't wish to deal with such bothersome personal responsibility at all. All most people want is for someone else, some trusted Authority, to figure out the rules and just tell them what to do! They don't want to have to think about things which they deem as trivial. They just want to know what the Law dictates so they can do it! Thus there is little cost to them personally to get a resultant peace, security, comfort, and freedom from struggling to have to 'do their own thing'. Your idealistic notions of personal responsibility and authority are laughable when looking at real-world behavior."

¹⁹⁵ **Lyle** (*folding his arms together defiantly over his chest*): "I beg to disagree! No institution, government, or set of laws exists without the consent of the people. No religious movement or group continues with-

out consent of its constituent members. No congregation of believers persists without the agreement of its people to do so. People do not exist to uphold laws, societies, or religions. All those Authorities exist because of and to serve the will of the people."

196 **Lawyer** (*throwing his hands up and laughing shrilly*): "So you fall into the deluded camp of those who claim that 'God' is an invention of man, made by man, to validate and give the selfish wishes of man a veneer of respectability beyond just 'I want this'? You don't see any God-given Mandates---just bottom-up conveniences!?"

197 **Lyle** (*angrily balling his fists down at his sides*): "Of course not! Our thinking-ability, our rational brains, our moral-ethical values, and our very ability to perceive a 'right' versus a 'wrong'...they all *do* come from God---but not as immutable dictates! I believe that God wants each one of us to *struggle* with what and why we are doing the things that we are doing! This is a critical part of walking the Golden Path! To just blindly accept some institution or writing as Ultimate Authority is *not* what the Lord wishes from us! The Holy Texts are not prescriptions for specific behavior in every situation... but rather are at their hearts are authoritative *guidelines* that drive us to *question* our own behavior and hearts! Instead of 'Books of Answers' they are indeed 'Stories of Questions'! Every single individual is indeed responsible for his/her own beliefs, decisions, and actions! I *cannot* say 'this book, person, and/or institution told me to do or say or think such-and-such therefore I am not responsible before God'! The Almighty Creator has placed within each of us humans the capability to think for ourselves. Sure, we should pay close attention to any continuing and accepted law or institution. Sure we should revere, study, and learn from our Holy Writings. Certainly, groups and society can make laws with which to regulate and govern their own behaviors. But responsibility and ultimate Authority before God *always* rests upon the individual. This is a key tenet of Creative-Theology®!"

198 **Lawyer** (*shaking his head to each side in mock exasperation*): "Oh, Lyle, what you say *sounds* very practical, pragmatic, and nonconformist! But it's actually just liberal nonsense! You say that each person should be his or her own little authority, with no need to believe in anything except the power of one's own mind... really? If you actually believe this, Lyle... then in effect you are denying *Faith* itself!"

199 **Lyle** (*backing up a step*): "Just because we all have to make and be responsible for our own beliefs, decisions, and actions... it does *not* mean we can't also believe in things outside ourselves. Since very little is absolutely 100% proven, faith is necessary! But *not* blind faith! Workable Faith is based on reasonable evidence from which one can then take a

considered, premeditated, thoughtful leap into the unknown. Failure to take that well-considered leap is, indeed, the ultimate 'sin'. Unconfronted mystery is *not* true religion! God is not interested in fools! Neither is God interested in short-sighted egotists, power-hungry predators, moral or ethical sloths, or theological cowards! A first and critical test of our spiritual character is to acknowledge the most important thing beyond our ability to 'prove': the existence of our Great Father, our Almighty Creator... the Unknowable Mystery that lies at the heart of all the great religions! Thus Faith extends beyond mortal constructs! Also, the concept of 'God' can readily be put into other terms or contexts than do the traditional religions. Divinity might be acknowledged in ways different from accepted spirituality. This high-concept can even be found in or based upon the immutable, unexplainable Laws of the Universe---or the awesome majesty and beauty of Nature! But without such a Faith in reality that's beyond our comprehension---whether declared or just substantiated by our actions---we are lost. With no attachment to the Golden Path we will fall. When we physically die, I believe---based on my own intuition, scientific knowledge, and the teachings of many of the Holy Texts---we will spiritually drift until our personal essence dissipates in the Black Pit. We will be forever damned to a Godless, empty void... *exactly what we decided to accept and act upon throughout our life here on earth*: a pervasive Negativity rejecting Faith that we---perversely and ironically---accepted *on faith*! So one way or another, Faith *will* decide our fate, whether to save us or to condemn us!"

200 **Lawyer** (*angrily standing up and pointing a trembling, yellow-gloved finger at Lyle*): "It pains me to say this, Lyle, since you are an articulate and well-spoken opponent... but you are an illegitimate, theological *bastard*! You *cannot* claim God as your spiritual Father! You are not a human-birthed child of God... just an animal! You rant and rave illogically, stupidly, and ignorantly! I may be a logically-minded Lawyer, but I am also a man of faith! We are *not* 'condemned' by Faith!! We are *saved* by well-grounded, solid, time-tested, society-certified, and true Faith! May God *strike you dead where you stand* for such odious disrespect to the foundations of our society! It is HERESY... and you, Sir, are a HERETIC!"

201 **Fanatic** (*jumping up also, excitedly waving his fists over his head*): "Yes! You are exactly correct, Lawyer! I knew indeed you were---at your core---a worthy *colleague*! We must stand together on established *Truth*, not self-willed silliness! Faith itself *is* time-certified, accepted Authority... *not* what's bouncing around in each person's confused little head! How would society function if each person just made up his or her own rules? Our civilization would crumble without established Truth! Lyle asked the child what he or she wanted! This is the most subtle and se-

ductive subversion of society! 'Truth' isn't something we decide to want or not want...it just *is*!"

²⁰² **Lawyer** (*regally sitting himself back down and patiently waving for the Fanatic to do so also*): "You make sense, Fanatic---as do I. But you and I are not on trial... it's Lyle. And the verdict must come from all of us. So, *Bystander*, how do you feel about Lyle's teachings now? Are you still somewhat intrigued by him, curious to 'make your own way'---now that you hear this new heresy on Faith coming from Lyle's own lying mouth?"

²⁰³ **Bystander** (*slumping down in his chair, his blue-masked head hanging forward, moaning*): "My head hurts...!"

²⁰⁴ **Lawyer** (*triumphantly*): "Do you see, Lyle? Do you see what you are doing to the child? He or she needs firm control, loving guidance, and a set & clear Authority! He, like most supplicants before God, requires firm and clear LAWS---not your mushy 'principles'! He needs only ask what his religion requires, not what it can do to further his/her own vagrant wishes!"

²⁰⁵ **Fanatic** (*gleefully clapping his gloved hands together*): "YES! YES! LOOK AT THE CHILD, LYLE! LOOK AT THE POOR SUFFERING KID! YOU CAUSED HIM OR HER THIS PAIN! IT'S ALL BECAUSE OF YOU!"

²⁰⁶ **Critic** (*sighing patronizingly*): "Both of you are just agreeing with what I've already said. The 'ultimate good' is not that which empowers the individual, but that which flawlessly *protects* society! This is a fact, accepted throughout human history. It is not the welfare of isolated individuals that provide security to us---it is *institutions*! We conservatives have known this from the dawn of time! Liberals like Lyle pretend to care for the individual yet work to destroy the very institutions necessary for individuals to thrive! And the organizations that best protects individuals are societally-certified groups bound by clear laws: whether a strong family, a viable company, a united nation, a secure religion---or all of them working together! 'Freedom' is only an illusion! Individuals 'control' their own fate only to the extent that they stay under the protective umbrella of multiple viable institutions! Lyle's subversive Creative-Theology® is not only wrong it is dangerous to individuals and to society! As you have so well pointed out, Lawyer... it encourages people to do their own thinking outside of established Authority! Thus, it exposes people to many threats and perils that they would never have encountered if they'd stayed safely inside the established norms! Plus, it encourages them to question and disobey any laws of society that in their own 'infinite' wisdom they deem to be inapplicable! Lyle says we should

flout the very Institutions that make society work! In defense of all that's Holy, Lyle should unanimously be *condemned* by this panel. We need to stop his evil teachings dead in their tracks... *now!*"

207 **Lyle** (*speaking fast and imploringly*): "I plead with you all to not make a hasty decision! I am not just trying to protect my own life, but the very long-term viability of religion and spirituality! The topic is too important for you to cavalierly dismiss my valid concerns! Critic, surely you see the faults running through inflexible, uncaring, hateful, self-righteous, dying Institutions! Yes, you are correct that Creative-Theology® is *not* just about preserving a comfortable, safe, simple, and easy environment for going about our routine affairs! Rather, Creative-Theology® is about how to *best* honor and show respect to the Almighty God! And in that process there must be a great *humility* on *all* our parts! I agree that so-called 'liberals' often err in attacking necessary institutions! Liberals need to modify their thinking in terms of what's practical, to be---in other words---'*practical-progressives*'! But you should also agree that conservatives often forget the hurt done to individuals in their zeal to protect viable institutions! Conservatives need to become---in similar other words---true '*compassionate conservatives*'! And, yes, we don't all need to become 'moderates' who can't envision extremes. We can retain our focus as so-called 'conservatives' or 'liberals' on either institutions or individuals. But we can never succeed if we destroy either individuals or institutions for the sake of the other! And we who are of a religious mindset also need to acknowledge that our Founders were neither conservatives, nor moderates, nor liberals! No, in the context of their times they undoubtedly were all RADICALS! They didn't want to modify the existing religious frameworks but BURN THEM DOWN AND START ANEW! These great Religious Founders took great leaps of Faith into the Unknown! To you my interrogators here at this table, I vehemently reject your labeling me as a 'liberal'! In the name of---and following the example of---my great religious Founder of my own inherited religion, I claim to be a Godly 'Loving Radical'! And no, it's not the 'love' of our Fanatic here at the table who 'loves' you enough to *kill* you if you don't bow down to him! This is a true Love that respects each individual: meaning IN TERMS OF THEIR LIVING THEIR OWN LIFE THEY KNOW BETTER THAN ME! Yes, this is a scary, 'radical' notion! But if that's true, then Godly Love---as defined by RURBAH---*won't* result in chaos and destruction! The message is clear! Each one of us, simply, don't know everything---no matter how lofty our position or status! None of us has all the answers! Likewise, there is no single Authority that can tell us how to mindlessly do everything in all circumstances! No Holy Text tells us how to always best use our own particular mix of talents and abilities in each particular situation! In fact, each situation is indeed unique and challenging! This is not 'relational morality' but mere practical application of our Holy Texts! That's because there are multiple

levels of Reality that go far beyond anything we are even capable of realizing! A tenant of Creative-Theology® is that 'Truth' is *always* MULTI-DIMENSIONAL! Simplistic, ritualistic, traditional, superficial 'answers' are recipes for disaster! For any so-called 'fact' there is *always* a deeper, higher, wider, more-complex, and more-substantial element to discover and learn! Consider our positional relationship to God! In comparison to God I---a certified, Ph.D. biologist--- suspect that we are not like dogs, or ants, or even one-celled amoeba! We are like... squirming, one-celled, mindless *bacteria*! Can we not all agree that all of us need to learn more and better in order to even *start* to be pleasing to the Lord!?"

[208] **Seeker**: "Well, I do want to get closer to God..."

[209] **Lawyer** (*dismissively cutting her off*): "—as do we all, Seeker! But the path to God is not by rampant, out-of-control individualism! It's not by asking 'What do you want?' All throughout human history, religions created doctrines, rituals, and traditions appropriate for their time and age. As such, the established Religions are powerful forces for conformity and stability despite a few well-publicized lapses. Lyle's rhetoric promotes *more* lapses, *more* failures of stability! His seductive words on 'fitting into any existing religion' are just planting seeds of conflict and chaos in otherwise smoothly-functioning religious groups! Our so-called 'humility' should be in submitting our personal egos to conform to the recognized Authority, *not* in each person blazing his or her own conflicting paths! Lyle's Creative-Theology® is just a 'recipe' for societal disintegration, *not* edification! It's not his 'major step forward in the spiritual growth of humanity'---but rather a huge leap *backward* to isolated cavemen all fighting and killing each other!"

[210] **Lyle** (*waving his hands about in the air attempting to get the attention of the panel focused back on him instead of the pontificating Lawyer*): "FREEDOM IS NOT AN ILLUSION! Freedom is a *gift* from God. How we decide to use this Gift is our biggest Test! Do we give it away to others? Or, just as bad, do we use our personal freedom to take away hope and joy from others? If we wish, I say we can *combine* our God-given freedoms within the facilitating, empowering framework of RURBAH---to build fluid, dynamic, and spiritually-powerful Crystal Cathedrals based on practical efforts! What reasonable God-seeking person would deny the validity to being reasonable, useful, respectful, beautiful, and honorable? Are those not great Godly Principles capable of producing good results? Thus we can together---despite our particular, different religious traditions---rise beyond the necessary human institutions to a higher plane where the Godly Principles and Efforts become their own enabling, empowering, and supporting Higher Super-Institution! We can work together to rise to this yet-higher plane of existence... or cower, as you say, in dirt-bound caves! Sure, we should 'conserve' that which

works! Of course we should! But we also as a society need the courage to explore beyond the horizon, to embrace that 'liberal' effort! And when that exploration is bound by the true Godly Principles of RURBAH then it will result in positive individual and collective movement forward! If we thus individually and collectively abide by the Five Pillars of Creative-Theology® then society will certainly *not* suffer disintegration from unrestrained fighting... but will, contrarily, *flourish* from productive cooperation! Families, schools, companies, organizations, established religions, and government will all be made better! Quality will be enhanced! AND SINCE IT ALL COMES FROM EMPOWERING EACH PERSON'S OWN WORTHWHILE, GODLY GOALS---THEN THE 'BUY-IN' EXISTS FROM EACH INDIVIDUAL PERSON FOR GIVING A FULL AND ENTHUSIASTIC EFFORT! What we must accept, then, is not unquestioned control by a self-righteous, privileged, egomaniacal few imposing upon us their own traditional framework... but the individual empowerment that comes from Almighty God! Yes, this is not comfortable---it is not safe, simple, or easy---but in accepting some danger, some puzzlement, and some difficulty comes true joy and productivity! God did not create mankind as a homogenous, walking-in-lockstep, obedient army of unthinking, identical robots! Where is the beauty or joy in me being an exact copy of everybody else? Where is the value in me just being another identical voice to everyone else? In *diversity* there is a great strength! Our many different talents, abilities, and capabilities can supplement and synergize with each other within the overlying framework of RURBAH facilitated by Godly Quality Leadership so that we can together be far better than we could in isolation by ourselves! And besides, making everybody else into a copy of me would be immensely *boring*!"

[211] **Lawyer** (*nodding firmly*): "Finally, we are in agreement. You indeed are getting to be very boring, Lyle---your arguments painfully repetitive. On that note, I think it's time we brought these proceedings to an end."

[212] **Fanatic**: "Here, here!"

[213] **Critic**: "Yes, let us stop this farce."

[214] **Bystander**: "I just want to go home..."

[215] **Seeker**: "I'm confused.... I need time to think..."

[216] **Lawyer**: "We've talked through all the issues. This trial has taken enough of our valuable time. Let's finish it."

. . . .

Pronouncement of the Verdict

217 The rain pounding down on the dome turned into snow... cocooning the protected peak in a swirling maelstrom of pure white;

218 Everything inside the dome was now dimly lit by a rainbow of glowing facemasks: *red, green, blue,* and *yellow* all glittering off the *diamond* facets of the Fanatic's mask;

219 Making the peak a kaleidoscope of flashing rainbows alternating with soft white... the dazzling, fireworks-like display causing Lyle to rapidly blink his eyes:

220 Losing his orientation, he seemed to be floating... lost in time trapped in an unthinkable, impossible situation... called-to-task on an idea, an intuition, and a possibility---on trial for his life!

221 The rotting & crumbling mass at the foot of the ancient tree bubbling and seething... then evaporated in a PUFF of black soot! ...returning the tree to only twisted, weathered branches and knotted roots:

222 A defiant sculpture of gnarled limbs thrust-out from a scarred trunk... holding on, a bare-minimum tribute to the stubborn tenacity of living creatures;

223 That where there seems no hope, no sustenance, no reason to continue... life somehow finds a toehold, drinking-in faint sunshine for energy... hanging on;

224 Fighting-back against mighty forces trying to hurl it off its tenuous perch... hoping for a chance to burst-forth in all its God-given potential:

225 But if to never flourish, yet remaining defiant to the end... finding victory even in defeat---a lonely, solitary flag waving high up at the top of the world.

226 **Lawyer** (*crossing his arms in stern finality*): "What say *you*, Critic?"

227 **Critic** (*standing up*): "Lyle is guilty of terminal arrogance. He ignores the gaping flaws in his own message. Perhaps there are some good aspects to his teachings. But, unfortunately, the negatives far outweigh the positives. It is a pity he cannot see the error of his ways."

228 **Lawyer**: "So you vote 'guilty'. And what, then, is your recommended punishment?"

229 **Critic**: "I humbly suggest that Lyle should be bound hand and foot---then thrown off of this high peak to smash to pieces on the rocks far below. Not a trace of his deeply-flawed doctrine should remain. He should vanish from this earth."

230 The Critic sat back down.

231 **Lawyer**: "Fanatic?"

232 **Fanatic** (*rising from his seat while simultaneously bringing out his long, sharp, glittering, silvery knife to hold tenderly by its black haft in his white-gloved right hand*): "GUILTY! GUILTY OF BLASPHEMY! Need I say more?"

233 **Lawyer** (*placidly replying*): "Perhaps a few words for the record in explanation would be appropriate."

234 **Fanatic**: "I am happy to set the record straight! Lyle makes God into a pale shadow of His true Self: something squishy and vague... definable in different ways by different people! Even worse, Lyle says that God's Will is interpreted through each individual's own experience and ideas! To the contrary, God is a great burning FIRE that CONSUMES the imperfect and disobedient! Certainly the concept of Divinity is *not* an excuse for 'empowerment' catering to our individual human whims! Rather, our God is our DEMANDING ABSOLUTE who gives us clear ORDERS by his Anointed Messengers and Holy Texts as to what all of us are to think, say, and do! There is no ambiguity! We have only to believe and obey! Anything else is heresy! Without a doubt, Lyle is a vile *Heretic* worthy of the most extreme condemnation!"

235 **Lawyer**: "And your recommended punishment?"

236 **Fanatic**: "The heretic should be *killed by my own hand* as I act---humbly, I might add, in the spirit of the Critic's fine words---as God's anointed agent! I will gladly with my very own blade *slice his throat from ear to ear*! Then you may do with his bloody corpse whatever you will... throw it off the edge the cliff as the Critic wishes, whatever! It will be of lesser worth than a pile of stinking dung!"

237 Before sitting back down, apparently by way of illustration, the Fanatic "whizzed" his blade through the air in a sizzling arc!

238 **Lawyer** (*turning his gaze to the next Judge*): "Seeker?"

239 **Seeker** (*dejectedly remaining seated, not looking at Lyle, her emerald-green mask turned downward, speaking in a barely audible, trem-*

bling voice): "I... like some of what Dr. Lyle says, but... what you claim about his possible effect on our orderly society... well, it makes me pause to declare him innocent. So, I guess... I think that..."

240 **Fanatic** (*angrily jumping-up, demanding attention*): "DON'T 'THINK,' WOMAN! IT DOESN'T MATTER WHAT YOU WANT! JUST DO WHAT'S RIGHT!"

241 **Seeker** (*her emerald mask jerking upward as she abruptly twists in her seat to directly face the risen Fanatic*): "*What* did you say?"

242 **Fanatic**: (*yelling in exasperation*) "CAST THE DECIDING VOTE, WOMAN! FROM THE CONVENING AUTHORITY OF ALMIGHTY GOD, THREE OUT OF FIVE VOTES ON THIS PANEL CONDEMNS LYLE AND DESTROYS ONCE AND FOR ALL HIS SATANIC DOCTRINES! MINE, THE CRITIC'S, AND YOUR VOTE MAKE THREE! SO LET'S END THIS FARCE RIGHT NOW! STAND IN SUPPORT OF THE WISE, MATURE, MALE LEADERSHIP OF THIS PANEL---THOSE THAT KNOW BETTER THAN YOU! JUST STAY IN YOUR GOD-ORDAINED SUBMISSIVE STANCE AND *DO AS WE TELL YOU TO DO!* CAST THE DECIDING VOTE!"

243 **Seeker** (*as the Fanatic arrogantly lowered himself back into his seat, she slowly turning back to directly face the Lawyer at the opposite end of the marble table---speaking now firmly and resolutely*): "Well... if that's what you think of me! Then I declare Lyle to be... innocent! Maybe his 'new' religion isn't actually all that new or different. But at least he's *trying* to help us advance closer to God, not just retreating into *arrogance* and *threats*!"

244 **Fanatic** (*his voice seething with menace*): "You lowly, stupid woman---*you* will be damned *along* with Lyle! You will suffer his fate! I'll slice your neck along with his! That is, unless you *change* your vote! Do so! Do so *now*, or else you will be judged a heretic along with him!"

245 **Seeker** (*now staring resolutely straight ahead*): "I... WILL... *NOT!*"

246 **Lawyer** (*quickly interjecting*): "---and what say *you*, Bystander?"

247 **Bystander** (*squirming in his seat, his head lolling back and forth, as if he were in great pain*): "Don't make me... don't make me do it... I can't do this..."

248 **Critic** (*speaking to the Bystander slowly and seemingly tenderly*): "It is good that you have this chance to prove your value to your community, Bystander. You may be just a youngster, but you can still clearly see

what's right and wrong! Don't be deluded by Lyle's faulty though seductive logic! The 'group-think' of centuries is far more powerful than your own confused ideas! If you follow the lead of the Fanatic and me you will find comfort, safety, and ease. Follow Lyle's example and you will sadly find yourself thrown into uncertainty, heavy responsibility, and painfully-difficult choices. Surely you don't want a spiritual life that puts its highest priority and emphasis on confusing, difficult, and dangerous 'work'---do you? Stay happily in your own established religion's dictates! They've stood the test of time! Your religion offers established Truth! Your parents are there, aren't them? You probably have other friends and family there also! You need only sit back, agree with what's taught, and follow instructions from those who know far better than you as to what's *really* right and wrong! The danger is minimal because you are securely on a safe path. It's not confusing because you know what's right and wrong! It's not difficult because you only need follow instructions! Since the Seeker failed in her duty, *you* can be the one to cast the deciding vote, right now! You'll be a young hero! Your religious leaders at your particular place of worship will be proud of you!"

249 **Bystander** (*looking up now, squarely into Lyle's unhidden, solemn face*): "But... but..."

250 **Fanatic** (*flourishing his glittering knife high over his head*): "CONDEMN HIM, YOU LITTLE *IDIOT*! You know nothing! You're just a child! There's nothing for you to have to think about! I and the Critic have already shown you what is true and right!   VOTE LYLE 'GUILTY'...NOW! Or do you want to join him and the Seeker in receiving my righteous wrath!?"

251 **Bystander** (*reaching out a trembling, blue-gloved hand to the Seeker, who grabs on tightly with her green-gloved hand*): "Well... I suppose... I guess... No! I'm *not* stupid! My life is my own, not yours! And Mr. Lyle is *innocent*! I'm not going to lie just to make things easier for me! All that you and the others tried to do---except for Ms. Seeker---was to try to make me into what *you* want! You just want to *use* me to get whatever it is that you want! He was *nice* to me, *really* nice! Nice for *my* good, not just for his good! HE ASKED ME WHAT I WANTED! Maybe I am just a kid---but I *can* think for myself! And I won't make Mr. Lyle guilty for something he is not! You should just let him go!"

252 **Lawyer** (*slowly standing up, firmly crossing his arms, and looking across the rest of the Judges*): "So, Lyle. It appears that your fate rests in my hands. The votes are now tied: two for guilty and two for innocent. It falls on me to cast the deciding vote. You can probably guess what my vote is... But I have no wish to harm you needlessly. I'll give you one last chance.   Will you now *recant* your illegal, disruptive philosophy---

submitting yourself to the valid, established, tradition-affirmed Laws and Precedence of Religion and Society?"

253 **Lyle** (*staring stoically forwards*): "NO!"

254 **Lawyer** (*shrugging sadly*): "Ok, then. You've clearly put yourself above the Law---when you are not! I have no other option than to pronounce you *guilty* of heresy. By commission and authority of the Almighty who assembled us here and proclaimed our mandate, this panel by a vote of three to two convicts you of flaunting the traditions, precedence, authorities, and established Laws of society. And in considering your punishment, I note that you are, indeed, the *worst* sort of criminal---one that recognizes no authority but his own! Even though you speak mild, slick words you are obviously capable of any perversity. When individuals take into their own hands total power they will inevitably become tyrants, rogues, and monsters. You, Sir, are a societal *monster*: one who richly deserves the *severest* punishment at the hands of this august panel of Judges!"

255 **Lyle** (*speaking softly, resigning himself to the verdict*): "So... just what is to be my fate, then?"

256 **Lawyer** (*now speaking matter-of-factly in an almost friendly tone of voice*): "You must be made an example. It is not enough that you be erased from history. We need to hold you up---in whatever memories or writings might come from this trial---as a reminder that we humans survive and function in cooperative societies, maintained by the Rule of Law. That 'rule' may be the law of a loving husband over his submissive wife and family; or the considered product of duly-elected legislators; or regulations from governmental agencies; or guidelines from standard-setting bodies; or the norms of societal behavior; or attendance and performance requirements of schools and jobs; or the moral mandates and traditions of established religions... whatever! The freedom of form and thought which you preach is just too extreme! As you yourself admit, you are a RADICAL! So in light of our findings, I decree your punishment to be the following: 1) that you be *bound hand and foot*; 2) that you then be *tied* to that useless, ugly stump of wood at our backs; and then, 3)---by ancient tradition of how evil witches and past heretics were executed---you are to be *burned alive!*"

. . . .

Sentencing and Punishment

257 **Fanatic** (*speaking happily and quickly*): "Yes! Excellent sentence, Lawyer! LET OUR ALMIGHTY LOVING GOD'S BLAZING POWER INCINERATE THIS SATANIC DISCIPLE! Yes, this heretic *should* be made an example! But burning him at the stake may be too swift! He may not suffer enough to deter others from making his same mistake! I volunteer to cut him up before we stake him! I can extend his suffering! He should feel the grief that his lies would have brought to thousands or millions of innocent souls! Lyle should experience a thousand cuts all over his body, and *then* to be burned alive!"

258 **Critic** (*quickly chiming in*): "Yes, I agree with the Fanatic! Those are very appropriate punishments! Lawyer and Fanatic, I see no holes in your logic! But.... perhaps I could suggest an addition? After burning Lyle at the stake, I say we should gather up his charred bones and toss them over the side of the cliff! That way there will be no burial, no memorial... no urn! His remains will be thrown away like those fancy fruits that sprouted from the tree only to fall and rot! Let there be no dignity or grace to his passing!"

259 **Lawyer** (*nodding repeatedly at the affirmations of Fanatic and Critic*): "Such is the will of this God-ordained panel. We will torture him with the knife, burn him at the stake, and toss his remains to the winds! Lyle, are you ready to face your punishment?"

260 Outside the protecting shield, the raging blizzard now abruptly abated... the clouds high up above them parting... revealing a spectacular night sky.

261 The surrounding, lower peaks stood out of the mists as dark Giants... their heads held high, proud, and solid---as seemingly eternal, impassive witnesses;

262 A full moon moved out from behind the last retreating clouds, casting everything into a dim silvery glow: highlighting an unworldly panorama of fogs and mountains... and above it all a vast sea of shimmering, twinkling stars spread out across the heavens: in Lyle's awestruck eyes, a diamond carpet of Divinity;

263 The Lawyer seemingly-politely awaited Lyle's answer... while it seemed that the Heavens also awaited Lyle's arrival: his weary footsteps on his long journey coming to an end; now facing his last trembling moments of hideous torture... but hardly worth noting compared to what truly awaited him in ever-higher levels of reality... convinced that his ul-

timate destination was more splendid, amazing, and prominent than anything else---positive or negative---found here on the earth.

²⁶⁴ Lyle took a moment to contemplate not just the majestic night sky but also his immediate environment... including the bare rock upon which he stood, the white marble table, the black-robed Judges, the skeletal tree looming behind them all, the sheer cliffs on all sides plunging down into cold swirling mists thousands of feet below...

²⁶⁵ ---just a few feet away in any direction a quick "way out" if he wished it... a fast sprint that no one there could stop---surely the Lord would let him breach the protecting dome... a leap over the edge to thwart the torture of the eager Judges... very tempting to escape the waiting horror... but...

²⁶⁶ **Lyle** (*taking a deep breath and squared his shoulders before replying to the Lawyer*): "When the Founders of the great traditional religions did not shirk from the penalties for their so-called 'heretical' beliefs, how can I who am less than they not follow in their footsteps? I choose to walk the Golden Path to its earthly end, whether it is easy or hard. I am ready..."

²⁶⁷ **Lawyer** (*shaking his head slowly from side to side, seemingly sympathetically*): "For the very last time, Lyle, I remind you that there is still time to recant your heresy. We, your Judges, are not evil or bad people! We merely stand in defense of society, true religion, and God's most-Holy Honor. We take no pleasure in inflicting upon you the terrible pain you are about to experience. We are not torturers. We will gladly let you go your way in peace if only you will publicly---here before man and God---repent the error of your ways! But, be perfectly assured, if you persist in your blasphemy against God, then you must be made a horrific example that will deter others from making your same mistake in the future... should others somehow know of you despite our best efforts to erase your life! Your crime is too dangerous to allow even a hint of legitimacy! Even some of your fellow Judges were almost deceived by your poisonous but seductive words! You played on Bystander's youth to cause him or her to question his or her elders! You twisted Seeker's noble desire to move ever-closer to God to cause her to doubt her traditions and think that her own thoughts might be more important than time-honored Dogma or abject submission to accepted male Authority! We cannot allow the chaos that might result if even-weaker minded people than that of the child and the woman here should hear your words! We have to stop your heresy right here, as dictated and sanctioned by the Lord! But if you'll just acknowledge how stupid and selfish you've been with this so-called 'Creative-Theology®' then you can go ahead and live out your little life in peace! Just admit you were wrong! After all, Lyle, consider the facts! No

one is interested in your 'new' religion! No one wants it! People are quite content and happy with their established traditions, rituals, doctrines, and ceremonies! As you stand here before us it has to be obvious even to your own devious mind that you are a total *failure*! Just admit the truth and you will be spared! If there were, say, thousands or millions of people clamoring for your new teachings or wanting to apply its dictates... then maybe you'd have a small case to make here! But there aren't and you don't! Why die in agony for something that nobody wants except for you? Spare yourself any more pain! Recant! Admit that your Creative-Theology® is just plain *wrong*!"

[268] **Lyle** (*struck to the heart with the truth of some of the Lawyer's chilling indictment, uncertain and starting to waver*): "I... I... I suppose... it's true that there's no one asking for what I have to give... no crowds clamoring for me to speak... few have even read any of my writings... You're correct, I suppose... I can see and admit where I've failed to-date... but... but... I am... I am *stubborn*! AND IT IS NOT JUST MY PRIDE OR SELFISHNESS THAT MAKES ME THAT WAY! *God* made me to be as I am! God put these images into my mind! God made me *question* things... but not for me to be cruel or disruptive... but rather to look to the Purpose, the Core, the Heart, and the AIM of what you and I claim to be doing! And if our actions don't match up to our rhetoric, then... then... surely there must be a better way!? Does not God want us to be and do ever-better in following Him, in seeking Him, and in perceiving Him? IS THIS NOT WHAT THE FOUNDERS OF THE GREAT TRADITIONAL RELIGIONS ALL TRIED TO ACCOMPLISH? I don't want to bother people who are content with their religion or spirituality! I'm not looking to impose anything on them or insist that they change their lives to suit my fancies! But there *are* people in the world like our Seeker---perhaps many of them---who are not satisfied with what's been handed down to them religiously or spiritually! They feel a gap, they see inconsistencies, and they know full-well that their talents are not properly utilized! They notice blatant hypocrisy! They see their Leaders falling far short of the aspirations of their own Founders! They see teachings from Holy Writings ignored, explained-away, or discarded by those who demand blind obedience! Thus they see noble Principles by their Founders twisted and perverted by their current religious Leaders! Also, they see the Godly-potential of God's followers unrealized while God's Creativity is *crushed* by those who should be appreciating it the most! The unsatisfied Seekers instinctively realize that Godliness is more than just conforming to the present dictates of one's society or placing Tradition above everything else or mindlessly trudging through the ceremonies of one's religion! GOD DID NOT PUT US HERE TO BE BIOLOGICAL ROBOTS THAT MINDLESSLY ACCEPT OUR GENETIC, TRIBAL, OR RELIGIOUS PROGRAMMING! The Founders of the world's Great Religions all spoke against the established 'truth' of their respective soci-

eties! They *also* faced outraged defenders of Dogma---like you---whether of the political or religious ilk! The accepted Leaders of their worlds condemned them also, just as you do now to me! I certainly don't claim to have the status of the Founders or be in conflict with their core Principles at all! And did they not *also* face disdain, rejection, imprisonment, torture, and even brutal execution? And were those terrible persecutions not done all for the very same 'reason' that you claim even here today as your primary justification---to defend the status quo? You *don't* ask the question: '*How can we be even better at following God?*' You *don't* ask: "*Could we possibly learn something useful from Lyle for moving even closer to God?*" You have not the slightest thought of: "*Maybe most of his stuff is junk, but could he have perhaps one small insight that would help us be and do better?*" *Instead* you ask the question: "*How can we stop anyone who dares question what we teach?*" YOUR GREAT SIN IS TO PRESUME UNQUESTIONABLE PERFECTION! Whereas the Holy Texts and the Great Founders raised existential Questions you brand anyone doing the same today as a heretic! To you, the very act off asking important questions is the very definition of 'heresy'! Using the excuse of being a 'conservative' who sees his number-one duty to 'protect the Truth' you belittle and destroy so-called 'liberals' who dare to say that God's Truth is dynamically 'multi-dimensional'! In your arrogance and selfishness to arrogate yourselves into Absolute Judges you attempt to FREEZE God into your designated 'box'... where you neatly define the characteristics of the *UNKNOWNABLE Mystery* which is 'God'---changing the Almighty into something you can easily grasp and manipulate and use to justify your own interests! You claim to defend society while in truth you are defending your own 'golden calf' *idols* that change religion and spirituality into your *own* petrified image! Your AIM is clearly *not* to help people use their God-given talents in pleasing God the best ways possible, but to make sure that everybody believes and does what Tradition has certified for maintaining your own physical, mental, and spiritual *comfort*! And your *biggest* sin---common to many religious Leaders, not just to you who stand on this peak with me today---is to *kill the joy* of your very own young-people in following God! The youth of religious congregations, like the Bystander, should be *embraced* and *enlivened* by their religious Leaders: to grow in leaps and bounds *by* questioning and careful experimentation! Instead, they are hammered into tight little boxes and ordered to say 'thank you' for their imprisonment! That's *you*! For the sake of maintaining your own position, power, and prestige---you *drain the Joy of God* from the people under your authority! Instead of growing the ever-present Positives to push-out the negatives, you obsess on the Negatives, killing the Positives! You are outraged that others have *splinters* in their eyes while ignoring the *logs* stuck in your own! You've changed Righteousness from a joyful Adventure moving ever-closer to God to a mean crusade attempting to condemn and stamp out 'sin'! You have no concern for 'throwing out the baby with the dirty bathwater' in doing any evil thing necessary to hide your own hypocrisy! You are happy to divide and destroy congregations over vague generalities, trivial practices, theoretical outcomes, slightly-differing doctrines, and personal preferences. You reject any proposal to do better for God because of so-called flaws---whether real or imagined---finding any excuse for casting it aside! You elevate Form over Purpose! You forget the great Godly Principles while insisting on their 'approved' specific application in the lives of all those under your control! You stifle Innovation in order to bore people with sanctioned-Stagnation---claiming that this very stagnation is what God wants from us! The great Initiators of the leaps-ahead-in-spiritual-growth throughout the history of mankind *were not you*! They were *me*! And I say that not because I am anything special, but because I AM AT LEAST *TRYING* TO FOLLOW IN THE EXAMPLE OF THE GREAT FOUNDERS OF THE ESTABLISHED RELIGIONS: TO *WALK* IN THEIR FOOTSTEPS, TO *THINK* AS THEY THOUGHT, TO ACTUALLY *DO* WHAT *THEY* TAUGHT... TO *BE* WHAT THE FOUNDERS WANTED THEIR FOLLOWERS TO BE! You and your ilk have ignored the harder teachings of your own religions! Where you could not just ignore those demanding Principles, you 'explained' them away! You are adept at 'proving' why your Holy Texts don't really mean what they clearly say! You've taken dynamic teachings and made them into static lists of rules---'do's and don'ts', 'rights and wrongs', 'true or false' dichotomies---that have perverted and dulled the original, scintillating Principles! You've changed sympathetic, helpful Love into cruel, dispiriting hate. You've chosen to rule not by mature, parental love---but by childish, selfish hate! You claim to love the 'sinner' so much that you are *happy* to crush, torture, and kill that person in the name of a loving God! You claim you are sad to have to silence, marginalize, and kick-out 'trouble-makers' while your black hearts dance with joy! In your zeal to tame and domesticate the life-altering Challenges of your own Founders you have nailed them to the crosses of your own inflexible doctrines! If the Founder of your Great Religion were to walk in the door of your place of worship, you'd quickly escort them out! You have *forgotten* the teachings of your Founders and instead enshrined Comforting Tradition in their place! In your quest to control the people under you, you've dictated the details of their unknowable futures! I SEE NOW WHY GOD SENT ME HERE TO THE TOP OF THIS BARREN PEAK! IT WAS NOT TO PUT ME ON TRIAL---BUT YOU! I AM HERE TO 'ROCK' YOU OUT OF *YOUR* COMPLACENCY AND ARROGANCE! BY GIVING YOU THE PRESTIGE OF BEING 'JUDGES' GOD IS TRICKING YOU INTO EXAMINING YOUR *OWN* POSITIONS! BY ALLOWING YOU TO 'INTEROGATE' ME, THE LORD IS FORCING YOU TO ACKNOWLEDGE QUESTIONING THAT YOU'D NEVER LISTEN TO OTHERWISE! YOU'RE NO LONGER 'PREACHING TO THE CHOIR' WHERE NO ONE CAN TALK BACK, QUESTION YOU, OR ARGUE WITH YOU! INSTEAD, YOU NOW HAVE THE DIVINE OPPORTUNITY TO SEE THE LIE IN

YOUR OWN PERVERTED POSITIONS! YOUR OSSIFIED DOGMA IS THAWED AND EXPOSED FOR WHAT IT IS---SELF-SERVING POISONS! But instead of being grateful to God for this opportunity, you are so in love with your own 'virtue' that you refuse to even acknowledge the possibility of your own corruption! You follow in the footsteps not of your Founders but in the despicable example of *their* murderers! It is those past religious and societal leaders who defiled their own Holy teachings, who thought they had the right to murder those righteous 'trouble-makers'! Where you should happily run to embrace moving ever-closer to your Founders you reject that very exercise as heresy! You brand anyone who dares question your beloved Traditions as evil heretics! You decry those that question your interpretations of your Holy Texts while you ignore whole parts and blithely add other convenient teachings at will! Rather than *face your own failings to live up to your own Founder's teachings*, you put *your* accusers to the stake---just as did the earthly judges of your Founders! But God saw fit by the martyrdom of the original 'heretics' to catapult His true overarching Cause to inspire thousands, millions, and even billions---causing them to 'grow-up' just a little bit more into true Godliness! Yes, few if any know of or listen to my particular religious-spiritual message. But there was a time when few if any knew of or listened to the revelations of each of the Great Founders! Knowing that God chose to use their failures to move billions of people closer to Himself... how can I just hang my head and quit when I face the same fate? How dare I shrink from the path God has set before me? How can I deny that which I know to be true just to avoid a brief flash of pain in order to live a few more cosmic micro-seconds? And just what is it that you offer me to recant the truth? Is it just to be one of you? You think that it is some great reward for me to become a little copy of you? Or is what you offer me the fantasy of thinking I have all the answers? Is it to lord myself over others? Is it to feel superior to other of my fellow humans? Or is it merely for me to feel comfortable right now at this moment? Or is it in a mere few, brief years to experience a more-pleasant death? Do you offer me anything that's edifying, inspiring, or productive? Whether you kill me here in agony or I die in a few years peacefully in bed is of no great matter! Either way in a cosmic instant I'm gone from this short life! I am not afraid of you people! You can kill my body, sure... but my soul is untouchable! It is enshrined in a Crystal Cathedral rising beyond your reach upon the ever-ascending Golden Path! And even though you may erase my appearance here upon this lonely peak, I know that God is greater than you! Somehow, in some way, I am convinced that the tenants of Creative-Theology® will continue beyond my death! And what I did here today will somehow be part of that legacy. So, if you still feel you must gleefully arrogate God's power to pronounce Final Judgment unto yourselves... *then do what you must!* I have FAITH in the true GOD that He can use any man or woman's earthly 'failure' to

His Glory---and from the ashes of that so-called 'defeat' He will bring Victory!"

²⁶⁹ At the end of Lyle's impassioned speech, the Bystander ducked his head down, weeping loudly. The Seeker turned to the smaller form beside her, cradling the child in her arms. The Critic, Fanatic, and Lawyer, however, as one *jumped* from their seats, *rushed* around the table, and menacingly *surrounded* Lyle...

²⁷⁰ ---*outraged* at his cutting accusations to *them*, they grabbed his outer shirt, ripping it off his body and tearing it into strips; also yanking up and off his undershirt to push him bare-chested down onto the icy rocks below their feet...

²⁷¹ ---firmly tying his legs together with strips of the torn clothes, forcing his hands behind his back, tying them so tight that the bonds cut into the flesh, his blood spurting out... circulation to his fingers blocked, his hands going numb...

²⁷² ---the frozen rocks sucking warmth out of his half-naked body, being dragged along the rocks, and then thrown up against the twisted, furrowed, tree trunk...

²⁷³ ---using his intact T-shirt to encircle both his neck and the wood behind him they knotted it tightly at the back of the tree, pinning him firmly to the rough surface;

²⁷⁴ ---as Lyle struggled to keep breathing, "*keep on keeping on*" to the very last... his vision beginning to blur, seeing the glint of a sharp knife held up in front of his eyes; hovering there, intimidating him, drawing-out the terror...

²⁷⁵ **Lawyer** (*his yellow mask glowing brighter and brighter, shimmering heat-waves now emanating from his black eye-cups*): "Almighty God has given me the Flame of Purity! Lyle, the same sunshine that glows from my face will burst forth and ignite both your clothing and the rotted wood at your back! In stark contrast to your pitiful lie that we have 'arrogated' righteous judgment---God's Power is clearly evident in me! Your ignorant tirade of a minute ago against me, the Fanatic, and the Critic is thusly proven to be wrong! YOU WILL BE CONSUMED IN A RIGHTEOUS INFERNO THAT'S FUELED BY THE POWER OF GOD HIMSELF! Your death will be a sweet offering to God Almighty! The smoke of your burnt flesh will rise up as sweet perfume to our Heavenly Father! The destruction of both you and this useless old tree that clings pathetically to the top of this hideous mountain will protect many innocent humans, far into the future! Your pathetic last hope of becoming

some sort of unknown, unrecognized, unwanted 'martyr' will be burnt up! Instead, innocents now and in the future will be inoculated against pursuing the twisted logic that confused both the simple Bystander and the misguided Seeker. Thus you will never raise the futile aspirations of many humans to think that they can be more than just followers. God in His Great Wisdom has decreed that only a few of us superior intellects are designated to be the Leaders. There are few Leaders and many Followers. You, Lyle, are *not* one of the leaders. You are nothing. Your arrogant quest to subvert the rules of the true God-ordained Leaders of humanity is at an end! Your blasphemous doctrines will die with you. No one will even know what you've written. Your words will be nipped in the bud, *un*-sprouted, *un*-flowered, and unrealized. Not one person will read any of it! And you will forever remain as you are now... a total failure! But... *one last chance* to you! You accuse us of glee at the prospect of killing you! True, we do feel joy at fulfilling the will of God and destroying evil! But we are sad to cause pain to anyone! One more time I insist upon proving that we three here who voted for your execution are not monsters! We are the true servants of God! So if you will just agree to become an obedient Follower of *us*---the so-called 'Critic', the so-called 'Fanatic', and me the so-called 'Lawyer'---then you can still be spared this awful death! Put your faith and talents to work in proclaiming established interpretations of Holy Writings---following time-tested, certified Doctrines-Rituals-Traditions---and in pleasing your properly-ordained Religious Leaders... and then you can live out a peaceful, comfortable, long life! This is your *last* chance, Lyle. Won't you please recant the error of your ways? REFUSE AND YOU WILL FACE THE FULL POWER OF THE CONSUING FLAMES OF GOD!"

[276] **Lyle** (*peering through bleary eyes straight ahead past the silvery knife blade at the hotly-glowing shimmering yellow mask, gasped weakly*): "If... that be... my path to Divinity... then I accept it... bring it on...!"

[277] **Lawyer** (*speaking regally and loudly*): "THEN LET NO ONE SAY YOU WERE NOT GIVEN EVERY CHANCE TO REPENT OF YOUR SINS... any last words, Lyle?"

[278] **Lyle** (*struggling to speak, coughing, and barely managing to gasp past the choking bindings on his neck*): "It's... been interesting... to be... here... but... I'm *glad*... to be going... home..."

[279] **Fanatic** (*laying the cold blade right alongside Lyle's nose*): "---but not before your blood drenches the rocks around us! You'll be glad for the cleansing fire when I'm through carving you up!"

280 ---as with a loud *implosion*, THE PROTECTING BUBBLE ABOVE THEM *BURST*... icy wind sweeping down across the peaks' top, tossing everyone around with its hurricane force;

281 Black-robed figures lurching and sliding, yelling-out in surprise, grabbing at Lyle and the tree, latching onto the heavy marble tabletop... momentarily, everyone stabilized!

282 Gasping for breath in the now thinned, high-mountain air... the Fanatic raised his blade, still determined to carry out the sentence of the panel... poised to *plunge* it into Lyle's neck when abruptly he was KNOCKED BACKWARDS...

283 **Bystander** (*kicking fiercely at the Fanatic who now lay sprawled on the rocks; the child grabbing-at the knife still held tight in Fanatic's hand, shouting against the howling gale*): "I WON'T LET YOU HURT HIM! LET GO OF THAT KNIFE!"

284 **Fanatic** (*struggling to right himself, to push away the shorter Bystander, shouting back at him*): "---ARE YOU CRAZY!?? LET GO OF ME, YOU LITTLE RUNT!"

285 **Bystander** (*grabbing the Fanatic now around his neck with an encircling small but fury-powered arm*): "I'M *NOT* LITTLE! HE TOLD ME THAT I'M *BIG*! GOD MAKES ME BIG! GOD WANTS YOU TO STOP TRYING TO HURT MR. LYLE! GOD BURST THE BUBBLE! *YOU'RE* THE WEAK, 'LITTLE' ONE, YOU *CREEP*!"

286 The Fanatic managed to jerk up to his feet, staggering in another burst of the icy wind... slipped! He lost his grip on the silvery blade which dropped and bounced...

287 ---the glittering blade sliding to a stop, falling down into a low crevice; the Fanatic frantically leaning over and grasping down for it as he simultaneously tried to beat-off the still-clinging child...

288 Bystander now with both his legs wrapped tight around the Fanatic's gut, his arms locked in a stranglehold at the Fanatic's neck right below the glittering, mirrored mask...

289 ---stumbling, Fanatic's left hand flailed around in a circle as he lost his balance... then managed to stop dead-still, looking down, shocked to find himself with the clinging Bystander on his back precariously poised at the very edge of the plunging cliff...

²⁹⁰ **Fanatic** (*screaming-out in terror, gasping in Bystander's relentlessly-choking grip*): "GET... OFF... OF... ME! YOU'LL MAKE US *BOTH* FALL!"

²⁹¹ **Bystander** (*still with his death-grip around the Fanatic's neck*): "*HAH*! NOT SO LITTLE, NOW, AM I!???"

²⁹² ---as with all his strength the Bystander doubled-forward, pulling the Fanatic's head down... as *locked-together they both tumbled over the edge of the cliff*:

²⁹³ ---in an instant vanishing together into the mists far below, a long SCREAM by the Fanatic lingering... punctuated by a faint, far-off "thud".

²⁹⁴ **Critic** (*clinging tightly to Lyle's feet, yelling over at the Lawyer who, though blown across the rocks in the blasting wind, still managed to cling to the edge of the heavy marble tabletop*): "YOU'LL NEVER GET YOUR PURIFYING FIRE STARTED IN THIS HURRICANE BLAST, LAWYER! I'M SENDING LYLE ON HIS WAY, AFTER THE FANATIC! I'LL UNTIE HIM FROM THE TREE AND JUST PUSH HIM OVER THE CLIFF!"

²⁹⁵ Lyle felt the strangling T-shirt ripped from around his throat. He slumped forward and fell face-first onto the hard rock. He felt himself being dragged, helpless. His legs were still tied securely, his hands bound as well behind his back...

²⁹⁶ ---slowly being dragged inch-by-inch against the hard rocks, face down, closer and closer to the edge of the small plateau... glimpsing the Seeker coming up beside him, as she staggered under the weight of a heavy crystalline chair...

²⁹⁷ ---which she sent SMASHING-down onto the back of the Critic who yelped in surprise as he was knocked to the rocks, frantically pushing himself away from the still-advancing Seeker...

²⁹⁸ **Critic** (*groaning in pain from broken bones, sprawled on his back, now facing up at the Seeker*): "WHAT ARE YOU DOING? YOU'VE GOT IT ALL WRONG! *LYLE* IS YOUR ENEMY, NOT ME! DON'T ATTACK ME! WHAT'S THE MATTER WITH YOU?!"

²⁹⁹ **Seeker** (*again laboriously lifting high the heavy stone chair, advancing inexorably on the downed Critic, speaking through chokes and sobs*): "NOTHING'S WRONG WITH ME! DEAR BYSTANDER WAS RIGHT! YOU NEVER SEE POSSIBILITIES, CRITIC---ONLY THE

RISKS! WELL, BY GOD, I'M GOING TO GIVE YOU WHAT YOU MOST DESIRE: *NONE* OF THE POSITIVES, AND *ALL* OF THE NEGATIVES!"

300 **Lyle** (*squirming over on his side to look up, vainly trying to loosen the strips of cloth binding his feet and arms, managing to gasp out a few words as the blasting wind rolled him onto his back*): "SEEKER... STOP... HE'S HELPLESS NOW..."

301 **Seeker** (*laughing through her sobs*): "SO YOU'RE STILL TRYING TO LIVE UP TO YOUR OWN TEACHINGS? SHUT UP, DR. LYLE! I'LL *NOT* BE HELD BACK BY HIS DISTORTIONS ANYMORE!"

302 She paused just above the groaning figure sprawled-out before her. Then she quite deliberately allowed the heavy chair to drop square onto the Critic's upturned head. Lyle heard the man's skull *crush* as his red mask bounced away across the rocks. Seeker turned away from the now limp, bloodied form to take a staggering step in the whistling wind menacingly toward the Lawyer as he pulled himself up by holding firmly onto the solid marble table.

303 **Seeker** (*staggering another step towards the Lawyer, leaning forward against the blasting wind, shouting out her words*): "---AND YOU, LAWYER, ARE THE WORST ONE OF THEM ALL! YOU SAY YOU'RE PROTECTING SOCIETY, BUT YOU CARE NOTHING FOR JUSTICE! YOU DEFEND WHOEVER PAYS YOU A SALARY! TO YOU, 'RIGHT' AND 'WRONG' ARE JUST ACADEMIC DEBATING POINTS! HOW DARE YOU CALL YOURSELF A 'DEFENDER OF GOD'S LAWS' WHEN YOU DON'T EVEN KNOW THE MEANING OF THE WORDS COMING OUT OF YOUR UGLY MOUTH?!"

304 **Lawyer** (*shouting back at her as he struggled to hold onto the marble table in the swirling, icy gusts*): "IF I AM SO WRONG, THEN WHY IS IT THAT GOD HAS GIVEN ME SUCH AWESOME POWER? HE APPOINTED ME TO BE IN CHARGE OF THIS PANEL AND IT IS BY HIS DIVINE WILL THAT MY MASK SHOOTS OUT HEAVENLY FIRE! YOU, 'SEEKER', ARE JUST A DISTRACTION! IT IS *YOU* THAT IS MERELY A 'DEBATING-POINT'! YOU ADDED *NOTHING* TO THESE PROCEEDINGS! YOU SHOULD NEVER HAVE BEEN HERE *AT ALL!*"

305 **Seeker** (*wavering in the powerful gusts, her forward motion slowing as the mind-numbing cold drained her strength... bending down stiffly to retrieve the Fanatic's knife from the small crevice into which it had fallen... holding the knife firmly by its solid black haft held tight in her small, green-gloved hand... the sharp point of the knife aimed straight at the Lawyer*): "GOD USES ALL SORTS OF EVIL THINGS TO TEACH PEOPLE, INCLUDING YOU! THE OPPRESSED CAN ONLY BE

HELD IN PLACE FOR SO LONG BY THREATS AND INTIMIDATION, LAWYER! THEN THEY WILL RISE UP AND *CHANGE* THE RULES! AND THE HATED OLD GUARD, LIKE YOU, WILL *DIE*! SO LET'S JUST HURRY IT ALONG, WHAT DO YOU SAY?! I'LL SHOW YOU RIGHT NOW WHAT A 'NOTHING' CAN DO...!"

306 **Lawyer** (*aiming his now-pulsating, yellow-glowing mask straight at her*): "I THINK NOT!"

307 ---as suddenly his mask gleamed *white-hot* and A TORRENT OF BLISTERING *FIRE* ERUPTED OUT...

308 ---and Seeker was caught in its full blast, instantly *set afire* from head to foot...

309 ---silently flailing-about, her black robes turned into red wings...

310 ---as, seemingly accepting her fate, she settled down to her knees...

311 ---and, bowing her burning head, she lifted up green-gloved hands to the sky...

312 ---as in mere moments the roaring inferno consumed her body...

313 ---and nothing was left of Seeker save a smoking pile of blackened bones and ash...

314 **Lawyer** (*gasping in the thin, high air as he laboriously rose from the table and staggered over to Lyle; coughing, dropping to both knees, grabbing protruding rocks to try and maintain his position against the howling wind. His yellow mask tilted upward to the heavens. He stared for a moment at the full, glaringly-white, night-sky moon... seemingly lost in thought...then yelled down into Lyle's face*): "SOME-TIME IT IS HARD TO FOLLOW THE RULES, LYLE! CRIMINALS ABOUND...WHO MUST BE *PUNISHED*! YOU, LYLE, ARE ONE SUCH. YOU CORRUPTED THE POOR SEEKER AND THE YOUNG CHILD, GOD REST THEIR SOULS. I DIDN'T WANT TO HURT HER... BUT GOD REQUIRED IT! YOU SEE, LYLE, JUSTICE STILL PREVAILS... IT SEEMS THAT MOTHER NATURE AND CIRCUMSTANCE MADE OUR JOB MORE DIFFICULT THAN IT HAD TO BE. I'VE DEPLETED THE POWER IN MY MASK SO I'LL NOT BE ABLE TO GIVE YOU THE SAME FATE THAT SEEKER RECEIVED... BUT PRAISE GOD I CAN YET FINISH MY TASK ELSEWISE..."

315 He slowly crawled over to what remained of Seeker, brushing-back still-glowing embers and pawing through the charred bone-fragments and pieces of burnt flesh...

316 ---triumphantly snatching-out Fanatic's knife, burnt but still sharp... wiping away soot on his own black robes as he crawled in the bone-chilling blast back to Lyle...

317 ---and crept up onto Lyle's legs, pinning him flat, the blade poised above Lyle's torso, aimed straight at Lyle's chest... the haft now held firmly in both of Lawyer's yellow-gloved hands, *his weight poised behind the blade to ram the dagger straight down into Lyle's heart...*

318 **Lawyer** (*his pulsating, yellow mask glaring directly down into Lyle's squinted eyes*): "AND SO YOU JOIN YOUR FRIENDS 'SEEKER' AND 'BYSTANDER' WHO SCORNED BOTH THE RULES AND THE APPOINTED RULE-MAKERS! GOOD RIDDANCE TO YOU ALL...!"

319 ---as with a yell of triumph, the Lawyer threw all his weight downward, *slamming* his entire upper body onto the knife pointed straight into Lyle's chest, driving the blade in to its hilt...

320 Lyle had all the breath knocked out of him but curiously felt no pain, looking directly into the black eye-cups covering the Lawyer's eyes...

321 It seemed to Lyle that *tears* were forming behind those enigmatic cups, moistening their edges... when the man abruptly jerked backwards and stared in horror down at his own hands...

322 **Lawyer** (*gasping weakly, such that Lyle could barely hear him*): "What?... But... How??..."

323 Both of the Lawyer's yellow-gloved hands were still firmly locked together around the black haft of the knife... but the Lawyer stared in disbelief, shaking his head back and forth, *moaning...*

324 ---as blood burbled out rich and red, spreading from a deep wound, the blade imbedded to its hilt *not* in Lyle's chest... but in the Lawyer's...!

325 Who, groaning in agony, slowly pulled the knife back out, inch by inch... then let it drop to the side where it clattered on the rocks, smearing them with a grim scarlet;

326 Weakly staggering to his feet, his hands now falling limply to his side, the Lawyer stumbled to the marble tabletop, collapsing face-first down

upon its surface, blood pooling around his crumpled form to drip-over onto the rocks...

327 ---as Lyle, stunned by the events of the last few minutes, LOOKED UP AT WHAT SEEMED TO BE A DESCENDING, GIGANTIC *TORNADO*... and the wind which before was a mere gale turned into a steadily-accelerating BLAST...!

328 Jarred from his stupor, Lyle---with his hands still bound behind his back---*groped for the dropped knife; clutching it in trembling hands then managing to work the blade up towards the bindings*, he started hacking and cutting at them...

329 ---finally feeling the cloth falling-away, he turned to his leg bindings, slashing them. He *jammed the knife securely between his belt and pants, realizing that up in the mountains that might be a good thing to have handy.... simultaneously crawling* to the tree, encircling the trunk with locked arms, and hugging tightly for dear life;

330 ---as the *roaring tornado* loomed above the peak, sucking away Seeker's ashes, lifting up the Lawyer's body and tossing it into the air towards Lyle who managed to grab at the black robes spinning past, yanking them off and holding them close...

331 ---as the corpse spun-away, lifted up into the maelstrom; Lyle with one hand wrapping the sticky fabric around his own bare chest...

332 ---now grabbing the tree trunk more firmly, daring to look upward, seeing *sheets of lightning* crackling and sparkling around all the sides of the descending black funnel... SMASHING into the peak with an incredibly-deafening "ROAR" as all went black around Lyle and he clenched his eyes tightly shut against the maelstrom...

333 ---as Lyle felt the tree trunk *squirm* in his grasp, warm up... growing, twisting... and the intolerable NOISE abruptly stopped. The thin air became wholesome. And in the jarring silence, Lyle tentatively opened his eyes...

334 Seeing in the now silvery, calm moonlight that the gnarled old tree had yet again *changed*... and HE NOW CLUNG NO LONGER TO HARD WOOD BUT PULSING, LIVING *FLESH*!

335 The tree trunk was now the base of a white-robed, wood-sandaled, sword-bearing GIANT covered with fabric-like *spun gold* hanging from shoulders to knees;

336 A broad, brown leather belt encircled the giant's waist; a loop in which rested the iron haft of a long sword, fully a foot across at its widest...

337 Lyle still scrunched-up upon one of its large feet, clutching at a muscular ankle, looking up into eyes high above him that were *not human*... just solid, golden, pulsating LIGHTS...

338 ---where, fully ten feet above Lyle's head, floated a mass of long, ivory hair... as if it were weightless in outer space... its long locks swirling freely about a massive head;

339 The celestial hair floating majestically about the living skull of a mightily-muscled, huge *Warrior*: sporting a long, thick, pure-white beard-mustache sprawling outward;

340 The craggy, ancient, wise, and kindly face calmly peering down at Lyle... huge, powerful hands lightly placed upon wide hips... rope-like veins pumping blood through bulging muscles;

341 Rippling with energy, vitality, power, health, and a wry humor the Giant's voice *boomed like thunder* heard from a safe distance:

342 **The Lord**: "GET OFF MY FEET, LYLE. IT'S TIME WE HAD A TALK."

. . . .

Judgment from God

343 Lyle scurried backwards on his rump, staring up in amazement at the Giant who took one large stride to loom above the marble table. Fully twelve feet long and weighing hundreds of pounds, the table had survived the tornado's blast but now was tipped onto its side.

344 The Warrior reached down with one hand and lifted the marble slab into the air "snapping" off its legs then "cracking" it in half twice. With incredible pressure the giant fused the pieces back together then "thudded" it down onto the rocks as a glistening, majestic *throne*!

345 Settling comfortably down upon it, the Giant casually motioned toward a crystalline chair from one of the judges which still remained on the mountain's peak, one of its legs caught in a crack in the boulders.

346 **The Lord** (*his voice deep and powerful*): "HAVE A SEAT, LYLE. BE COMFORTABLE."

347 **Lyle** (*weakly pushing himself up on trembling legs, wobbling over to the crystal chair, pulling it free, righting it, and then sitting down on it facing the awesome Giant*): "Yes, Lord..."

348 **The Lord**: "ARE THERE NONE REMAINING TO CONDEMN YOU?"

349 **Lyle** (*looking down in fear, just now beginning to grasp the significance of what was happening, speaking in a soft voice*): "No, Lord."

350 **The Lord**: "THEN I SHALL DIRECTLY JUDGE YOUR WORDS AND ACTIONS. YOU MUST ANSWER TRUTHFULLY AND FULLY. DO YOU UNDERSTAND?"

351 **Lyle** (*trying to think clearly, in a state of shock from all that had already transpired*): "I... will do my best... Lord..."

352 For a while there was silence...

353 Lyle was acutely aware that the wind was gone. It was still cold, but not freezing. In fact, Lyle felt like he sat before a welcoming, warming fire.

354 It dawned on Lyle that he was in the very presence of Divinity. Surely it was not the fullness of the Lord, just some sort of a representation. And certainly it was not the entirety of the Lord, just a tiny fraction of His substance.

³⁵⁵ But there at the top of the world, in the stillness of a moonlit night, Lyle knew he was blessed to experience that which few other humans had ever done before him:

³⁵⁶ ---to directly converse with the Source of all inspiration and creativity... the all-knowing, eternal, omnipresent, Almighty God of everything!

³⁵⁷ **The Lord**: "SO, LYLE---ASK ME *YOUR* QUESTIONS."

³⁵⁸ **LYLE** (*uncertain of what to do*): "Lord?"

³⁵⁹ **The Lord**: "YES, I KNOW WHAT IS IN YOUR MIND. YOU NEED NOT ASK ME WHY I'M ASKING WHAT I ALREADY KNOW! BUT YOU MUST BE CAPABLE OF SPEAKING EXACT WORDS TO HAVE ANY HOPE OF ACTUALIZING WHAT YOU PERCEIVE. YOU MUST BE ABLE TO CLEARLY ARTICULATE THEN CONFRONT EVEN YOUR OWN DOUBTS. THIS IS PART OF YOUR TEST---WHICH WILL DETERMINE HOW I CHOOSE TO USE MY *SWORD*!"

³⁶⁰ The Holy Giant loosened the loop at his belt, lifting up his mighty sword that shone coolly in the moonlight, its sheer size startling to Lyle... its edge glinting, razor-sharp;

³⁶¹ The giant laid the sword tenderly across his lap, which extended a full six feet from hilt to its tip, seeming to pulsate with a life of its own: brilliant, lethal, and final...

³⁶² **Lyle** (*now fully realizing that more than his physical life hung in the balance, indeed his eternal relationship with God... so he spoke carefully and thoughtfully*): "Lord, why are you not talking just from the floating Golden Light, as you did when you first brought me here?"

³⁶³ **The Lord:** (*smiling now as He looked out with deep satisfaction over the nighttime expanse of moonlit, silent, retreating mountain peaks*): "I LIKE THIS PLANET. IN ALL THE MANY PLANETS OF THIS ENTIRE UNIVERSE IT IS ONE OF MY FAVORITES. IT SADDENS ME THAT YOUR SPECIES HAS SO LITTLE REGARD FOR ITS CONTINUING BEAUTY. BUT AS TO YOUR QUESTION, LYLE, APPEARING LIKE YOU I CAN BE MORE EXPRESSIVE AND PERSONAL. USING THIS FORM WE CAN TALK SOMEWHAT ON THE SAME LEVEL, SIMILAR TO WHAT YOU SO NICELY DID WITH THE BYSTANDER! I LIKE HOW YOU TALKED WITH THAT CHILD. DO YOU RECOGNIZE THIS BODY?"

³⁶⁴ **Lord** (*hesitating before answering*): "No, Lord."

³⁶⁵ **The Lord**: "GOOD. IT'S PATTERNED AFTER THE CARTOON THAT MY SERVANT MICHELANGELO DREW OF ME ON THE SISTINE CHAPEL'S CEILING. BUT THAT WAS A MERE SHADOW OF A PALE SHADOW OF A FAINT SHADOW: A HUMAN-SIZED OLD PERSON, ALMOST AN INSULT TO ME! THAT IS NOT AT ALL HOW YOU SHOULD THINK OF ME. STILL, IN THAT CLEVER ARTIST'S STRIVING, HE DID CAPTURE A SMALL DEGREE OF MY DIGNITY. BOUNARROTI REMINDS ME A LOT OF YOU, LYLE."

³⁶⁶ **Lyle** (*taken-aback, not sure if the Lord was giving him a compliment or not, but choosing the former*): "Thank you, Lord."

³⁶⁷ **The Lord** (*sighing with pleasure, still peering out over the beautiful nighttime landscape*): "GO AHEAD, THEN. ASK YOUR NEXT QUESTION."

³⁶⁸ **Lyle** (*struggling to sort out in his mind all that had just happened*): "Yes, Lord... so... so... You were the Tree all along...?"

³⁶⁹ **The Lord** (*his laugh a deep, resonant rumble*): "OF COURSE! I WAS THE TREE... AND THE TABLE, THE CHAIRS, THE MOUNTAIN, THE CLOUDS, THE RAIN, THE WIND, THE PLANET, THE SUN, THE MOON, THE STARS, SPACE, TIME, ENERGY, SUB-SPACE, AND FAR BEYOND---ALL THAT AND MUCH MORE! THEY ARE *ALL* 'ME'...'ALL ALONG', JUST AS YOU SAID!"

³⁷⁰ **Lyle** (*ducking his head in chagrin at his abysmal ignorance*): "Yes, Lord. Forgive me, Lord!"

³⁷¹ **The Lord** (*sounding amused*): "DID I NOT ORDER YOU TO SPEAK FULLY AND TRUTHFULLY?"

³⁷² **Lyle** (*raising his head*): "Yes, Lord, you did."

³⁷³ **The Lord** (*now appearing stern and a bit impatient*): "THEN PROCEED WITH YOUR FINAL QUESTION."

³⁷⁴ **Lyle** (*gathering his courage, carefully concentrating on each of his words*): "The Seeker and the Bystander... they were both innocent---it was my fault they had to be here, not their fault at all---Why, Lord... *why* did they have to die?"

³⁷⁵ **The Lord**: "WHY DO YOU THINK?"

376 **Lyle** (*nervously clutching his hands together in his lap, furrowing his brow with intense concentration*): "I... I suppose... it was to teach *me*... something..."

377 **The Lord** (*tipping his large head to the side as if keenly interested in Lyle's reply*): "TEACH YOU *WHAT*?"

378 **Lyle**: "Well, I guess... that my words are not just an interesting exercise in theological abstraction, but might affect real lives... that it's possible someone, someday, might actually read what I say and have reactions---either positive or negative... and that their reactions could then affect other people in turn... that if I'm not careful then people may get needlessly hurt..."

379 **The Lord** (*nodding encouragingly*): "AND WHAT ELSE?"

380 **Lyle** (*feeling a bit more at ease to speak his mind*): "Well... I feel that all of what I've said and written---particularly what I stated tonight in my defense---was the truth as I see it. And, assuming that I'm correct in that belief and not just engaging in self-congratulatory delusion... then there are times when doing and saying what is 'right' may actually do more harm than good. If I were to heedlessly proceed to disrupt people's existing relationship with you just to show how supposedly 'smart' I am, or to demonstrate how 'clever' I am to discover some 'new' wrinkle in how to best approach you... then perhaps I am myself violating the Five Pillars, particularly the 'Respect' provision, and deserving myself to be cast into the Black Void..."

381 **The Lord** (*narrowing His golden-glowing eyes, His rumbling voice sounding gentle but serious, as a father talking to his young son*): "SO, HAVING A GLIMMER OF THE TENUOUS AND SYMBOLIC SUBSTANCE OF EVEN YOUR MOST CHERISHED CONCEPTS---DO YOU NOW THINK THAT IT'S BEST THAT YOU *NOT* TAKE THE RISK OF TROUBLING ANYONE, THAT YOU JUST *QUIT* WHAT YOU ARE DOING?"

382 **Lyle** (*speaking glumly and sadly*): "Well, Lord... I suppose that Bystander and Seeker did what they did out of their own free well... they were not forced to come to my defense... but that's little consolation to me. It was *my* words that prompted them to put themselves in danger... I *am* responsible for their deaths..."

383 **The Lord** (*imperiously crossing his hugely-muscled, bare arms*): "YES, YOU *ARE* RESPONSIBLE AS THEIR PROVOCATEUR, LYLE---WHETHER DELIBERATE OR TANGENTAL. BUT YOU NEED NOT FEEL TOO BAD. THEY, LIKE YOU, WERE HERE IN THE SPIRIT. IN

A FEW MINUTES THEY WILL BE WAKING UP IN THEIR OWN BEDS, SAFE AND SOUND. THEY'LL REMEMBER HAVING HAD A PARTICULARLY-VIVID NIGHTMARE. PERHAPS THEY MAY EVEN DISCOVER THEMSELVES TO BE A BIT WISER THAN WHEN THEY WENT TO SLEEP. OTHERWISE, THEY WILL CERTAINLY NOT BE HARMED. I CHOSE NOT TO PUNISH THEM FOR YOUR WRONGS."

[384] **LYLE** (*a wave of relief easing his mind*): "Thank you, Lord! You are very generous. Thank you!"

[385] **The Lord** (*his resonant voice now soundly, ominously, more accusatory*): "BUT I TAKE IT YOU HAVE NO SUCH CONCERN FOR THE CRITIC, THE FANATIC, OR THE LAWYER?"

[386] **Lyle** (*chagrined to realize he had actually been glad when the Critic, Fanatic, and Lawyer met their horrible ends*): "Well... I suppose not, Lord... but... weren't they our *enemies*?"

[387] **The Lord**: "DO YOU SO QUICKLY FORGET YOUR OWN WORDS? ...NOT TO MENTION, THOSE OF THE GREAT FOUNDER OF YOUR INHERITED RELIGION, TO '*LOVE* YOUR ENEMIES'?"

[388] **Lyle** (*now hunched over in his seat, groaning as if he'd been struck with a baseball bat in his gut*): "Yes, Lord... but... but... they were *arguing* with me! They were *laughing* at what I was saying! And then they tried to *kill* me! ...and worse yet, they harmed *innocents*! I know the theoretical Teaching, of course, to 'love even your enemies'... but *why* should I love such vile creatures as they?? How could I possibly have any *real* 'love' towards them? Yet... oh, wait a minute... oh, yes... oh, my Lord... I see! It's so *clear* now! You're right, Lord, as always! My *own* words explain it all! It's your Holy 'Connection' isn't it? It's what I was telling Seeker... about *Connectivity*! They... are... ME! And I... am... THEM! --- which, I see now, is why the Lawyer killed himself when he tried to kill me! What he did to me he did to himself...!?"

[389] **The Lord** (*nodding with the hint of a wry smile at the corner of his imperial lips*): "OF COURSE. IT IS NOT HARD TO UNDERSTAND. *WHY*, THEN, DID YOU FORGET YOUR OWN TEACHINGS?"

[390] **Lyle** (*speaking now in a small, weak, frightened voice*): "Because... I'm weak... I'm stupid... I'm ignorant... I'm blind... I'm selfish... I'm egotistic... I'm scared... I'm unfaithful... I'm mistrustful... I'm vengeful... I'm hateful... I'm a hypocrite... I'm a failure... I'm a sinner... I'm a mud-eating, slime-covered worm... I'm not fit to call myself a Godly person... I'm certainly not worthy to be in your Presence, Lord..."

³⁹¹ **The Lord**: "YES. ALL OF WHAT YOU SAY IS TRUE. YOU STAND CONDEMNED BY YOUR VERY OWN WORDS AND ACTIONS. YET WHAT DOES THIS SELF-REVELATION GIVE TO YOU?"

³⁹² **Lyle** (*now daring to look straight into the glittering, unblinking, golden orbs beaming down at him*): "It... gives me... *clarity*! ---knowing from where I truly am starting. And... *gratitude*! ---for the awareness of who I am. And for the ability to perceive deeper than mere superficial certitude... *opportunity*! ---to go forward and upward, knowing that I start out at such a low and shameful state. And because there's so much room for me to improve and try to do better... *humility*! ---to realize that somehow You still care enough about me to allow me a chance to learn better despite my evil failings. Also, it gives me a deep *shame*! ---at my arrogance to think I could somehow speak for You!"

³⁹³ **The Lord**: "BUT IF I *WERE* TO GRANT YOU THE POWER TO SPEAK IN A LIMITED, INDIRECT MANNER FOR ME---EVEN SO FAR AS TO PASS GENERAL JUDGMENT ON OTHERS---WHAT WOULD YOU THEN DO WITH THE CRITIC, THE FANATIC, THE SEEKER, THE BYSTANDER, AND THE LAWYER? IF, AS YOU GUESSED PARTIALLY CORRECTLY AT THE LAST OF YOUR INQUISITION, *YOU* WERE THE TRUE JUDGE OF THOSE IN YOUR JURY... WHAT IS THEN THE PUNISHMENT YOU WOULD LEVY UPON *THEM*?"

³⁹⁴ **Lyle** (*pausing for a moment before answering; nervously wetting cracked lips with his tongue, before finally speaking from pure conviction*): "I would... punish them... by *taking them all into myself*... so that the things which they found so striking in me would nag at them, be undeniable to them, and compel them to re-evaluate everything... but *also*... make ME re-evaluate *my* life, *my* obedience, *my* service, and *my* love to You..."

³⁹⁵ **The Lord**: "HOW SO?"

³⁹⁶ **Lyle**: "Well... if they were all truly inside of me... then first of all I would remember to *be the Critic* looking for flaws---but always directing the hardest questions first at myself, envisioning even the most remote possibilities for failure; so that by detecting and overcoming those flaws I can make myself be and do ever-better! Second... I would remember to *be the Fanatic* willing to take extreme positions---but not forgetting that all actions have consequences for which I am responsible; that I might not needlessly hurt others in my zeal. Third... I would remember to *view myself as a Seeker* continually looking to improve---but tempering my impatience with those who may not share in my Vision; that I might, if possible, inspire them to come along with me on my journey. Fourth... I would *be more aware of myself as a Bystander* witnessing the initiatives

of others---but not quick to automatically reject things just because they are different from my own traditions, heritage, and thinking; looking for the value in extending my ability to think, feel, do, and prioritize differently! And Fifth and finally... I would not forget to *be the Lawyer* respectful of precedence and existing sensitivities---but daring, whenever useful, to take outrageous leaps of faith; that what I help build does not disrespect or waste the efforts of past Seekers upon whom the foundations of society are based."

397 **The Lord**: "SO YOU DARE TO HOLD ONTO YOUR ARROGANCE?"

398 **Lyle** (*remembering the Lord's initial commands to be truthful and complete he tossed caution to the winds, speaking respectfully but with strong conviction*): "Yes, Lord. I do retain the arrogance of stepping forward where, perhaps, no one has gone before. But I do not do that by choice. I do it by compulsion. I understand that the urge to *be and do ever-better* comes not from my animal-self which is ruled by fear. Also, it does not come from my own selfish desires---which would rather have me retreat to my 'cave' and enjoy whatever I've already got. Instead, I believe that the compulsion to make progress---forward and ever-upward---comes from *you*! You made me this way on purpose. And as much as some people want to deny your existence, I can see that evolution---energy-driven processes fueling more-complex, upward development---of everything in this wonderful Universe is part of your great Plan. I'm not sure exactly why you did all of this... I suspect it's beyond my brain-power... but I want to do my part, whatever that part may be. My fondest wish is to somehow---in my own little way, in whatever brief time remains to me in this fragile physical existence---to be pleasing to You!"

399 **The Lord** (*lifting up a thick eyebrow inquisitively*): "SO YOU THINK YOU UNDERSTAND YOURSELF, DO YOU? *YOU REALLY KNOW WHAT YOU WANT?*"

400 **Lyle** (*feeling his momentarily enthusiasm draining away, replaced by a cold apprehension*): "I... I think I do... I guess..."

401 **The Lord** (*tossing his big head back and snorting derisively*): "YOU 'THINK'... YOU 'GUESS'... WHILE JUST A MOMENT BEFORE YOU KNEW WITHOUT A DOUBT?"

402 **Lyle** (*gulping in confusion, averting his eyes looking down fearfully at the rock beneath his feet, feebly protesting*): "But Lord... how can I know myself...?"

⁴⁰³ **The Lord** (*standing up from his throne, lifting high his mighty sword, holding the haft firmly in both of his boulder-like fists*): "I'VE HEARD ENOUGH. IT'S TIME TO MEET YOUR FATE, LYLE."

⁴⁰⁴ **Lyle** (*reaching down with his hands to grasp the edges of his rock-hard chair, steeling himself to his fate, bowing his head in abject submission, and squinting his eyes looking downward*): "Yes, Lord... as You will!"

⁴⁰⁵ From his peripheral vision, Lyle saw the blade plummeting down driven by the Giant's huge, powerful muscles... "CLANGING" loudly as it *smashed* into rocks, *shattering* stones and *splitting* boulders...

⁴⁰⁶ ---a great "GRINDING" and "ROARING" filling Lyle's ears as the entire mountaintop CRACKED in half... the peak upon which Lyle sat *swaying* back and forth as if in a great earthquake...

⁴⁰⁷ ---*tossing* Lyle from his seat onto hard rocks that writhed beneath him like snakes... both the marble throne and the crystal chair bouncing to the edge and plummeting over the cliff...

⁴⁰⁸ ---Lyle also slipping across the smooth stones of the mountain peak toward the edge... desperately latching-onto a protruding rock to stop his slide, wincing against the spray of dust and stones exploding upward forming great grey clouds above him...

⁴⁰⁹ ---the terrible swaying slowing, stopping, Lyle managed to stagger to his feet tottering at the very edge of the precipice, looking down and around in awe, the obscuring clouds of debris parting... Lyle turning to see the Giant standing straight and steady in the middle of what remained of the peak...

⁴¹⁰ ---his flesh turning *wooden*, shrinking, twisting; his arms becoming out-reaching *branches*; his legs merging into a thick tree *trunk*; his toes lengthening, punching-downwards as cable-like *roots*...

⁴¹¹ ---and the Giant's great white swirl of hair turning upward into *leaves* sprouting-out in a waving crown of glorious, sun-drinking GREEN; his deep voice ECHOING as if from a great distance...

⁴¹² **The Lord** (*his voice softer now but still rumbling like a distant thunder*): "---YOUR JOURNEY CONTINUES, LYLE. IT IS STILL DANGEROUS, BUT NOW YOU HAVE AN OPTION TO HAVING TO CLIMB DOWN SHEER CLIFFS."

⁴¹³ **LYLE** (*grasping at the tattered black robe still hanging around his chest; gasping as he realized there indeed was now an alternative to leaving the peak via a thousand-foot drop... a ragged crevice now descending at an angle into the bowels of the high mountain; whispering in relief*): "Thank you, Lord..."

⁴¹⁴ **The Lord** (*now barely audible; the Giant's voice fading-away into the surrounding moonlight*): "AND LYLE, THIS 'Creative-Theology®' THING OF YOURS...?"

⁴¹⁵ **LYLE**: "Yes, Lord?"

⁴¹⁶ **The Lord**: "IT HAS MERIT. KEEP AT IT."

⁴¹⁷ And with those final words, all that remained on the peak was Lyle looking at an ancient tree now bursting with life---both he and it lit by pale moonshine from the sinking orb above---and a foreboding newly-cleaved crevice leading down...

⁴¹⁸ A cool breeze wafted over Lyle as he stood there, raising his gaze to look outward, viewing with wonder the first tints of yellow on emerging cloudbanks... accompanying the sun just peeking up over the horizon...

⁴¹⁹ ---spreading waves of yellow, orange, and red aggressively pushing-back lingering blackness; the mountain-range emerging now lit in a warm and peaceful glory...

⁴²⁰ ---as Lyle's interrogation came to an end... in actuality, though, the start of a long journey home: HIS LIFE BEGUN ANEW, AS UNCERTAIN AS BEFORE, BUT NOW WITH A FRESH ENTHUSIASM *anchored* in a deepened awareness, *tempered* by caution, and *driven* by just a hint of Divine Love...

- -

Lyle 31:1-458

THE MEANING OF LIFE

Down the precarious slopes

¹ And so Lyle began his long trek back to civilization, wrapped in the torn black robe now secured about his upper body; a hood fashioned from it to protect his exposed head against the icy cold; clutching the sharp knife in his right hand as a rock-climbing piton...

² Climbing down the treacherous split in the mountain, from crumbling rock to broken boulder; perilously lowering his aching body hand-hold by hand-hold down thousands of feet; marveling that one slip would send him spinning down into the mists...

³ *So precarious this fragile thing called biological life... ended in a second by sudden fall, car crash, heart attack, or bullet fired in anger or mistake;*

⁴ Blood pumping, his breath inhaling-exhaling, muscles contracting all so easily *stopped* by a moment's slip of the foot, a missed handhold, or a crumbling ledge...

⁵ And leaving *what* behind... just a lifeless body wrapped around some boulders awaiting ants, eagles, or rats? Would the sum total of his life be just a short feast for hungry scavengers? Would anything remain beyond a recycling of biological molecules?

⁶ That which so bravely and heroically struggled for transcendent Meaning and Significance---for Purpose, Answers, Illumination---that dared to wrestle with the Devil, even to stand in the very Presence of the Lord... what was it all for if the same nagging Questions remain *unanswered*: *"Where did we all come from?" "Where are we going?"* and *"Why are we here?"*

⁷ ---just a mere few moments... and it would be as if Lyle had never existed: vanished into the hungry bellies of vultures, a rotten meal broken down by enzymes; transformed into the structures of bacteria, fungi, worms, birds, or lizards! The organic molecules of Lyle remolded into many other manifestations of biological life...

⁸ ---*yet always one with the underlying Substance, the spiritual cement connecting everything not just metaphysically but actually*:

⁹ Where each single thing is a part of the other, a grand subliminal communication network in which the death of one *does* affect everything else;

¹⁰ Where one is dissolved another is made... a grand recycling of souls broken out to be sorted, cast aside or gathered-in;

¹¹ *Biological lives but vehicles for spiritual growth and purification... a choice made by self-and-God-aware intelligent life-forms*:

¹² ---shown not by intentions, emotions, or beliefs... but by every moment's purposeful actions.

. . . .

Resting at the foot of the mountain

¹³ Bloodied, bruised, and exhausted... Lyle finally made it down to the base of the mountain, looking up in amazement at the towering slopes he'd somehow managed to safely descend through;

¹⁴ Wishing that instead of the Fanatic's knife---that he now secured back beneath his belt---that he had a cell phone; indeed, that he'd had his cell phone with him when the Lord swept him away to that mountaintop peak: so that maybe now he'd just call for, via some circling satellite, a nice mountain rescue... maybe a helicopter to whisk him away back to civilization...

¹⁵ But nothing so easy would help him out of his present troubles... he slumped down to the ground, totally drained;

¹⁶ Battered and bruised from the number of short falls he'd suffered climbing down the mountain, every muscle screamed out with pain and fatigue;

¹⁷ Absently noting that the sun was sinking behind the tops of the surrounding mountains; knowing that he might yet die of exposure, hunger, or injuries;

¹⁸ Everything becoming very still and quiet... entirely isolated from civilization... Lyle becoming acutely aware of himself hunched-up and huddled in a fetal position:

¹⁹ Seemingly granted an amazing gift of heightened senses he could feel, see, hear, smell, and taste the *desolation*... the silence... distilled on his lips as salty sweat and acid bile—a rare "mindfulness" of the moment;

²⁰ *Marveling that even in his suffering and desperation it was an amazing experience for his learning and advancement...* unwillingly placed at one with nature; receiving harsh lessons on human limitations; meditating on personal fragility within the scope of the entire, wide universe;

²¹ Such that where there should have been panic and fear, Lyle felt strangely at peace---yes, weak from hunger, exhaustion, and minor wounds---yet at the same time *exhilarated*:

²² Perhaps only the result of still-lingering adrenalin from recent events; but more likely *the certain knowledge that the Lord was present not just theoretically or theologically... but tangible and real!*

23 So Lyle relaxed his body and mind... laying on a patch of soft soil instead of hard rocks, sucking cold air deeply into his lungs, a prickly brush next to him pushing into his side, patches of snow at his feet, and towering mountains over his head;

24 Surely the native Americans---and many other tribal cultures around the world throughout history---understood what he was experiencing... *not just an awe at the complexity and beauty of nature, or marveling at the infinite forms of animate and inanimate matter, but in seeing God everywhere*:

25 Where Nature and the Laws of the Universe become Holy Hands and Fingers... nurturing and cradling the delicate dynamic systems of biological Life;

26 *Allowing the fierce, unyielding interplay and competition necessary for evolving thinking creatures arrived at the advance state of being self-and-God-aware*;

27 Capable of receiving and appreciating God's greatest Gift: Life as a dynamic canvas where art is expressed in self-replicating organic matter... the ultimate expression of Divine Creativity formed in the Father's spiritual image... a purposeful Creativity;

28 *Sprouting wherever in the Universe conditions are permissive... a tenacious searching, growing, ever-advancing, fluid, diverse, grasping-upward for the light---relentlessly seeking survival and dominance in both body and mind; a few favored species blessed with the ability to go even further...*

29 And as Lyle continued to ponder on biological immensity, pulling the torn robes closer around himself... he drifted off into an exhausted, shivering, but *triumphant* sleep.

. . . .

Across the frozen glacier

³⁰ The next morning Lyle awoke weak, stiff, disoriented, half-frozen, and *sick*! He was shivering uncontrollably, felt congestion clogging his lungs, and a fever in his brow confusing his thoughts. Plus He couldn't feel his feet or hands. But somehow he managed to lever himself by his elbows and knees up to his feet... only to immediately fall back down. So he just crawled forward down the steep slope, until he started rolling and bouncing... desperately managing to stop his slide, jerk up to his feet, and stagger onward like some frozen zombie... woodenly stomping his legs and beating his arms against his sides. Finally starting to get feeling returning to his extremities, he could woozily ponder the present mystery...

³¹ ---*why would the Lord spare his life on the mountaintop only to let him freeze, starve, or die from exposure on the lower slopes?*

³² And as he staggered along, coughing, trying to clear out his clogged lungs... Lyle looked out over a daunting vista: between surrounding gigantic mountain cliffs there flowed a vast sheet of gleaming-white, solid ice... over which he'd somehow have to find his way if he were to live;

³³ Somehow to locate a passage out of the mountain range, find food and shelter, get medical help... returning to humanity in safe valleys beyond;

³⁴ Picking up cold handfuls of snow he stuffed them into his mouth to melt... grateful for the moisture but fearful of hypothermia... the cold mouthfuls causing him to shiver violently, causing him to become more and more *scared*;

³⁵ Knowing that unless he found something solid to eat soon he'd die, the constant exercise trying to stay warm burning-through his fat stores, leaving him drained of energy... causing him to stumble, fall, and not get up;

³⁶ Looking down at his thin-soled shoes he realized that they were contributing to his freezing feet; he paused, tore off parts off of the robe wrapped around his upper torso, and tied the strips around his feet to simulate boots;

³⁷ Staggering onward onto the glacier, his feet feeling a bit warmer, he was soon hopelessly lost in a dazzling maze of ice sculptures... each step uncertain, deep holes and crevices in the glacier covered with light snow waiting as silent traps to swallow him up; preserving his carcass for centuries, eons, perhaps emerging eventually as an ancient 21ˢᵗ-century "ice man"---hardly the acclaim he'd sought!

38 A notebook in his back pants pocket perhaps his only writings to survive into the far frozen future! The future scientists would see addresses, random ideas, a grocery-list... curiosities carrying no weight, utility, or beauty... none of his lifetime's attempt at Godly Creativity... only the legacy of a desiccated, ancient corpse...

39 Lyle laughed out loud, the strange sound echoing eerily amongst the tower ice spires, trudging dutifully forward while wanting to just sit down, take a break, and drift off into a 'short' nap... "I'M LOST!" he shouted, the sound of his voice sucked-up by the surrounding glacier... "WON'T SOME ONE PLEASE HELP ME!?" he yelled, knowing that there was only him in that desolate expanse... "SHOULD I JUST LIE DOWN AND GIVE UP!?" he queried loudly to no one in particular before his voice was clogged by a fit of deep coughing...

40 ---but knowing full well that if he gave into the exhaustion he'd never get up again... he'd just peacefully drift off into a "warm" hypothermic frozen *death*...

41 Lyle dragged a club-like cold hand across his face... a "slap" to keep himself attentive... not to be seduced by the incredible beauty of the sweeping curves of the ice sheet surrounding him---so perfectly blended and molded by millennial winds...

42 *All of time, space, and energy collapsing down to the present magic moment... such that Lyle was surprised to not feel cursed to a miserable, unheralded ending... but, unexpectedly, he again felt immensely blessed*!

43 Trudging-slipping forward where perhaps no human had ever walked, somehow determined to carry on the proud endurance of biological life:

44 To persist, continue, find a way... not obsessing on the impossible quest, but only on what lay beyond the next curve, the next slippery ice sheet, the next hump, the next snow plain... trudging on and on *one step at a time*... forcing himself to sing forcefully, as loud as his heaving lungs would allow: "I AM YOUR CREATION BEAUTIFUL AND BRIGHT... FILLED WITH YOUR SPIRIT BURSTING TO GET OUT... NOT JUST EMOTIONS BUT TANGIBLE DELIGHTS... PUTTING WHERE WAS NOTHING---SOMETHING VERY NICE..." ---knowing that brave words matter little, but that the song gave him an irrational exuberance to advance yet one more trembling step...

45 ---*not so much as an endurance race to the end but as a fantastic perpetual Adventure... even if to finally fall, never to rise again; but having drunken-in every incredible moment, savored each new and wondrous experience whether pleasurable or painful*!

⁴⁶ Looking up at the darkening sky... realizing the sun was almost down... Lyle's reveries broke. Despite his brave song, now he again felt full-blown fear, his survival instinct kicking in full-blast---realizing that he'd not last another night out there on the ice;

⁴⁷ Seeing to his side a glint of green in the distance... there between two cliffs a narrow pass evident, leading off of the glacier... struggling nearer... resolving in his view into a thick forest beckoning him to keep going, though he felt so exhausted and cold the next step did not seem possible;

⁴⁸ And to keep himself motivated he again shouted up at the sky, as he steadily wavered onward: "*PLEASE GOD, IF YOU'LL LIFT THEM UP---I'LL PUT THEM DOWN... IF YOU'LL PICK THEM UP---I'LL DROP THEM DOWN... IF YOU'LL RAISE THEM UP---I'LL PUSH THEM DOWN...*" until, amazingly, the snow beneath his feet was gone as he trudged off the glacier into a thick, protecting forest...

⁴⁹ ---where, falling to the ground, he rolled under a thick bush, drew his knees to his chin, wrapped his arms around his shins, and in a fetal position *fainted* into a deep sleep punctuated by jarring, fleeting Visions:

⁵⁰ Seeing himself seated on a warm, safe, and pleasant commuting bus going to work in the early morning, using his time productively typing on a laptop computer nestled in his lap... glancing out at thick traffic while recording a marvelous spiritual odyssey... *retreating from the duties and struggles of the moment into Imagination---the delicious caldron of a Godly Creative mind---from which everything else blossoms...*

. . . .

In a Garden of Eden

⁵¹ Suddenly Lyle was jolted completely awake, every nerve ending tingling, sensing that out in the darkness a deadly danger was creeping closer. Sure enough---from off in a distance---came the loud howling of *wolves*;

⁵² Hunching himself down, pulling himself closer together, careful not to make a sound, his heart racing, clutching at the knife at his belt, Lyle hoped to escape the attention of the hunting pack... safe and hidden under his leafy bush, shivering... waiting out the long night...

⁵³ ---until, in the dim, misty morning, desperately weak, Lyle managed to grab some overhanging branches of the bush and pull himself to his feet... small green leaves on the bush in his hands... he grabbed some off the bush and began to ravenously munch on them... *spitting them out* as the bitter, acrid taste made him cough and gag; exhausted from the long, scary night... fevered and coughing...

⁵⁴ Stumbling onward into the deep woods Lyle heard *rustlings* and *cracklings* as birds swooped through the overhanging canopy; small underfoot creatures *scampering* out of his path... as he pushed himself through wild growth.

⁵⁵ Lyle knew he had to find some sort of food---berries, nuts, anything---something to put in his aching belly that wouldn't be immediately vomited up...

⁵⁶ And then he pushed through thick undergrowth into A PEACEFUL MEADOW WARMED BY MIST-FILTERED, YELLOWISH MORNING LIGHT... in the middle of which was a wide, shallow, gurgling creek... Lyle tottered over, sank to his knees at its edge, cupped his hands, and greedily splashed-up and sucked-down the cold, delicious fluid...

⁵⁷ Then he weakly grabbed-at a few small fish which easily evaded his grasp; but noticed at the other end of the meadow *something half-hidden in the high grass, brown and red*! Crawling over to it he discovered the half-eaten carcass of a medium-sized dead deer, remnants of its entrails spilled out across the ground.

⁵⁸ Perhaps it was the prey of the howling wolves from the night before... not yet stinking, fairly fresh... Lyle without hesitation used his knife to slit-open the skin of the still-intact neck and slice out ribbons of red meat... gobbling it down with whatever congealed blood, ants, and flies were on it...

⁵⁹ It was better than the best-barbequed steak he'd ever eaten! It was soft, warm, and filling. Lyle swallowed all he could manage. Then he made a pouch of part of the robe and filled it to overflowing with as much meat as he could slice out and carry with him... his own heart overflowing with *gratitude*!

⁶⁰ ---thinking that somehow the Lord was still watching out for him. When it seemed he would freeze to death on the endless glacier a way opened up to let him get off the ice and into the forest. *And now, about to collapse from starvation, he was presented with a bloody feast... apparently provided to him courtesy of the very threat he'd feared so much in the blackness of the previous night*!

⁶¹ "*Thank you, Lord...*" Lyle softly stated, moving onward into the dark forest with newfound energy---perhaps things were finally getting better. Indeed, there was hope... "What do I want? What do I want? What do I want?" he whispered to himself, delirious with relief...

⁶² "IT SEEMS LIKE THE GARDEN OF EDEN..." Lyle exclaimed, marveling to himself as he lay back into the soft green grass at the side of the gently-flowing creek: "IT'S SO PEACEFUL AND QUIET... SO BEAUTIFUL---EVERYTHING FILLED WITH MARVELOUS SOFT YELLOW MORNING SUNLIGHT FILTERING DOWN THROUGH SURROUNDING TREES... WITH YELLOW AND WHITE FLOWERS SURROUNDING ME! IT SMELLS SO FRESH AND CLEAN...!"---warming his heart... making him feel pleasantly sleepy, his belly full of meat...

⁶³ "*Perhaps I can stay here forever...?*" Lyle wondered aloud. "*Maybe that's what the Lord wants for me to do... a return to the Garden? I can learn to fish. There's clean water. Everything I need is here! Is this what I want? I could be at one with Nature! I can build me a cabin out of fallen branches and logs. I can roam the surrounding forest... find edible nuts, berries, and such. There are no Critics here to pester me, no Fanatics to attack me, no Lawyers to constrain me---neither Bystanders nor Seekers for whom I have to take responsibility! I can just turn my back on civilization and live as one with the Lord! After all... it's a noble, time-honored pursuit: to be a Holy Hermit! I can devote all my thoughts to meditation and spirituality---with no need for difficult application or dealing with irritating people!*"

⁶⁴ "*I don't have to go back...?*" Lyle sighed, closing his eyes. "*To hell with civilization---they've no need for me! THIS IS WHAT I WANT!*"

⁶⁵ Drifting off to sleep, Lyle's eyes suddenly jerked wide open! He heard a soft "growling" coming from the trees lining the idyllic meadow... driving

a spike of fear deep down into his heart! *The pack was back*! *They knew he was stealing their meat*!

66 Now their *desert* would be *him*! Lyle jumped to his feet and spun to face at least a dozen of the brutes! They advanced carefully, drooling, their teeth on display, *growling* ominously... readying to leap on him, overpower him, dismember him, and rip *him* to shreds!

67 Remembering the weapon at his waist, Lyle *whipped out his knife and brandished it angrily* at the closest wolf... which charged him, apparently not realizing the knife was dangerous! *Lyle slashed the wolf across its nose* as it yelped and dropped back... the other four animals undeterred, prancing closer! Lyle jammed his knife back into his belt and *grabbed-up a small log sticking up out of the grass*, and swung it around his head. He *yelled* at the startled pack: "YOU WANT ME!??" he screamed at them. "YOU THINK YOU CAN TAKE ME!?? WELL COME ON!!! COME AND EAT ME! I'LL STICK IN YOUR MANGY THROATS, YOU OVER-GROWN DOGS, YOU'LL SEE!!!"---as, swinging his log wildly, he abruptly *advanced* on the wolves at his front... they growling back at him, wavering, then reluctantly retreating back into the woods...

68 ---Lyle, still screaming macho taunts, pounded his large tree branch onto the ground... finally dropping the small log, sitting on a boulder, gasping for breath as he threw back his head and laughed loudly until his throat hurt...

69 ---*realizing that in mere moments his thin veneer of civilized behavior had been totally stripped away*. "Good one, Lord!" he yelled-out, as his merriment turned into tears of relief. He was back to being a primitive "cave man" eating raw meat---battling fellow scavengers for pieces of a fresh carcass... descended in just a couple days from spiritual heights to bare survival-mode.

70 *But, amazingly, here he was---still alive and kicking*! *Life was good*! All it took to transform his hopes was some raw meat fueling his muscles, some stream water to slack his thirst, and a good fight... to convince him that *Life was not just a benign beautiful flower, but rather sported the demeanor of a carnivorous beast*:

71 *Ready and willing to destroy and use the surrounding life totally selfishly*... a rampaging monster set loose in a permissive environment;

72 Not limited to civilized constraints adorning, decorating, and peacefully discussing reasonable options... but ready to FIGHT AND KILL, SEEK ONE'S OWN... OBLIVIOUS THAT OTHERS SHOULD STARVE OR PERISH, THE HIGHEST PRIORITY TO GET ONE'S NEXT MEAL...

AND THE NEXT ONE AFTER THAT! For, after all, humans are evolved apes not meant for peaceful gardens but savage forests!

73 *How quickly we forget the short distance from our animal heritage...* in developed nations replete with grocery stores, art galleries, the Internet presenting the knowledge of the world at our fingertips, and formal religious establishments nobly housed on almost every corner of our towns... blissfully oblivious that all of our splendor is fueled by our digestion breaking down the substance of once-living creatures gobbled greedily into our bellies.

74 *Indeed, Lyle now realized without a doubt that there is no "Garden of Eden" where the lion lies down with the lamb*! He was lucky this time. But the wolves would soon learn that a loan adversary armed with only a single knife and club could be quickly overcome by a smart pack... just like that lone deer...

75 Again Lyle began to weep... this time crying uncontrollably... his hand on the warm pouch, patting it with affection, gratitude, and respect---the result of the deer's *sacrifice...*

76 ---an innocent animal going about its daily existence, captured by ripping teeth sunk into it haunches... in its last few terrified moments feeling its flesh torn from its back, neck, and head;

77 Now the deer was transformed into fuel for wolves to fight, to mate, to produce cute little cubs, and them to continue on living and reproducing... and for Lyle to likewise survive for yet another day out in the wild, hoping to make it back home and peck out more "words of wisdom" on the Meaning of Life in his "*The Book of Lyle*" manuscript:

78 Made possible and greatly facilitated by a sticky mass of ripped-out deer meat smelling rankly at Lyle's side... a blood mass of undeniable reality!

79 "Yes, Lord, I see how far I have to go..." he whispered, wearily pushing himself back up to his wobbly feet. THE GARDEN WAS NOT THE END OF HIS JOURNEY---JUST AN ENTICING TRAP HIDING SAVAGE BEASTS... And so he woozily trudged out of the beautiful meadow, pushing his way back into the thick underbrush of the tangled, dark, and ominous woods... suffering yet more scrapes and bruises;

80 ---carefully inching himself down slopes where a misstep could result in broken bones with no medical help available. Crippled, he'd be easy prey for the predators out in the woods.

⁸¹ *But now a deeper fear began to nag at his mind... that SOMETHING ELSE was out there... something relentlessly mechanical... an Evil that was chillingly-uncaring... far more dangerous than the pack of wolves...* silently moving up behind him to tap him on his shoulder... whipping out his knife he whirled-around to confront it and just glimpsed *something...* vanishing back out of his sight... "WHO ARE YOU? WHAT DO YOU WANT?" he yelled into the dark forest, brandishing his weapon... but there was no answer...

⁸² In the total isolation and gloom of the deep forest, Lyle could sense it always present, always waiting, always poised to *snap his neck* in an instant... sending a shiver down his spine and causing the small hairs at the back of his neck to stand on end...

⁸³ ---convinced that the ominous Presence could without hesitation or a second thought kill him in an instant... sensing it coming up again, now "thudding" along behind him, *shaking the trees*!

. . . .

Down the river

[84] Lyle broke into a terrified run, smashing-through low-hanging branches without any thought or plan as to the direction he was going... using his knife as a machete to slice away the brush in front of him...

[85] ---while a "swooshing" and "stomping" came closer and closer behind him and he hurtled through a stand of thick bushes only to find himself *hanging in midair, the ground vanished* from beneath his feet! And then he was flailing-about *falling straight down*...

[86] ---"slammed" hard into a mass of seething, rushing, ice-cold water; he was instantly submerged, whirled-about, struggling in terror to right himself... head emerging, gasping for breath, twirled-about, and *smashed* into rocks;

[87] ---glimpsing the shore, fighting towards it, managing to grab an outhanging root, clinging desperately against the swift current until he could drag himself up out of the pounding water onto a tiny flat dry area just a few feet wide;

[88] Drenched, icy-cold, and shivering uncontrollably Lyle saw above himself the towering, foreboding wall of thick trees that loomed on each bank... while between them raged a deep, surging, white-rapids mountain river;

[89] Lyle allowed his body to relax on the narrow shore, starting to get his labored breathing in check, laying on his back, trying to feel if any bones were broken... glad to not discover shattered bone shafts skewering his flesh, but knowing he'd been battered very thoroughly before escaping the rushing river; grateful that he still clutched tightly his horde of raw deer meat... *but his knife was gone, lost to the raging waters! He was now defenseless!*

[90] Should he survive to the next day he'd barely be able to move from the extensive battering and bruising... but completely soaked in the icy water he knew he had to find shelter fast or he'd not make it to the next day; if he lay there much longer---with no knife left for defense---he'd be easy prey to the wolfs or the larger Threat that'd driven him into the river in the first place...

[91] Forcing himself to stand, groaning at the pain in his right leg where he'd smashed it into rocks in the river, grabbing up a thick broken branch to use as a crutch, limping along down the narrow bank, figuring that following the downhill-flowing water would be the fastest way to find civilization;

[92] Perhaps also the best way to escape the ominous Presence that had chased him into the river: knowing without a doubt that it was still out there in the woods... patiently watching and waiting...

[93] Coughing and shivering, Lyle noted the sky turning orange...night was near...stumbling along beside the *roar* of the savage river that'd nearly killed him:

[94] Hardly some peaceful, gentle, idyllic source of meandering life-fluid... the river was a *raging maniac*, slamming itself relentlessly against the rocks of the earth;

[95] *Carving out for itself a track consistent with gravity and erosion... a tangible expression of the very Laws of the Universe in unconscious FURY*:

[96] Animals falling in having to do the same as Lyle, to sink or swim... offered neither pity nor malice, the River just "was" formed by snow melting on the high mountain slopes, running down the path of least resistance;

[97] Rushing back to its ultimate home in the sea... then to evaporate in the sun's warmth to condense in the atmosphere as clouds... to then fall back yet again as rain or snow...

[98] Purified by its journey to the sea leaving behind accumulated salts, dirt, and contaminations... rain returning it to the earth as clear water... life-giving or life-taking as delicious drink or smashing & drowning floods...

[99] ---right beside Lyle, splashing and crashing, wetting the great black boulders he climbed over them at his feet, surging up onto Lyle's cold ankles, making the rocks slick... seemingly wanting to make him slip, to drag him back down, to drown him and sweep his carcass away... *it seemed an unwitting ally of the Presence dogging his footsteps?*... Lyle grabbing at supporting bushes to the side to keep from falling back into the swirling waters...

[100] ---*Lyle knowing without doubt that he existed at its pleasure... dependent on its substance, slave to its presence and whims... dictating his poor, fragile, delicate, ephemeral life*:

[101] ---biological constructs arrogantly thumbing their collective nose at the vacuum of outer space; arrogantly assuming thermonuclear stellar bonfires are tamed energy sources...

102 ---without thought using the pull of huge hunks of matter to make its own territory, defying the threat of ever-advancing Time to capture each moment...

103 ---*an expression of conscious Significance in a burning-out universe that here, for just a brief cosmic moment, there was THOUGHT... no matter how limited, how brief, or how bestial... defining "US".*

104 Wanting more than anything else to make it out of the oppressive woods before the sun sank---to leave joy-drainers, fear, and dejection behind; convinced that the ominous Presence out there in the gloomy forest was still relentlessly pursuing him---Lyle became more and more anxious, hobbling rapidly along the slick riverbank;

105 ---and just as it was getting darker, Lyle finally saw the trees thinning... as he and the pounding river both emerged from between the high peaks that led back to the mammoth glacier; and he walked away from the river into rolling bushy meadows... wild grass reaching up to his waist, low foothills dropping away in front of him into gathering evening mists... and there, sticking up bravely in the wilderness, was one lonely structure... a building! It *beckoned* to Lyle, urging him to *hurry*...!

. . . .

Stopping by a church

[106] So Lyle slogged doggedly onward through the wild meadow growth. As night descended, he was happy to come upon a one-lane, country dirt road;

[107] He followed it along to the structure he'd spotted earlier: a small house-like structure set-upon a hill. At its top was a cross. Lyle realized it was a little church building, sitting there all by itself;

[108] Finding the front door unlocked, Lyle wearily dragged his exhausted body inside---shuffling into one small auditorium filled with primly lined-up pews, a podium, and a small fireplace with wood stacked neatly next to it.

[109] Discovering a pack of matches in a cupboard on one of the four walls of the auditorium, Lyle managed with shaking hands to strike one... keeping it going long enough to light up some crumpled paper, getting logs starting to glow... then collapsing gratefully on the floor in front of a warming fire:

[110] *That essential step forward made by primitive humans---a happy accident enabling rather than destroying its discoverers---domesticated flame...* protecting him from the cold, wind, rain, and savage animals. Lyle should have felt safe; but as he drifted off to sleep he was still haunted by that brooding "Presence"...

[111] ---it's ominous, unseen manifestation even stronger than previously... *not* left behind in the primeval forest, but inexplicably there *with* Lyle even in the little, empty church---not lurking in the shadows but dancing unseen in the fireplace:

[112] The blazing fire, however, not revealing the form of the Presence... but Lyle could *hear* it: as raspy-faint whisperings, scampering, a cackling laughter off at a distance; and *feel* it as a lingering heartache that prevented him from having a healing sleep... rather, a fitful tossing---tortured by brief fever-driven nightmares---frightened beyond belief...

[113] Lyle got up in dim morning light, the fire burnt out, coughing, hurting all over, and staggering from whatever virus was raging inside his exposure-weakened system... but grateful to still be alive. He wanted to try and go back to sleep now that he'd survived the night's awful demons... but the light from outside kept him from doing so. So he dragged himself to his feet, feeling mentally drained and physically torn-apart. Staggering around, he found no phone, but did discover a small bathroom at the front of the building. There, he was able to wash up a bit.

¹¹⁴ Once again he wished he had a nice, freshly-charged cell phone from which to dial for help... knowing that he was still stranded, but closer to finding his way back home if he didn't die from exposure on the way;

¹¹⁵ And beneath the podium he discovered a large paper box containing a welcomed treasure: several bottles of Welch's grape juice and a package of flat crackers;

¹¹⁶ Surely it was the makings for the congregation's Sunday morning communion service... but he needed it more than they! It would be a very satisfying breakfast. First, though he bowed his head in prayer... giving heartfelt thanks. *"Dear God, I thank you for all your many blessings that you give to me continually. From this little congregation of your people I receive this gift of nourishment. I thank you and thank them for this food. I see here your mercy and divine providence. Where I thought I was about to be captured by... something bad... I see yet again your divine help and guidance. It has retreated away from me... at least for a while. Help me to defeat it, whatever it is! Help me learn what you'd have me to see! Help me be what you want me to be... whatever that is... Amen!"* Then he quickly wolfed-down all the communion-fixings, hoping the congregation would understand...

¹¹⁷ Then he felt guilty about stealing their communion service. Did he have to ravenously eat and drink *everything*... not even leaving a crumb or drop behind!? But he suddenly realized that his wallet was still intact in his back pants pocket. Grabbing it out and looking in it he discovered all his money was long blown or swept away save a single, soggy twenty dollar bill protected in one of the "hidden" compartments. Lyle placed it into the empty communion-service box as token payment...

¹¹⁸ Then, before returning to his long trek back to civilization, he sat down on one of the pews to try and let his body-mind-spirit relax for just a few minutes. In the silent, empty auditorium which might hold at most a few dozen people comfortably, there---dimly lit by the morning sun shining in through several windows---he visualized a dedicated group of believers meeting in the single room. Probably they'd be from widely-scattered farms all coming to that central, isolated location. Sure it was far away from town... but it was, as well, nestled gloriously at the foot of God's majestic snowy mountains. It would be a marvelous gathering-place to worship the Lord!

¹¹⁹ Lyle could hear them in his mind singing grand old hymns, intoning a collective "amen" to a fervently-preached country sermon... cozy and warm in the winter with their wood-burning hearth, fanning sweat in the summer with windows opened wide to let in each cooling passing breeze;

[120] Occasionally baptizing one of their maturing youth in the river up the road; setting out tables for a Sunday "pot-luck" social; kids playing around the building after church; grown-ups chattering sharing the news of the week; a place to encourage each other with mutual triumphs and struggles:

[121] The crops coming in nicely, a tractor broken beyond repair, a new baby, some cattle sold for a good price... glad to see each other and be comforted yet again together hearing and honoring the New Testament's "grand old story";

[122] Completely content to stay within the pages and boundaries of their religious traditions; not knowing or caring that things could be even better, even more rewarding...

[123] "*DO I WANT THIS?*" Lyle loudly spoke into the empty chamber, his voice faintly echoing back from the high ceiling. "*Is this where I should be, Lord?*" he gulped, putting a hand to his fevered brow. "*I could be a preacher for some small group of a few dozen people! I could probably convince them to follow my 'strange' new teachings! I'd have people who'd listen to me and treat me like I was some great teacher! Or... maybe politely sit silently while I bored them with my lectures! Yes... my own little 'congregation'... really? Just change the 'set-point' a bit on their beliefs? Establish a new set of rituals? Really? But people do seem to like it...*"

[124] Lyle was troubled that the Bystander might have come from there: set-into an inherited stasis of conservative unquestioning contentment... where belief was easy, safe, and simple... complacency and compliance accepted as complementary comfortable habits;

[125] Lyle realizing that *biological Life was certainly a struggle driven by fierce pressures to adapt, change, and evolve; but not by choice... rather species are happy throughout the geological record to achieve dynamic balance, maintaining a mellow stability wherever possible*;

[126] *Not* looking to undergo the trauma of lurching to a radical new set-point; the present "status-quo" quite sufficient... sometimes maintained for many eons!

[127] And why not? If, indeed, essential needs are met, reproduction proceeds apace, things are generally "ok"... why not dismiss the rare dissenting voice as that of a troublemaker, enemy, or fool?

¹²⁸ Where gentle folks are totally satisfied with their uncomplicated lives feeling no need to acknowledge shades of gray---where decisions are set-into sharp relief as "yes or no", "right or wrong", or "black or white"---and superficial answers readily, quickly, and satisfactorily settle complex issues;

¹²⁹ Hit with the same predictable problems well-tolerated on a well-worn path---not wanting to reach out to some demanding "Golden Path" nor construct any confusing, uncertain "Crystal Cathedrals"---with no thought at all of pursuing some "greater grandeur"...

¹³⁰ Where one's Faith is predetermined, constructed from settled tradition and long-established doctrines... where fresh ideas are often confusing, unhelpful, upsetting, and even dangerous:

¹³¹ If indeed the "heresies" do disturb productive equilibriums... then why even consider "improvement" if what one already has is not only "good enough" but perfectly fine?

¹³² *Lyle was sobered, thinking that maybe here on his journey back to civilization he'd found an unwanted answer: that evolution of mind & spirit often came at too high a price*;

¹³³ *When increased complication is not necessary for continued survival, perhaps further evolution was just too expensive a luxury... best to bow to yet another biological imperative, that of conserving that which works*: causing the respectful visitor with fresh ideas to quietly back off...

¹³⁴ Realizing that new religions, fresh spiritual paradigm shifts, or revolutions often are the festered fruits of bloody chaos, fighting, destruction, and death:

¹³⁵ *If so much pain would truly result from reigniting the eternal war between conservatives and liberals---a frequent cause of the "splitting" of many a small congregation---would "Creative-Theology®" be worth such a terrible cost*, perhaps to leave this little "Church of the hills" in ruin? Lyle pondered, greatly disturbed... "*Is this what you wanted me to learn here?*" he whispered into the quiet, looking up in confusion at the worn wooden beams of the small auditorium's high ceiling. "*Are the thoughts you've put in my head just academic theory, at best?*" he appealed to the walls of the little church building. "*Where I see practical implementation, is that incompatible with the real purpose of small churches like this one: providing and perpetuating comfortable religious tradition? And even if that should prove boring and unproductive for the participants, is their mere presence sitting in worship in this small auditorium sufficient... even though things could easily be so*

much better?" There was no answer to his queries. But the questions remained, hanging discouragingly in the air...

¹³⁶ *Lyle had an uneasy feeling that he was missing something important... that in the little congregation's ready acceptance of even a helpful status quo---the implacable Presence he still sensed in the building was triumphant!* But... how could that be? Perhaps his vision of a throng of happy kids playing tag at a "pot-luck" social was somehow a clue? *Did those kids when reaching the "age of accountability" readily march to that cold mountain river to be "buried with Jesus" in baptism? Or was this little mountain church really a dying institution populated by a few stubbornly-lingering old people?* Surely there was no fitter place for Tradition to remain relevant than in an isolated farming community nestled high up on the foothills of a mountain range? But... the world was now simultaneously a lot bigger and lot smaller than any single dispersed farming community, wasn't it? Although he had no cell phone with him, Lyle knew that it and similar electronic gadgets were ubiquitous... bringing a wide world of awareness, knowledge, and entertainment to even the remotest corners of the planet... hardly the means for encouraging youth to unthinkingly accept religion in the form of boring Sunday sermons? But... maybe he was too pessimistic, too idealistic, or too critical? Was he seeing trouble where there was none? Was that what he needed to recognize and accept? *It was so hard to reach a healthy balance between the Critic, the Fanatic, the Seeker, the Bystander, and the Lawyer*! THEY JUST WANTED TO KEEP ON FIGHTING WITH EACH OTHER INSIDE HIS HEAD! NO! NO! NO! NO! *Agggghhhhhhh*!!!! Shrugging in exasperation, Lyle angrily forced the loudly-arguing voices to the back of his mind!

¹³⁷ He needed to take action---to get going! So he stood up, limped on aching legs outside the building, and then determinedly continued his slow trek on down the road, not looking back... but stewing in his own juices: what remained of his clothes filthy and dirty, stinking along with his pouch of rotting meat! Only God knew how far he'd have to walk. He might need that nourishment, vile as it was becoming. He walked with renewed strength, however, grateful for the respite at the little country church---but with a heavier heart: more *conflicted* than he'd ever before been...

¹³⁸ In the warm morning sun trudging down the one-lane, country road slouching over, dejected, dragging his feet---angrily kicking up clouds of brown dust... hard to think around the fever still burning in his body: "*Why is everything so difficult?*" he yelled-out to no one in particular...

¹³⁹ ---which further dirtied the wrappings that were still tied around his battered shoes... thinking that at the little church building he'd perhaps

come to the real end of his journey: a resigned acceptance of his own personal failure... *"I'm too weak, Lord..."* he whispered. *"I'm a weak vessel..."* he moaned, shivering, feeling totally drained of energy, feverish and aching all over... *"I don't know any more what I want... if I ever did... what lies beneath my boast---my supposed desire to please You... is it just abject selfishness?"*

. . . .

Talking with a truck driver

140 Suddenly a shrill *"screeching"* and *"honking"* broke his train of negative thoughts, causing him to hastily jump off the dusty one-lane road to let some onrushing vehicle pass by...

141 Looking back over his shoulder he saw looming right behind him an open-bed, rattling, beat up pickup truck with a hefty large lady up in the cab. Lyle saw her waving a big hand cheerfully at him, but was so stunned by the sudden apparition that he didn't even respond back...

142 ---which rumbled on down the dirt road past Lyle before coming to a full stop. Looking back, the driver leaned from an opened window. Her round, pudgy face smiled cheerfully at him!

143 Lyle saw she was wearing a faded blue-white-green checkered flannelled shirt. She had short grey-white hair on her head. On her beckoning hand was a well-worn leather glove...

144 **Truck Driver** (*speaking loudly in a shrill but friendly voice*): "HEY, WANT A RIDE?"

145 **Lyle** (*lurching forward to catch up, then painfully climbing up into the opened back bed, managing to yell back*): "YOU BET! THANKS A LOT!"

146 **Truck Driver** (*leaning across from her wheel to swing open the loudly-squeaking cab's opposite door while yelling-out an invitation*): "NAW! COME ON UP FRONT WITH ME! AH DON'T BITE!"

147 **Lyle** (*gratefully dropping back down off of the truck's bed, going around to the cab, and stiffly climbing up inside---wincing from complaining, sore muscles*): "I'm afraid... I'm pretty gamey... I really don't mind riding in the back... (cough)..."

148 **Truck Driver** (*laughing loudly*): "Ah've smelt worse than you, young man. No need for you-all to bounce around back thar with them crates. And sounds like you've got a cold! Get on in here where it's warmer, once I crank back down the window, that is!"

149 **Lyle** (*happy to oblige the nice lady, sinking into the tattered but comfortable fabric of the wide flat seat*): "Sounds real good to me, Ma'am... real good, indeed... (cough)... I am a bit under the weather, that's for sure... hope I don't give you some virus..."

¹⁵⁰ Lyle felt around for seat belts to buckle, didn't see any, stopped and settled back.

¹⁵¹ **Truck Driver** (*chuckling as she forced complaining gears to engage*): "Ain't no nevermind, fellow---I've got the constitution of a mule! And there ain't no seat belts in mah truck! Ah don't believe in them. Ah took 'em out! Too many folks ah've seen crunched-up stuck in their smashed-up cars on these here steep mountain roads. Maybe they could've been thrown free! But they weren't!"

¹⁵² **Lyle** (*wincing at the mental picture her words invoked, mumbling absently to himself*): "---yah, and maybe decapitated passing through the windshield..."

¹⁵³ **Truck Driver** (*obviously having heard what he said, her cheerful grin instantly replaced by a frown*): "You want a ride or not, mister?"

¹⁵⁴ **Lyle** (*hastily putting his hands together in a prayerful gesture while lowering his head in submission*): "Oh, I'm very sorry, Ma'am! I'm a bit messed-up... not thinking straight at all. I'm kind of... feverish... I'm *so very grateful* for your kindness to me! I didn't mean to sound arguementative..."

¹⁵⁵ **Truck Driver** (*grinding the gears as she started the truck forward, loudly gunning the motor*): "Well, ok then---and the name's 'Burt', not 'Ma'am'! I'm the 'delivery boy' around these here parts. Ah takes all sorts of stuff out to the farms. Ah've been doing it for more years than ah kin count. Ah just got rid of some boxes of horse feed to the Simpsons up the road. Now ah'm heading back to town. We'll be there in about an hour. Suit your fancy, stranger?"

¹⁵⁶ **Lyle** (*leaning back against the warm fabric at his back, wonderfully relieved at not having to continue his grueling solitary march; all his aching, tensed-up muscles relaxing; wanting to just melt into the comfortable seat but his head filled with feverish visions keeping him wide awake*): "That... is... so good to hear, Burt. And my name is 'Dan'... Dan Lyle. It's very kind of you to give me a ride. In fact, you are a sight for sore eyes, for sure... I don't think I've *ever* seen anyone so beautiful in my whole life!"

¹⁵⁷ **Truck Driver** (*throwing her head back and belching out a loud belly-laugh*): "Hah! Ain't nobody accused me of thet in years, young fellow. I'm a bit too old and fat to be 'beautiful'! But *you* shore look like somethin' the cat drug in, that's God's truth! And what the hell is that torn-up, bloody thing you're wearing---not to mention that God-awful smelling thing in your pouch?"

¹⁵⁸ **Lyle** (*speaking sheepishly and jerkily as he was bounced in his seat by the truck hitting holes in the dirt road*): "Uh... well... I got into some... trouble... and this old cloth was all I had to... keep me warm. The pouch... well... that's my food. It's some raw deer meat... I cut it out of a carcass some wolves left behind... and... and..."

¹⁵⁹ **Truck Driver** (*shaking her head, chuckling*): "---'and', Dan, you just up and chuck that whole smelly mess out of the window! And then reach down under the seat and pull out my traveling box. I've got bottles of water and lots of Twinkies in it! And while you're at it, pull out a pile down there ah've got bound-up in some twine. It's some old clothes I keep in the truck for emergencies. Ah've got some beat-up old pants, undershirt, and a flannel shirt like the one ah gots on here, plus a light coat. Best you also toss out the window those rags you got tied around your upper parts. Put my stuff on! Don't look like your pants are in too bad shape, though, but the rest is in dire need of replacin'! My stuff is dry, warm, and clean. Sure it's just raggedly old work clothes. But you're welcome to them!"

¹⁶⁰ **Lyle** (*weakly pulling off the remains of the bloody, black robe with its attached lump of congealed, decaying meat----rolling down the window and reluctantly tossing them both out*): "Thank you, Ma'am. I really appreciate it..."

¹⁶¹ He reached down under the seat, fumbled around until he felt the indicated items. He slipped into the warm clothes as the truck continued bouncing down the rutted road, felling almost back to being a civilized human.

¹⁶² **Lyle** (*leaning back in his seat as he munched on a sweet Twinkie sponge-cake while sipping at some bottled water, easing the flow of gunk up out of his lungs, slowing the urge to cough and sputter*): "Ma'am, you are a real life-saver! And I totally meant what I said about you being beautiful! Not only are you a super-beautiful person, but you're also a Saint! These Twinkies are *so* good...!"

¹⁶³ **Truck Driver** (*casually steering with one hand as with the other she stuck a fat cigar in her mouth and lit it up*): "Yep, them thar Twinkies are damn fine food. They taste good and last forever. They're my 'survival' chow! And, ain't you the sweet talker, calling an old bag like me 'beautiful'! Oh, mind my manners... you smoke, Dan?"

¹⁶⁴ **Lyle** (*breathing-in the wafting, pungent smoke in the closed cab*): "No, Ma'am. But your cigar does smell rather good to me right now. It's

very... friendly... sort of like a warm fireplace on a cold night---drives away the demons!"

¹⁶⁵ **Truck Driver** (*peering knowingly over at him as the truck continued bouncing down the rough dirt road*): "So... you sayin' you got a *devil* after you? Is that it? You got something evil on your tail that's lookin' to catch you?"

¹⁶⁶ **Lyle** (*involuntarily jerking his head to the side to peer nervously back behind them... still feeling that oppressive Presence but seeing nothing zooming up from behind!*): "I... hope not. I try to walk the Golden Path, Ma'am---I mean, Burt! But... no matter how careful you try to proceed, there's always something bad sneaking up to kick you in the seat of the pants, isn't there? I'm really not superstitious, just a bit cautious..."

¹⁶⁷ **Truck Driver** (*now narrowing her eyes, suspiciously*): "So... what is this 'Golden Path' that you mentioned? You one of them religious nuts we occasionally get around here after having gone on some sort of 'pilgrimage' off by yourself into the wilderness?"

¹⁶⁸ **Lyle** (*laughing weakly*): "Maybe so, Burt. I've been trying real hard to figure that out myself. Yes, I do have some 'new' religious ideas I've been trying to sort through. And those concepts did take me into your mountains for I guess what you'd call it a 'retreat'... to try and get my head straight. And... maybe I am just some kooky 'nut'. But somehow I still think there's something to what I've spent a lot of time studying and writing about. It all has to do with fully 'empowering' ourselves and others for moving ever closer to God: for doing what the Lord most wants from us other than just repeating boring rituals; and from those actions to build up a traveling 'Crystal Cathedral' that's kind of like a spiritual 'portfolio' except it's show-casing the Effort rather than just any end results... all part of the upward spiritual trail I call the 'Golden Path'... But I guess I'm rambling. I'm a bit feverish, not thinking too straight. I doubt that any of this makes sense to you... Sorry..."

¹⁶⁹ **Truck Driver** (*squinting sideways at Lyle while keeping an eye on the winding road*): "We get all sorts of types up here, Lyle: *criminals* looking to take advantage of us 'simple' folks, *psychos* on some 'mission' that makes sense only to them, *hunters* looking for a quick trophy, *crazy city-folks* trying to escape what's in their own heads, and sometimes... *religious fanatics* looking to convince us they seen the 'truth' and we need to agree with them! I don't think you're a criminal, hunter, crazy person, or escapee. But you jist might be one of them psychos with twisted-up mentalities who don't see the world like it really is---who get lost in their own fantasies! Or, then again, you might be one of them '*mission-*

aries' types presuming that we ain't smart enough to figure out the 'true' way to follow God. I see you ain't a nut, that's for sure. But you might be something even more dangerous: what ah calls an *'intelligent visionary'*! Yep, I've seen 'em all... Kooks are easy to dismiss. But smart, slick talkers like you can cause real trouble with their sly visions! Seems to me that this 'Crystal Cathedral' religion of yours might fall in that thar later category... is ah rat, Dan?"

170 **Lyle** (*sighing with a wry grin on his face*): "Could be, I guess, Burt. But the 'vision' I have of a personal 'Crystal Cathedral' is a place that God enjoys visiting---that's completely honest and open! It's not some closed-down stone fortress like the medieval castles. It's not some insular 'cult' that tries to trap people. Instead, it's a 'transparent' Temple! The regular 'castle' protects nobility like Kings, Queens, and other rulers---keeping them hidden away and safe from the 'peasants'. Cults are prisons that try to enslave people to some person or ideology. Instead of those perverse things, the Crystal Cathedrals I envision are 'people' buildings where we can see how well we connect and work with each other to try and accomplish the very best things. It's a Castle for the People, like you and me, to help each other advance on the Golden Path!"

171 **Truck Drive** (*snorting in derision*): "Most of us 'peasants' don't think much of fancy notions like 'Crystal Cathedrals' Lyle! That sort of talk around here will get you nowhere! Besides, we're jist common folks up here that don't belong in no fancy Castles, even if such things did exist...!"

172 **Lyle** (*firmly interrupting, briefly energizing himself with the intensity of his conviction*): "---which is a mistake! In *God's* sight, we are *all* royalty! Each in our own ways is already---or can become---the best types of Leaders! Each of us not only can have, but *deserve* to own, our own Crystal Cathedrals! *Each* of us can be a King or a Queen... a Prince or a Princess... who has our own well-deserved 'Castle'---and is respected and appreciated by the highest certifying power of all: Almighty God!"

173 **Truck Driver** (*taken-aback by Lyle's spirited defense*): "Hmmmm... kind of strange! Those are some uncommon ideas, fer shure! In fact, what yore sayin' sounds like something from them oriental-type religions! Are you, maybe, one of them thar 'Buddhist' people??"

174 **Lyle** (*shrugging*): "Actually, Burt, I'm a Christian. I was raised by a Christian family from a baby to go to church each and every week, study the Bible, and believe the teachings of Jesus. That's my 'traditional' inherited religion. So I'm a Christian who believes in Jesus' teachings! I'm not Hindu or Islam or Jewish or Confucian or Buddhist or whatever other religion... but also I'm *more* than just an adherent to the inherited

faith in which I was raised: thinking of myself as a 'Creative-Theologist' in *addition* to being a Christian; though probably, sadly, at this time the *only* one in the world! So---to give you the thumbnail summary---I've developed something that's religious but not the regular top-down, patriarchal, command-and control structure. What I call 'Creative-Theology®' is something I've developed where the Leaders practice Godly Quality Management and are more 'facilitators' than preachers, if you know what I mean."

175 **Truck Driver** (*shaking her head in the negative*): "Nope. Got no idea at all what you mean. But it does sound kinda interestin'... tweaks my brain-matter! 'Course ah kin see where regular preacher-types and church people would label you as a nut-case, fer shure! But I'm different! I'm a little nutty myself! So is it just some ding-bat idea of yours or is there some rubber meetin' the road to it?"

176 **Lyle** (*happy now to find someone interested in at least listening to his ideas*): "If you are asking if it is just some philosophical theory or can it actually be done---the 'how' is, indeed, very practical. It has to do with so-called 'Quality' tried-and-true Principles and Mechanisms. Some of the best businesses out there in the 'real' world use these methods to achieve great success. And it's not just for businesses! It's all about how to best motivate and help people to work together in any social group to achieve more than they could in isolation. It's all very practical, achievable, and operational. The problem in applying it to religion, though, is that the whole notion of it is different from how religions normally work. So, yes, a lot of typical church folks---both leaders and members---would see this as completely foreign to what they do! For instance, instead of 'protect the Truth' being the AIM for the church Leaders, their main objective in Creative-Theology® becomes *helping their people use their God-given talents together attempting to do great things to the glory of God*! The short version of that AIM is: 'Together express our Godly Creativity!' As such, Creative-Theology® could revitalize faith, energize believers, intrigue their youth, and better-achieve their most-cherished personal and collective goals!"

177 **Truck Driver** (*not sounding all that convinced*): "Uhm... right... now ain't that somethin'? So when you say 'empowering'... just *who* are you talkin' about, specific-wise?"

178 **Lyle** (*speaking quickly and fervently*): "Women! Children! Minorities! People not in command! Those with different ideas! The Dreamers! The Builders! The Seekers! The Poor! Those low on the social ladder! Old folks! The Restless! The Questioners---all of the people that presently feel they lack the power they need to do worthwhile creative things with their particular talents!"

¹⁷⁹ **Truck Driver** (*shrugging*): "Well, I guess we could use some more of that.... Most churches that I know *are* kind of stuck on their own version of the 'truth' and their own way of doin' things, that's fer shore. Plus they typically ain't none too good at helping anyone who's not to their particular taste or outside the stuff they do or that don't take to being ordered around! Course it's kind of unrealistic ta think any existin' religious rulers who are happy with what they've got would want anything different, no matter how better it might be. But it does sound like you know what you're talkin' about, Dan, got to give you that! You ain't just some dumb nut. You sound like an educated guy. I suspect you is definitely one of them 'intelligent visionaries', that's for shore! So I guess the main question is: are you a *dangerous* troublemaker or a *helpful* troublemaker? It'd help me to know which one you is by knowin' if anyone important has endorsed this crazy notion of yorn?

¹⁸⁰ **Lyle** (*smiling sadly, thinking back to his recent 'mountaintop' experience*): "Well... I thought so! But now... well, I'm not so sure anymore. It seems like I'm being educated on the negatives of rocking the boat. And I certainly don't want to do more harm than good! To answer your specific question, though, I've got no desire to be a 'dangerous' troublemaker! So I'm thinking that maybe I should just shut up about this stuff and not bother anyone with it anymore---and even stop wasting my time writing about it! I can still implement it myself, I guess, as my own personal religious philosophy. That way I'll benefit from it while not bothering anyone else with my 'crazy' notions..."

¹⁸¹ **Truck Driver** (*nodding her head in affirmation*): "Hmmmm... your last words there are rather intriguing, Dan. The 'evangelizers' I've met in the past were none too humble, that's fer shore. I never did take to people who thought they knew better than me how to run my own life! They always made me feel like I was dumb... and didn't give a hoot about what I thought, just that I should listen all excited to their lecturing of me so that I could take it all in lock, stock, and barrel---to believe and do what they in their great 'wisdom' told me, whatever that was! Heh!"

¹⁸² **Lyle** (*nodding*): "Yes, that's so true. Probably some of them were really good-hearted sorts sincerely trying to help people, convinced that they did in fact know 'the' Truth from God! After all, if everyone who thought or did differently religiously than you were actually 'damned' by God then I suppose you would be doing them a service to beat them over the head with your 'salvation'. But---even if they were right in their ideas---you can't force things on people! The day of converting people with the 'sword' is pretty much over. Today, to successfully help people expand their thinking you have to give them what *they* agree is useful! It that's

truly done, however, I still think that some people will gladly accept a helping hand!"

¹⁸³ **Truck Driver** (*nodding in agreement*): "Huh! Ok... well said, Lyle. So is your 'Golden Path' supposed to do that---give something that people will agree they really need?"

¹⁸⁴ **Lyle** (*sighing sadly*): "Yes. I think so... But... maybe like the typical 'evangelizer' I've got myself fooled on what other people really need? Or maybe the 'Golden Path' is just an 'Eastern' type of idea that doesn't fit in with most of our Western-society type of thinking? Or maybe formal religion is just the wrong vehicle to use for this approach to Godliness? Or... well, I just don't know! I'm really confused. I'm convinced that these ideas are valid. But *how* to proceed with them...?"

¹⁸⁵ **Truck Driver**: "Anything written on this that people could read for themselves... maybe people like me?"

¹⁸⁶ **Lyle**: "I've written things about it, yes. But none of it is published yet. Someday I hope to have my own spiritual adventure summarized in a book I'd call '*The Book of Lyle*." Maybe you'd be in it with me, Burt! I might even write into it the conversation that we're having right now! And then I'd like to publish another additional book to lay out the particulars for implementing it all which I think I'd call '*Creative-Theology®*'. Also, I've already written and self-published a book on the Quality Principles and Mechanisms that underpin it all, titled "*In Search of Quality, Principles and Mechanisms*'. That and my other stuff are at my website LylePublishing.com. I've also another website specifically on my Creative-Theology® things called Creative-Theology.org. So, yes, I guess I do have some things available that other people could read, and more on the way... assuming I just don't toss it all out to the side of the road like that bloody robe I was wearing---and quit wasting my time!"

¹⁸⁷ **Truck Driver**: "Well, you shore did need to get rid of that blood mess, that's fer shore! And to be honest with you, Dan, I don't know if ordinary people would ever read things like yore talkin' about---even if you had *me* in it! Hah! My experience is that most Christians don't even read their own Bible, let alone other religious stuff. They just go to church and put up with a boring lecture as their religious 'edjumication'. And if they had to go to some 'website'... that's jist way too much trouble, Dan! But personally I give jist about anything a fighting chance to perk my interest. So... is there anything you can quote to me right now that's in your 'Creative-Theology®' stuff, so ah kin get a sense of how it percolates on mah brain?"

¹⁸⁸ **Lyle** (*pursing his lips together for a moment in deep thought*): "Well... there are some things I like so well that I've memorized them... so, how about this..."

¹⁸⁹ **Lyle** (*lowering his voice and projecting his voice dramatically*): "WHEN I LOOK AT YOU I SEE *MYSELF* LOOKING BACK AT ME...

¹⁹⁰ THERE BEHIND THOSE CURIOUS EYES A VERY REAL PIECE OF *ME* RESIDES...

¹⁹¹ SEPARATED BY SPACE AND TIME, CONNECTED DIRECTLY IN THE SPIRIT...

¹⁹² SUCH THAT IF I HURT YOU IT BRINGS HARM TO ME; WHILE HELPING YOU MAKES ME HAPPY...

¹⁹³ NOT JUST ENLIGHTENED SELF INTEREST BUT A GENUINE SYMPATHY, EMPATHY, AND LOVE."

¹⁹⁴ **Truck Driver** (*seeming to relax a bit*): "Huh... that's kinda purty... You some sort of poet or something?"

¹⁹⁵ **Lyle** (*closing his eyes and now speaking more softly in his normal voice*): "You might say so..."

¹⁹⁶ **Truck Driver**: "You ever wrote anything famous?"

¹⁹⁷ **Lyle** (*quietly laughing*): "No... sad-to-admit, nothing of any note. Like I said, I've tried to sell some of my books by self-publishing them--- but nothing's 'took'. I've been continually writing creative stuff ever since I was a little boy. But over my whole lifetime I've earned maybe a few hundred dollars total from my creative writings."

¹⁹⁸ **Truck Driver** (*nodding in sympathy*): "Yep. Your sad story is pretty common, Lyle. I've known a few unsuccessful writers like you around here. They keep at their little poems and 'books' and what-not, but there ain't nobody interested in either publishing, buying, or reading them! So, just out of curiosity, how much did you spend out of your pocket to get those few hundred dollars over your lifetime of writing?"

¹⁹⁹ **LYLE** (*looking out to the side of the cab as green meadows swept past; noticing that the morning sun was quickly fading, gray clouds accumulating above*): "Oh... probably out of my pocket around fifty thousand dollars, not counting the many hours of my time put for free into the work itself..."

200 **Truck Driver** (*laughing in a knowingly-friendly way*): "Shore doesn't sound like much of a business plan. How do you manage to live and support your family?"

201 **Lyle**: "Well, first of all it's just me. I've never got around to having a family. Too selfish of my time, space, and whatever little money I've got... I guess. Not to mention that families often have tough times with a failed would-be 'artist' for the father... who's trying to work a regular job plus do creative things on the side which takes up pretty much one's whole life, leaving a family to suffer neglect... But fortunately my creative writings are... I suppose---just a 'hobby'. I've earned my keep as a Biologist working at various jobs: in hospital clinical laboratories, in higher education, and in government agencies."

202 **Truck Driver**: "You do strike me as a loner... probably introverted too, huh? Maybe explains why you got stuck with weird ideas no one except you cares much about? 'Course not burdening a family with your compulsions might be notched-up by some to *un*selfishness, don't cha know! But did you do any writing at those 'jobs' you speak of?"

203 **Lyle**: "Yes, Burt, I sure did. So I guess—as you are kindly reminding me---that's where whatever writing skills I've got have actually earned me some money: writing up reports, research plans, product reviews, communications, e-mails, lectures, presentations, and scientific papers published in scientific journals... that sort of thing. And... yes... that's real observant of you. I am indeed an 'introvert' that loves to sink into my own little writing world. I'm aware of that and---I think---I'm healthily suspicious of my own world-view... so I don't take too strongly my own conclusions as to how things should be... (sigh)..."

204 **Truck Driver**: "Huh. That's unusual, Lyle. Most of the 'gurus' ah've picked up here were certain they had the 'truth'! I like that you've got a bit of humility in you! Makes me want to hear more about what got to say! So did you ever discover anything important in your money-earning 'research' work??"

205 **Lyle** (*ruefully sighing*): "I tried, Burt. To the side of the jobs that I managed to get in risk assessment, teaching, hospital tests, and regulatory questions I worked on some great ideas of mine for better treatments for cancer and diabetes. And a couple times I thought I was on the trail of something big. But each time, Mother Nature did *not* agree with me! She laughed her guts out at me while kicking me in my rear end and slamming doors SMACK in my face. I always tried to do my best at whatever job I was being paid to do in the lab or wherever---thought I succeeded at that ok, my bosses seemed happy with my work---but, no, sadly, I discovered nothing important. No 'Noble Prize' for me! Either I

wasn't smart enough or Lady Luck did not smile on me. I tried real hard to come up with those better treatments for cancer and diabetes, even things that might have been 'cures' if they'd worked. But in regards to those things directly helping sick people, I failed. However I don't feel my failure is something to be sad or ashamed about. I did my very best under the prevailing circumstances! I gave it a hell of a try, but Mother Nature *hated* me!"

[206] **Truck Driver**: "Well, Dan, on behalf of all the sick people of the world---ah thanks you fer tryin'! I'm a diabetic myself, 'type two' they tell me. The Doc keeps tryin' to get me to lose some weight, get more exercise, and quit my smokin' habit. But I figure at my age the harm's been done. I'm too old for fancy 'lifestyle' changes to make much difference. I figures ah might as well jist enjoy the time ah got remainin' ta me and not worry too much about staying healthy forever!"

[207] **Lyle** (*speaking tentatively and carefully*): "So... did you ever try to quit... the smoking, that is?"

[208] **Truck Driver** (*taking a long drag at her cigar, then lifting it up before her face with her right hand, looking straight at the glowing tip before putting the moist butt back into her mouth*): "Hah! You're a meddlin' introvert, ain't yah? Sure, lots of times. But ah could never kick it. It always brung me back. It's just something ah gots to do is all. Ah tells young-uns, particularly my grandkids, not to start. If it takes aholt of you, you're trapped. That's whut ah tells them. You can't get free. Least wise that's true for a lot of us. Some folks, ah knows, manages to quit with no problems. But not me! Some of my young-uns get the message. Some don't. Kind of breaks my heart ta see some of the ones ah likes the best goin' down my own sad road. You'd think kids could learn from the mistakes of their elders... but they don't! They's jist as stupid as I wuz at their age! One of my grandkids, in fact, took up smoking behind the barn when she was just eight years old---jist like ah done! Her name's 'Missy'. Her daddy tried to get her to stop it. But Missy just stood up straight and said 'Granny does it, don't she?' 'Course I know she wuz jist makin' a damn excuse for doin' what she wanted ta do. But still, it makes me feel bad. She's a teenager now and smokes like a chimney. Again, jist like me at her age! But, like you say, I done my best to warn her and the others. We each gotta make our own decisions, what's right and wrong fer our own lives. Don't you think so, Dan?"

[209] **Lyle** (*nodding jerkily as the vehicle continued bouncing down the single-lane dirt road, struggling---since there were no seat beats---to not slide off the seat, getting woozier from his verbal exertions and escalating fever, feeling sweat dripping from his hot brow*): "Yes. Ultimately we can't make others do anything, except to give them good advice and

a good example. But to me it sounds like overall you definitely helped your kids. I'm sure your warnings mean a lot coming from someone who's been there, is there, and can't escape. You're not just some 'preachy' public service ad on TV... you're someone that I'm sure they love and respect."

210 **Truck Driver** (*speaking with a catch in her voice, after swallowing hard*): "Uh...well that's real kind of you to say, Dan. Maybe ah haven't got all mah kids warned off of this nasty habit, but some did listen to me, fer shure. Ah feels you understand where ah'm at... not many folks try to get into other people's heads, especially religious types. They jist pass judgment.... And even if they don't say it out loud, ah kin see it in their eyes. To lots of them I'm jist a chain-smokin' fat old hag with yellow teeth, who coughs up a bit of blood now and then, who hates going to public places where ah cain't smoke, and spends tons of my meager money on buying these damn 'cancer sticks'. But I don't see that disgust in yore eyes. Jist what is it that you're tryin' to do, Dan? Why are you *really* out here in the middle of nowhere?"

211 **Lyle** (*looking straight forwards, soberly, at the winding, now rapidly-descending dirt road*): "Well... that's good question, Burt. Why am I 'really' here? Wow. That's actually one of the Big Three Questions: 'How'd I get here?' and 'Where am I going?' and 'Why am I here?"... I suppose I share that puzzlement with everyone: 'Why do we do what we do?' or 'What drives us?' and 'Why do we do good things?' or 'Why do we do bad things?' and 'What controls us?' or 'Do we have at least some free will?' And I guess for myself---in addition to having a nagging itch to figure things out---I also have another inward compulsion to answer that tough 'selling question': 'How do we change things for the better when most around us are happy with the status quo or gave up hoping and trying a long time ago?' So... to answer the question as best I can... I was forced to be here by an inward compulsion. Where I could have just lived my life doing regular stuff... instead I've got an 'itch' to write things, even to the exclusion of regular family-type pleasures... trying to figure things out! It'd be a lot easier if I was content just adding a few more regular science fiction novels, or cook books, or management books etc. to the latest books being published... But God made me the way I am to write strange things! It's all His fault!"

212 **Truck Driver** (*scratching her head with her left hand while casually steering with her right hand*): "That's some heavy stuff there, Dan! You some sort of a preacher? Is that why you wuz really comin' from the Church of the Hills? You fixin' to try and get them to give you an invite ta go give a sermon there? But... if that's so... you shore don't talk like any preacher ah ever heard before! What is it you really want, Lyle?"

²¹³ **Lyle** (*smiling*): "Thanks, Burt. I take that as quite a compliment. No, I'm not a preacher. But maybe I am 'some sort' of a *Teacher*... hopefully the *best* sort of a teacher who doesn't just give speeches but actually 'facilitates' the best type of learning. And... as to what I *really* want... well... I'm starting to question my motivations... recognition? Praise? Success? Acknowledgement I exist? Meaningfulness? It's really hard to get into my own brain..."

²¹⁴ **Truck Driver**: "'Facili...*who's*'???"

²¹⁵ **Lyle**: "Oh, sorry about that, Burt. There I went and used the Quality Management unfamiliar terms. A 'facilitator' is a person who *helps* other people be able to get to where *they* want to go. The best motivation of all is from inside. A trained Facilitator know the techniques and good methods for getting at what's inside of us, then letting it loose in a way that doesn't hurt oneself or others---channeling it to actually help ourselves and others---especially when people need to work smoothly together. Does that make some sense to you, or am I just jabbering again?"

²¹⁶ **Truck Driver** (*pondering a moment before answering; taking a long pull at the cigar then blowing out a cloud of white smoke*): "Maybe. So you're sayin' you don't just condemn people and order them to get their lives right by your standards, like regular-type preachers. Instead, you-all sayin' you help them ta somehow *themselves* see the bad and how to figure out fer *themselves* how to get better? Or, contrawise, ta help them see whut's good and how to get it?"

²¹⁷**Lyle** (*smiling at her clear statements*): "You've hit it on the mark, Burt. That's what I try to do with my books. But, unfortunately, I haven't mastered the part of getting people to see the need. So far, no one's interested in reading my books. But I still am able to do some limited creative facilitation for kids where I go to church. That's rewarding. I suppose if I can somehow help just one person to actually move closer to God then I've not totally failed. It's like you and your grandkids. Maybe you are trapped forever by your own addiction to nicotine, but you've probably kept dozens of others from the same fate... if not by your words then by your *bad* example of how hurtful the addiction can be to a person's life!"

²¹⁸ **Truck Driver** (*frowning in irritation, but not looking angry*): "Hmmmm. Don't mince your words, none, do you, Dan?"

²¹⁹ **Lyle**: "Sorry if I was offensive, Burt. You remember when you first asked me if I smoked---that I didn't mention at all the many negatives, but instead found a way to positively acknowledge my being in 'your house' and subject to your rules, which includes smoking 'in house'.

However, I'm a 'Ph.D.' Medical Biologist. I know full well what all that burnt smoke and addictive drug is doing to your cells and tissues. It's pretty horrible. I've also seen the end-results too often in hospitals where I've worked. Very gruesome! In fact, I *hate* tobacco."

220 **Truck Driver** (*narrowing her eyes in puzzlement*): "So why ain't you lecturin' me to quit!?"

221 **Lyle**: "If you want, I'd be happy to give you some lectures that would curl your eye-teeth! But I respect you too much to try to force you to live up to whatever 'standards', as you say, that I may have for my own life, my own 'house'. Also, I know from a physiological and genetic perspective how it can be almost impossible sometimes to get rid of addictions. In fact, I believe that I have those 'addictive genes' in me as well! I regard myself as being the best type of alcoholic---one that's never taken the first drink! Even minor things can quickly 'take control' of my life and dictate my actions. During graduate school I unknowingly got hooked on pain killers, caffeine, and fatty foods! That's because I was so stressed-out I felt sick all the time and took to taking an Anacin pill every hour and a half. And then to keep my guts from rotting-out from all that constant aspirin usage I unconsciously started eating lots of smooth, fatty foods! So now I avoid all the addictive drugs, even caffeine, because I'm so susceptible to them! Also, it took me years to get rid of the fat I laid onto my body during those years---which hops right back on me if I give-in to my fat addiction! So I understand from my own life how hard it is to get rid of addictions, even minor ones, whether behavioral or chemical! It's not just a matter of how 'strong' is our willpower. There's a lot more going on than just making a conscious choice! Addictive drugs get into our brains and subvert cell signaling pathways! They create their own need by taking over synaptic biochemical systems in which the body stops making the normal chemicals that keep us in balance! So just to feel 'normal' people have to have that external drug! People can become true slaves to their addictions, losing control of personal choice! The power of 'mind-over-matter' only extends so far!"

222 **Truck Driver** (*abruptly changing the subject*): "So where'd you come from, mister?"

223 **Lyle**: "Oh, sorry if I was getting too worked up on the tobacco-nicotine topic, Burt. I didn't mean to seem to be 'nailing' you in particular. It's just that nicotine is such a good example of how us puny little humans let our genetics dictate our actions, even to doing things that seem in our best immediate interests but can have terrible long-term results. We often don't realize how much of our life is spent dancing to the tune of our genetic programming: in other words, just being smart animals. A big part of religion is supposedly to rise above our animal na-

ture. But then, perversely, religion often devolves into being just another way to satisfy our genetically-programmed survival instinct! But to answer your question, Burt, I'm just a regular person. I grew up in California, went to Europe when my 'Uncle Sam' insisted I had to go into the military back during the 'Vietnam War'---going into the U.S. Air Force with a guarantee to do hospital work as a medical laboratory technician---then, having survived the war effort, went to graduate school back in California, and finally had some jobs culminating at the Food and Drug Administration on the East Coast of the United States. That's where I work now, as I'm simultaneously going through these additional experiences. So as we already discussed, I suppose that I went on a 'retreat' into the mountains here... was hiking all by myself, lost my supplies, got lost myself, then barely survived going across the glacier up there, discovered your 'Church of the Hills' and spent the night there. Then you kindly picked me up in your truck! And here I am talking to you! There it is---a summary of my life!"

[224] **Truck Driver** (*squinting knowingly*): "Yep. Here you are... and me too! Maybe God put us together here in my truck for some reason! It's sort of what that little church does, also...! You know, they leave their church building open on purpose. It's actually right neighborly of them to help out the occasional passing 'hiker'---I call them 'bums'---I suppose you ate the communion?"

[225] **Lyle** (*embarrassed*): "Uh, yes I did... but I left all the money I had in its place?"

[226] **Truck Driver**: "Well I guess that's somethin'. Not many bums'd do that. So why didn't you just call for help on your cell phone when you got in trouble up in the mountains, as you claim?"

[227] **Lyle** (*even more embarrassed*): "Uh, well, I didn't bring one. You see I don't like people calling me in the middle of trying to accomplish my high priorities. Also, I like having my own space... guess that's another reason I've managed to stay single---too selfish to give up even closet space! And here I was on a 'retreat' from civilization, so it just seemed best to..."

[228] **Truck Driver** (*frowning as she forcefully interrupted him*): "---so let me get this straight... you say you went all by yore lonesome without even some pretty gal as a climbin' companion up into these high mountains without any way ta call fer help if you got into trouble?? You're tryin' ta tell me thet you ain't smart enough to turn off your cell phone but have it available to use in emergencies? Real mountain climbers got those special phones that reach up to satellites! And what the hell are you doing up here this time of year anyway? We get the hippie hikers in

the spring and summer, some in the fall---but never in the dead of winter! And they jist love to come along with their girlfriends and boyfriends fer companionship! Heck, I've even seen 'Jesus' up here with his backpackin' 'Missus Jesus' hobblin' along at his side, poor thing! Just what sort of an idiot do you take me for, Dan? I certainly didn't size you up to be a *liar*!"

[229] **Lyle** (*sighing ruefully*): "Alright, Burt. You got me... I didn't tell you everything... which will explain why I may seem 'atypical' to your regular mountain-retreater! So... ok, then...you want it... so here's the full truth of the matter. First of all there's no lady with me because, well, even though my genetics certainly make me like them well enough, they don't seem to think much of a snake-loving biologist! My houseful of snake cages---even though they are all harmless, nonpoisonous, 'pet-store-snakes---protect me quite well from most romantically-inclined females! Also, their genetics tend to have them see 'romance', naturally enough, as the means to helping them make and raise children! Now I've nothing against children---wonderful things at their best---but again, that's a huge responsibility that burns up huge amounts of time, energy, and money! If I took on those heavy responsibilities I couldn't give my artistic urgings their full due, no matter how futile that effort may be. So that's the reason I haven't settled down with some pretty girl... too selfish! I prefer a houseful of pet reptiles---tortoises, lizards, and snakes---to a wife and kids! There! I said it! But the real reason I'm up here alone with no equipment is that... I didn't choose to be here... It's just like I said before about my compulsion to try to figure things out! I was *forced* to be here, because... well, you see... uhm... I know this may sound a bit crazy... *God* brought me here! He brought me here 'in the spirit' to put me on trial for heresy! I had a big trial up on the highest peak in front of a panel of my peers where they condemned me to death. But then God sort of... *pardoned* me... I guess. It was all kind of confusing... but I somehow managed to climb down and here I am... without a cell phone or much anything else! And more questions than ever..."

[230] **Truck Driver** (*turning her head to stare at Lyle for a moment in amazement, before bursting out laughing*): "Hah! Good one, Lyle! You really had me going there! *God* grabbed you up and stuck you up on a mountain's peak! *Hah!* Ok... I see you don't want to tell me what really happened. I get it. People have their reasons fer doin' what they do, some obvious and some private. And I ain't pryin' into your private life! Yore love-life ain't somethin' ah'm interested in---though there might be a lovin' girl somewhere willin' to read some of yore crazy books! Now, puttin' up with a houseful of pet *snakes* is somethin' else again...! You jist keep gettin' stranger and stranger, Dan! Well, a lot of things, I guess, can cause people to end up hobbling down this mountain road needin' a ride. But, whatever really brought you here, you *is* obviously on some

sort of 'spiritual quest', that's fer sure. So I guess I'm asking---just out of my own curiosity, mind you---if up in them big old mountains of ours... did you find what you wuz lookin' fer?"

231 **Lyle** (*relieved that his host had not tossed him out of the truck when he told her the full truth of how he'd gotten to be there in her cab*): "Ok, Burt... I *am* searching... and as to 'did I find the answers?'... I don't know. We're back to those 'big' questions again... perhaps that have no answers we can comprehend! Maybe I did find some answers... But, like I said, I think I ended up with more questions than I started out with! It's very confusing... I guess I was looking for some direction or affirmation. I sure didn't get a ringing endorsement from on high... but I did, I think, maybe get some encouragement. But then how to move forward from there became a blur... Perhaps that's the main point of it all. Life isn't just getting to some arbitrary Destination. Even when we occasionally do manage to climb up to some high Peak... we can't stay there---it's too rarified and dangerous!---and we've quickly got to descend back into the valleys! Also, though, life isn't just a Journey to some destination, as mystics like to put it. Instead, maybe life is... more of a *Struggle*... where we try to make God happy by using His Gift that He has given to each of us: a God-like '*Godly Creativity*'. And through that intensely-enjoyable practice of our God-given talents attempting to do worthy things... maybe we learn what's good and bad inside of us: cleaning, refining, and growing our spirits! But any sort of cutting-off or grafting into ourselves is bound to be very painful! So it's kind of like going back to the old notion of the 'gods' of Olympus looking down on us, amused by our sufferings! But, instead of laughing at our struggles, I believe that the Great Creator is *pleased* with our attempts---however feeble or futile---to put something where before there was nothing... that is reasonable, useful, respectful, beautiful, and honorable! Just making that *attempt* elevates us beyond being mere smart animals. It is counter-intuitive to our immediate survival instinct. Instead of staying safe doing what's simple, easy, and safe we choose instead to attempt that which is dangerous, hard, and complicated! Instead of seeking comfort we seek to be uncomfortable! It's irrational! But as an empowering personal philosophy it is very powerful. Nonetheless, though, my compulsion to push it beyond me to others may be doomed. Maybe that's the main lesson I need to learn here. Maybe the most 'respectful' thing here is to use these concepts to shape my own personal effort at godliness while *not* bothering other people! So maybe I should just give up, stop trying to change things, and just live my own life without worrying about connecting with other people. That would make things a whole lot simpler. Also it might be a lot less frustrating and a lot more fun for me! I could take whatever little extra money I might have and instead of using it trying to advance this new religious methodology that no one wants---to instead spend it on stuff all for *me*! There's something to be said for a ruthless selfishness! Come to

think of it... I might be able to build in my own home a projection system to watch incredible movies and concerts 'full-size', all of which I would find tremendously enjoyable! Or I might do like other of my friends do---go on marvelous but very expensive vacations all around the world! I could just stop trying to fund out of my pocket my weird book projects that no one has any interest in and use that money totally for myself! Yes! How about that? Maybe that's what I *really* want!"

232 **Truck Driver** (*nodding thoughtfully as they bounced along, picking up speed as the downward slope increased even steeper*): "Nice speech, Lyle. You make a good case for giving up. But... ah suspects... you're back again to that there 'compulsion' thing---you *have* to do it, don't you?"

233 **Lyle** (*growling in frustration*): "*Damn* it! You're *right*! That stupid inward compulsion *drives* me to keep on trying... whether I ever get any overt success or not! Does that make me into my most despised enemy, Burt---a Fanatic? Have I lost all touch with reality? Am I just rolling along powered only by my self-generated fumes?"

234 **Truck Driver** (*snorting as she chomped down tightly on her cigar, spitting out her words*): "Hah! So you're sayin' you've got yore own 'fumes' problem? But seriously, Dan, you definitely in my book *are* way out there on the fringes of reality! But it dies put you right out there with *Jesus, Buddha, Confucius, Muhammad, Moses, Abraham*... and jist about all the rest of the great religious icons in history! Ah's done my share of readin' about the history of the world, Dan. We got a nice little library in town where I go and cozy up with all sorts of strange books that otherwise just gather dust on the back shelves. Plus, I love to read 'Time' magazine and see what's out there now-a-days also. That's why I enjoy picking up nuts, bums, and kooks like you---because I get a different perspective on things! You got what ah've read is called a '*righteous insanity*' that afflicts a favored few who are *cursed* to wander the world always unhappy with how things are! You cain't jist settle down and be content! You got an itch you've gotta scratch! You got to try to *change* things, *mix* things up, and *be better*---even when things are pretty much 'ok' ta start with! You see problems where others don't! You see 'opportunities' where others jist shrug and accept the 'status quo'! Ah may be myself jist a grade school dropout thet 'edjumicated' myself... but so wuz Abraham Lincoln---and see what happened to him! That's right! He became President of the United States of America, changed society for the better, and got a bullet through his brain for his troubles! So, yes, Lyle, I think ah understands where you be comin' from! Yes, it don't make much sense---but to you that don't matter! You still gotta do what you gotta do! In fact, ah knows that feelin' all too well myself! I cain't get my own life together but I still cain't help but try and change my grandkids fer the bet-

ter... I gotta have my own damn cancer-stick but ah don't want my cut little kinfolks to get hooked on it also! So I jist keeps on a-naggin' at my young-uns' young-uns'...hah! Now ain't that a trick..."

235 **Lyle** (*a bit overwhelmed*): "Well... see what I said about you being a beautiful person? Not only do you pick up us 'hippy' hikers but you *listen* to us as well---when no one else will! For a 'seeker' that's the biggest gift you could possibly give to me. You're a lot smarter than you make out to be! And, by the way, thanks for your great compliment. I don't think of myself on the level of Jesus, but I do think that God talks to each of us and prods us each to try to be our best. And I'll bet you don't drive down these back roads because you get paid a fortune to do it! How much of what you do is 'charity' work---done just to help people out of their troubles?"

236 **Truck Driver**: "Well, now that you mention it... that's right perceptive of you. Some of what I do is for nothin' but token payments. A lot of folks out here are dirt poor... just hangin' on. Or they are old folks whose kids have moved off. They ain't got much money. Ah do like's to help them out a bit... get their groceries, give them a ride in to town to see their doctors, that sort of thing..."

237 **Lyle** (*nodding*): "I thought so. All of us do bad things, Burt, both to ourselves and others. That's because we're all of us just sorry old, grubby humans who screw up. It's not something I'm proud of about myself, but it is part of what I am. I'll screw up until the day that I die. There are faults in me that I can't get rid of, no matter how many preachers lecture me on them. But---just maybe---I can also rise above my animal nature to now and then do things that are helpful to me and others: doing that which makes good sense, has a positive outcome, doesn't hurt other people, is beautiful, and of which I can be proud. I suspect you also do the same."

238 **Truck Driver**: "Well, maybe so. But probably not as much as ah should do... and not as much as I'd like!"

239 **Lyle**: "So then Burt, those motivations in you are also at the heart of Christianity. I like to say that Jesus was a Creative-Theologist who would have heartily endorsed 'Creative-Theology® '. Are you perchance a church-goer yourself, perhaps a member of that little congregation back there?"

240 **Truck Driver**: "Hah! I went there a few times but the preacher twern't none too happy with me. Ah guess ah asked too many uppity questions. For him the definition of 'heresy' seemed to be to ask 'why?' Ah just didn't swallow his line---hook, bait, and sinker---like he wanted

me ta do. So I guess I'm damned to hell, huh? Least wise that's what he told me! Lessen ah repents of my evil ways, go to his church regular-like, and do the things he said I had to do... well, then ah wuz headed straight fer the hot spot!"

241 **Lyle**: "I think we'll both find out eventually that God is a lot more sympathetic and understanding to us little humans than many preachers preach, Burt. Of course that doesn't excuse any bad things I do, especially when I know better. Do you want to hear a story that, though very illustrative of this point, you might find a bit offensive?"

242 **Truck Drive** (*snorting in derision*): "Why the hell not? The only thing I get out of picking up you 'hippy hikers' is the off-the-wall conversation. So you might as well lay it on me! 'Course you *are* provin' to be one of my *dangerous* hitch-hikers... but ah ain't scared of you! Ah never picked up one that stunk as bad as you! Ah kin still smell that mess of rotting meat you wuz carrying with you! So you've already made a powerful impression on me! Might as well give me the full blast! So go on, don't hold back! Hit me with everything you've got!"

243 **Lyle** (*laughing out loud*): "You know, Burt, back at the church... and before that in the woods... I felt there was something coming after me... something cold and deadly. It wasn't just some animal, like a wolf. I don't know exactly what it was but it scared me worse than I've ever been scared. But whatever it was, I feel that you rescued me from it when you so kindly stopped and picked me up. So I sure don't want to make you mad at me. Consequently, then, I'm not sure I should tell you this story or not..."

244 **Truck Driver**: "Dang it, Lyle! *Spit it out!*"

245 **Lyle**: "Alright then, but remember that I warned you! It's about my Dad."

246 **Truck Driver**: "He alive?"

247 **Lyle**: "Passed on years ago."

248 **Truck Driver**: "Sorry ta hear thet..."

249 **Lyle**: "Thanks, Burt. Anyway, my Dad smoked also."

250 **Truck Driver**: "Yeah?"

251 **Lyle**: "Sure did. Of course that was back when I was a kid, when just about everyone smoked---back in the 1950's. Why not smoke? Every

hero in the movies or on T.V. smoked! The ads on billboards, T.V., or the movies all said how great it was! If you wanted to be a real 'cowboy' he-man or a sophisticated lady you smoked!"

252 **Truck Driver**: "So, then, as a kid, you wanted to smoke?"

253 **Lyle**: "Of course! In fact, at the grocery store in my town you could buy candy cigarettes in a little pack that looked just like the real ones! They were made out of colored sugar. They were slender white cylinders with a red tip. You stuck them in your mouth. They dangled from your lip. And you sucked-away on them like you were the cowboy hero in the movies and ads! And they tasted very sweet and delicious! I really liked them, as a kid! Plus, like I said, my very own Dan smoked! So I figured just matter-of-factly that as soon as I was allowed to do so, I'd be smoking too!"

254 **Truck Driver**: "Ok, so what happened?"

255 **Lyle:** "Well, one day my Dad came home from seeing the doctor with a bandage on his lip."

256 **Truck Driver**: "On his lip, you say? Must have looked strange to you..."

257 **Lyle**: "Sure did. I didn't know what was up. He never mentioned it to me. But my mother told me what it was."

258 **Truck Driver**: "A tumor?"

259 **Lyle**: "Yes. It was right there at the exact spot that his cigarette usually dangled. He'd grown a benign tumor on his lip, the start of cancer. He played with fire and it burned him..."

260 **Truck Driver** (*snorting*): "Humph! So what happened then?"

261 **Lyle**: "He never smoked again. Never! Not cigars. Not cigarettes. Not snuff... nothing! And that made a big impression on me. He didn't have to say a word to me about not smoking. I figured it all out by his actions. But without him quitting cold-turkey like that... well, I don't know where I'd be today. Probably I'd have started out young---with the other kids behind the bleachers on the playground at school. I saw them there! But I was never tempted to join them. But if I had done so, I don't know what that would have done to my present health, my life goals, whatever influence I have over others, or my positive impact on young people. All I know for sure on the subject is that I had tremendous respect for my father. His example of doing whatever it took to kick his

life-long smoking habit was proof that smoking was not all that the movies, T.V., and billboard ads were saying it was. Smoking wasn't just another sweet treat."

262 **Truck Driver** (*snorting in amusement, taking another long drag on her now-stub of a cigar*): "So, am I supposed to get some lesson from your story that I don't already know? Maybe that crack you made about *'playin' with fire and getting' burned'*?"

263 **Lyle**: "Oh... sorry about that crack, Burt. I guess I'm still trying to relate it all back to me... FIRE can enable the start of civilization---or a conflagration destroying everything in its path! But... back to my Dad... It's just a story, Burt. And, like you said, it's late in your life. But people are still learning from you. You have a lot powerful influence especially from young people who look up to you... even kids that never asked you a thing about smoking."

264 **Truck Driver** (*taking a last long drag on the stub before rolling-down the window a bit and tossing the remnants out*): "Ok! I agree it's something to think about---that is until about fifteen minutes from now when the craving starts in again and I light me up a nice fresh Camel's cigarette from my pack in the glove compartment. Like I said before, some people can quit without much trouble. Maybe your Dad was like that. But I'm not. Quitting is *not* an option for me. I jist *have* to have it!"

265 Both of them became quiet. Lyle was glad to sink back into an exhausted silence as they continued bouncing down the dirt road. The fever was kicking-up in his head again, making his vision bleary... THANK GOD HIS FIERY TRIALS WERE ALMOST OVER---HE DIDN'T KNOW HOW MUCH MORE HE COULD POSSIBLY STAND...

266 Then up ahead, Lyle managed to make out the meadows to their sides ending at a steep decline...

267 Burt applied squealing brakes to slow their speed as they swung out into a narrow, two-lane, paved road.

268 Though the sky was still overcast and gloomy---seemingly in the evening now after their long dialogue---in reality it was still early in the morning! No other cars were around. Off to Lyle's right, out of the window, right next to the road, he saw a steep slope beyond which the vista of the high mountain chain loomed. To their left, directly against the road, rose a sheer vertical cliff.

²⁶⁹ The paved road dipped sharply, the truck picking up speed as it raced down the decline...

²⁷⁰ **Truck Driver**: "It's only about twenty minutes to town, Dan. We jist gotta make it down this steep part. It's real twisty... we'll go slow! Lucky mah brakes are in fine order... puts quite a strain 'em! I just got them checked-up a week ago! Some drizzle's startin' to fall, so the road'll be slick. But we'll be fine! Mah tires ain't more than four or five years old, well... maybe six or seven... but they've been down this here decline thousands of times before! It's kind of fun, lots of quick turns! It's sort of like one of them *roller-coasters* at a 'theme' park... Hah! You like to have fun, don't cha, Dan! This is the best part of my route!"

²⁷¹ **Lyle** (*elated to finally be minutes away from returning safely to civilization, but still with the nagging feeling that something wasn't quite right... that something terrible was coming closer and closer: that malignant "Presence" returned to hover now right above their careening vehicle!*): "Uh, you've a fine truck here, Burt. It's a real classic, for sure. And if you can drop me off at any motel or hotel that'd be super... or, come to think of it, maybe a doctor's office would work also! I think I (cough) need some antibiotics or something... or at least a good night's sleep. Maybe then I can sort my thoughts out better, figure out what I really want... And I'm all out of cash, but if you'd wait around for a minute I'm sure I can find an ATM to use my credit card on. I insist on paying you for your time and gas!"

²⁷² **Truck Driver** (*lowering her voice, speaking firmly*): "You tryin' to *insult* me, Lyle?"

²⁷³ **Lyle**: "Oh no! Certainly not! But I want to make it clear I'm not one of those 'hippy bums' you've referred to that only gave you conversation..."

²⁷⁴ **Truck Driver** (*fiercely frowning over at him*): "You already gave me more than jist jabbering! Maybe I'm not changed miracle-wise into some church-goin' smoke-quitin' saint, but you've got me thinkin'. Also, I got to admit you make me feel a wee bit important. I like that. You got a gift, Lyle. You know how to lift people up, encourage them instead of jist beat them down! And, come to think of it, maybe you should listen to *yourself* more often instead of bein' so negative on your achievements! Ain't you the one preachin' that 'success' isn't that important---it's the *effort* that matters?"

²⁷⁵ **Lyle** (*blinking, bemused, his hot-shivering body/brain not processing well what she'd just said to him*): "Uh, well... but that doesn't answer what I really want deep down..."

276 **Truck Driver** (*tensing in her seat as she snapped her eyes back forward*): "*Uh-oh!!*"

277 **Lyle**: "What...??"

278 **Truck Driver**: "Hang on tight! The brakes just went out!"

279 **Lyle** (*startled, looking down to see her foot banging uselessly on the limp brake-peddle as they suddenly picked up speed*): "But... you said you just got them fixed!"

280 **Truck Driver**: "Not fixed. I got them 'looked-at'. They told me they wuz good fer a few more months! Guess not!"

281 **Lyle** (*swallowing hard as he grabbed onto the dashboard in front of him, shouting over the roar of the speeding-up engine*): "CAN YOU SHUT OFF THE ENGINE AND GEAR DOWN?"

282 **TRUCK DRIVE** (*growling as she jammed the gear stick around with a big hand, wincing at the "screeching" coming out of the gear box*): "WHAT THE HELL YOU THINK I'M DOING? MY FOOT'S OFF THE GAS AND AH NEEDS THE CONTROL OF THE ENGINE RUNNING. DAMN! AH THINK THE GEARS STRIPPED! WE'LL JIST HAVE TA STEER THE CURVES AS BEST WE CAN!"

283 The truck whipped around a curve, barely hanging onto the road...

284 ---as Lyle gulped, looking out over a steep drop "whizzing" by under his window.

285 Immediately to their left was the sheer cliff going up, nowhere to pull over on that side. To the right was the slope plummeting down...

286 The road before them, cut-out of the cliff, descended rapidly...

287 ---another sharp curve coming up right in front of them as the truck sped faster and faster...

288 Desperately wishing Burt hadn't taken out the seatbelts, Lyle was thrown to his left against Burt as the cab missed the turn, spun over to the right, and *leapt* beyond the edge of the narrow road into open air... "CRASHING" and "SMASHING" as it hit hard rock, "*CRUNCHING*" its way down the steep slope...

[289] The last thing Lyle remembered of the fall was Burt's puzzled look beside him as she still clung tightly to the wheel trying to steer through thin air, the entire world spinning around them...

. . . .

At a bar

²⁹⁰ Lyle looked up at the overcast sky, absently blinking red out of his eyes... on his back, his right leg twisted under his body; convulsing, feeling tentatively at a cut above one eye and gashes on both cheeks...

²⁹¹ He staggered up, thankful his legs still worked though they hurt terribly, particularly the right one that'd gotten twisted---dazed and looking down the steep rocky slope at a tiny-looking little truck squashed-up down at the bottom, smashed against some big boulders... its back end on fire!

²⁹² ---when the gas tank *EXPLODED* and THE TRUCK WAS CONSUMED IN A ROARING BLACK CLOUD OF *SMOKE AND FLAMES...*

²⁹³ **Lyle** (*painfully starting to slide down the slope in the direction of the burning wreckage*): "Oh my God! Burt! I'm coming..."

²⁹⁴ **Truck Driver**: "Don't... get all... shook up... I'm... over here..."

²⁹⁵ **Lyle** (*tripping to his knees then crawling over to her crumpled body sprawled a few yards from him on the slope*): "Jesus, Burt. You're banged up pretty bad..."

²⁹⁶ **Truck Driver** (*weakly laughing while coughing up bright red blood*): "Hah! See... I told you... them damn seatbelts would... kill you..."

²⁹⁷ **Lyle** (*tears of relief welling up in his eyes to find his new friend still alive and "kicking"*): "Getting thrown out through the windshield didn't do us much good either, Burt..."

²⁹⁸ A gash sliced right across her forehead. The skin hung down in a flap. She was hunched-over on her side, clutching her ribs with her arms.

²⁹⁹ Both of her legs were twisted at strange angles, mangled and bloody.

³⁰⁰ **Truck Driver** (*coughing up more blood*): "Sorry... for the... rough ride... Lyle... looks like you weren't so lucky after all... having me pick you up..."

³⁰¹ **Lyle** (*gasping for his own breath, tearing a strip of cloth from her sleeve and wrapping it around her forehead as he talked*): "There, Burt. That'll stop the bleeding on your head. I don't suppose *you* have a cell phone on you, do you?"

³⁰² **Truck Driver** (*smiling weakly*): "'Course ah does, Dan! Ah uses it... all the time! It's in... the glove compartment... *hah*!"

³⁰³ **Lyle** (*looking in disbelief down at the flaming heap at the bottom of the steep slope*): "Right... well, I guess that won't help us much. I'm all bruised up, but I can still move. Maybe I can carry you back up to..."

³⁰⁴ **Truck Driver** (*wincing in pain*): "No! I'm... I'm hurt bad... Probably some busted ribs stickin' in mah lungs (*cough*)... ah cain't feel mah legs... maybe broke my back... no, jist leave me here. I'm no good to anyone no more anyways... my times up. You jist save yourself..."

³⁰⁵ **Lyle** (*angrily yelling at her*): "DON'T YOU TALK LIKE THAT! YOU JUST HANG ON, BURT! I'LL GO GET HELP! I'LL CLIMB BACK UP, FLAG DOWN A PASSING CAR. EVERYONE'S GOT CELL PHONES! THEY'LL CALL FOR HELP. WE CAN GET AN AMBULANCE HERE IN JUST A FEW MINUTES! OR SOMEONE WILL SEE THAT HUGE FIRE DOWN THERE AND STOP TO CHECK IT OUT!"

³⁰⁶ **Truck Driver** (*now speaking faintly with increasing difficulty*): "Today's... a holiday... 'President's Day' ah think... ain't many cars out this way even on a regular day, Dan... today you could wait fer hours for one to come by... and the fire's gonna be gone quick once all the gas in the tank is burnt up (cough)... maybe all day long no one'll come by anyway... best bet's for you ta walk down to the truck stop... it's only about five miles, half way between here and the town that's down in the valley... the bar's got a land-line phone... but don't worry about me. Ah think ah'm on that 'Golden Path' of yours... and it sure is beautiful, yes sir..."

³⁰⁷ Her voice trailed off and she was unconscious. Lyle took off the light jacket she'd given to him and placed it over her still-breathing upper body.

³⁰⁸ Then he looked up the slope, shuddering at the steep climb, realizing that in his present condition it wouldn't be easy just getting back up to the road! And then, how long would it take his weakened, banged-up body to make it an additional five difficult miles by foot?

³⁰⁹ Poor Burt was right. She didn't look like she'd last that long. So he'd better get to it... though the last thing his feverish, weakened, and battered body needed was a steep climb...

³¹⁰ Finally having somehow managed to painfully climb all the way up to the road, Lyle limped along favoring his aching right leg... yet again resorting to singing songs he'd written for his "Book of Lyle" to try to keep himself alert, distracting himself from his fevered exhaustion: "I'VE

GIVEN IT A GOOD TRY, NO REASON TO BE SAD OR CRY; EXPERIENCED LOTS OF POWERFUL THINGS, SEEN MY SPIRIT SOAR AND FELT IT BLEED; HELD NEWLY-HATCHED SNAKES IN MY HANDS, AVOIDED CONFLICTS OR TAKEN A STAND; BEEN TO THE TOPS OF MOUNTAINS, SAILED THE SEA...TOSSED BY A HURRICANE OR BALMY BREEZE: DOING BATTLE WITH MOTHER NATURE, MOST TIMES DEFEATED BY HER CRUELTY; YET OCCASIONALLY SHE'S TAKEN PITY, SMILED ON ME, AND LET ME SUCCEED: GRUDGINGLY GIVING UP SOME PRECIOUS SECRET, ALLOWING ME NEW INSIGHT... A REVELATION THAT'S AMAZ-INGLY EXHILARATING, THE GREATEST FUN OF ALL; WHERE BEFORE THERE WAS NOTHING YOU'VE MADE A WONDERFUL FANTASY REAL; SO EVEN THOUGH PAINS & DISTRESS MAY INCREASE---WHILE VULTURES CIRCLE FOR THEIR GORY FEAST---I'LL HAVE TO PROCLAIM IT'S BEEN QUITE A RIDE..."

[311] His voice trailed off as he kept hobbling along. It was much easier going downward on the paved road than it was struggling up that slope! But his throbbing head felt like twice its normal size. He was tempted to just sit down and slump over, take a much-deserved rest, perhaps a short nap, despite his brave song maybe to just *give up*... now quite willing to sink down into an exhausted, woozy sleep...

[312] No! He had to keep going! He couldn't stop! If he stopped he'd never get started again! He needed to sing out even LOUDER... to keep his spirits buoyed and determined!

[313] **Lyle** (*belting out the words in short bursts, as forcefully as he could, between fits of hacking and coughing*): "I AM YOUR CREATION BEAUTIFUL AND BRIGHT...!

[314] FILLED WITH YOUR SPIRIT, BURSTING TO GET OUT...!

[315] NOT JUST EMOTIONS BUT TANGIBLE DELIGHTS...!

[316] PUTTING WHERE WAS NOTHING---SOMETHING VERY NICE!"

[317] But the brave words on the cold mountain road sounded hollow, muted. They would be great sung or recited in a small group of healthy, happy folks in a room. But in the middle of this senseless tragedy, out in the vastness of nature, they seemed *empty*...

[318] So Lyle stopped singing entirely, concentrating rather on just keeping each wavering step coming after the other... one after the other... staying on his staggering feet... not falling down... next step, next step, next step...

³¹⁹ And as he doggedly trudged down the pavement he looked upward at grey, roiling clouds... getting more and more *angry*... his mood turning as ugly as the darkening sky... finally lifting up his fists to the sky, and *screaming-out* as loud as he could:

³²⁰ **Lyle:** "LORD!?? WHY IS ALL THIS HAPPENING!? WHAT IS IT THAT I SHOULD LEARN?? *TELL ME*! I TRY TO DO YOUR WILL---BUT ALL THAT HAPPENS IS PEOPLE GET HURT!

³²¹ WEREN'T WHAT THE SEEKER AND THE BYSTANDER SUFFERED ENOUGH? WHY MORE? WHY DOES BURT HAVE TO DIE!?? SHE'S A SOLID PERSON, GOOD-HEARTED!

³²² CAN'T YOU JUST TAKE ME INSTEAD? I LEARNED THE LESSON OF THE LITTLE MOUNTAIN CHURCH! MAYBE ONE OR TWO PEOPLE IN THE WHOLE ENTIRE WORLD MIGHT BENEFIT A BIT FROM 'CREATIVE-THEOLOGY®', BUT I'LL NOT TROUBLE THE REST IF THAT'S WHAT YOU WANT! MY DUMB BOOKS WON'T BE PUSHED ON ANYONE WHO DOESN'T WANT THEM!

³²³ I'LL JUST FADE AWAY, TAKE MY PLACE WITH ALL THE OTHER FAILED 'GURUS' DOWN THROUGHOUT HISTORY! I PROMISE NOT TO TROUBLE OR BOTHER YOUR ESTABLISHED, SUCCESSFUL RELIGIONS IF YOU'D RATHER ME NOT!

³²⁴ I'LL NOT ROCK THE BOAT OR THROW A CURVE BALL OR CRASH ANOTHER TRUCK! I GET IT! I SEE WHAT YOU'RE TELLING ME! PLEASE DON'T HURT ANYONE ELSE BECAUSE OF MY DELUSIONS OF GRANDEUR! LET YOUR FIRE BURN ME UP!"

³²⁵ But there was no answer from the sky expect for a few far-off flashes of lightning, rapidly growing nearer... So Lyle lowered his head and just kept on plodding forward, struggling to put one foot in front of the other... wincing from the pain each time his right leg pushed down...

³²⁶ Until, finally---stumbling through now-streaming sheets of rain and brutally-cold gusts of wind---he saw a roadside café on a wide outcrop beside the road, with a fluorescent sign flickering on-and-off: "BAR AND GRILL, TRUCKERS WELCOME".

³²⁷ Lurching eagerly forward, Lyle limped up to and banged with both fists on the solid-wood front door. Only after knocking for a while with no response did he notice there was a small, painted board secured to the door which read: *"Closed for Holiday"*.

328 Lyle stopped pounding his fists on the door, wiped the rain out of his eyes, and yelled up at the sky: "OH, COME ON! WHAT SORT OF RESTAURANT CLOSES FOR A HOLIDAY?" ---apparently an isolated, small mountain bar all by itself five miles from town did so. Lyle slid around the slick wall to a window while icy wind and torrential rain slammed into both him and the building. The window had *solid black bars* over it---no way to get past them even if he somehow broke the glass behind the bars! But squinting through the wind-whipped rain, rubbing away grime on the glass behind the bars with his sleeve, he could just make-out by close lightning flashes what looked to be *a phone hanging on the wall* to the side of a bar counter. So he continued to work his way around to the back of the building, trying to see through the torrents of rain drenching him... but everything was barred up solid! The doors were impenetrable. The ground-floor windows were all covered with thick black grills. Obviously, they'd had problems before with would-be burglars out there isolated so far away from the town! "HELP ME OUT HERE LORD!" he screamed up at the dark clouds. "COME ON! CUT ME A BREAK! THIS PLACE IS A FORTRESS! I'VE GOT TO GET INSIDE TO USE THAT PHONE!"

329 And then he noticed a high, small, bathroom window that was unbarred! He found a crate, located a large rock, and dragged over a garbage can... then clutching the rock in one hand managed to stack the garbage can precariously on top of the crate and clamber up on both of them... tottering precariously in the pounding rain... shakily reaching up to the closed, small window---and SLAM the rock with all his strength into the glass above him...

330 ---SHATTERING the window inwards, banging-out most of the remaining last glass shards, grabbing the window's edge, and laboriously dragging his body up inch-by-inch, then squirming forward jamming his body through the narrow opening... then falling ten feet down, twisting and CRASHING into the concrete floor below him... "Auuugggggghhhhhh!!!" he screamed, clutching his right leg that he'd unfortunately landed on... "I broke it... I broke it... I broke it..." Lyle moaned, rolling in pain in the darkness. After a while the horrific pain lessened a bit, enough for him to feel along his lower leg to see if a bone was poking through... nothing... maybe just fractures... He'd hurt that leg in the car crash but now it felt definitely broken. Also, his left arm was terribly bruised, swelling... Painfully he felt around, grabbing the lip of a toilet seat with his right arm, getting up on the toilet, sitting, feeling around in the gloom... a broom! Using it as a sort of crutch under his right armpit he levered himself up---hobbling, searching for a light to turn on in the darkened interior...

331 Clicking a light switch he got a bulb hanging down from above to turn on. *"Oh, thank God..."* Lyle gulped, trying to ignore the blazing pain in his broken right leg, hopping on his left leg to a dirty sink to grab its edge, steadying himself... seeing his reflection in the mirror behind it... *"Oh, Lord!"* he gasped, seeing reflected back at him the image of a haggard, hollow-eyed, scraggly-bearded, long-haired apparition coated with clotted blood from jagged cuts... *"I'm a bloody mess..."* he groaned, reaching down to turn on some water to try and clean his face with... But the light above suddenly flickered-out! "OH, COME ON!" he cried-out, "NO, NO, NO!"... Fumbling in the sudden gloom back along the wall over to the switch... up-and-down, up-and-down... he got nothing! Probably the now constantly-BOOMING lightning had blown out some fuses or a transformer... maybe even downed a power line from trees or their branches falling in the gale-force wind howling outside...

332 Lyle slowly lurched out of the bathroom, continuing to use the broom as a crutch, into near-total darkness in the building's interior, feeling his way along a wall. He inched into the front bar area he'd glimpsed through the front windows. He felt the edge of the bar counter that was closest to the back wall. He followed along its backside, running a shaking hand under the countertop. *"There's got to be a flashlight in here somewhere..."* he moaned, feeling with his trembling left hand past piles of papers and various other items stored beneath the bar countertop... his right hand laid on top of the countertop bumping into a large object... probably the cash register... feeling deeper beneath that "strategic" area he jerked out whatever was stored there onto the floor at his feet... when "BANG!"---*a loud explosion startled him, making him drop to the floor... followed by a cascade of glass crashing down all around him*, puncturing his head and arms... the searing pain in his leg almost making him black out... then getting his breath back and fumbling at what was now strewn beneath his knees... recognizing the feel and form of a HAND GUN he gingerly lifted it up by its handle... *"Jesus Christ!"* he gasped. *"I could have killed myself!"* Leaving it there beside the register, in great pain levering himself back to his feet with the dropped broom, continuing to fumble his left hand beneath the countertop... "Ah! There it is!" he gasped in relief, feeling in the storage opening a familiar cylindrical object, pulling it out and flicking it on. Suddenly a shaft of weak light illuminated the area around him---revealing beside him part of the big mirror behind the lined-up glass bottles that'd been blown into pieces by the bullet from the gun... and, yes, there on the wall at the end of the bar was indeed a phone! "I'VE GOT YOU NOW!" he cried-out in triumph, lurching over to it, lifting the receiver and punching-out "911"... but... but... it was just as dead as the electricity! No dial tone, nothing! *"NO, NO, NO!"* he screamed-out in disgust and anger, *slamming* the receiver against the wall repeatedly. "I FINALLY GET TO A PHONE AND THEN IT'S *DEAD*!? REALLY??? *REALLY???* WHAT ARE YOU DOING TO ME,

LORD???" he sobbed, as, drained of energy Lyle dropped the receiver to dangle on its cord... then hobbled his aching, bleeding body over to a booth and sat down... *"The phone line must be downed, along with the power lines!"* he groaned to no one in particular. He felt helpless... his leg swelling and throbbing... drained of all strength. Somehow he'd managed to make it all the way up the slope at the site of the wreck, then all the way down the road to the truck stand! There it was impossible to get into the locked-down fortress of the restaurant---but he still found a way! His leg was broke but he still found the phone! He'd done everything he possibly could do on his own! But all of that struggle and heroic effort didn't make any difference at all! Nothing mattered! Nothing at all mattered now... There was no way he'd be able to make it the miles down the road to the town on his broken leg in the near-hurricane that was pounding the walls of the small restaurant, blackening the windows... and according to the sign on the door, they wouldn't open the bar until the next day.... Lyle knew without a doubt that his fate---and that of Burt---was now totally beyond his own control. She'd surely not survive exposed on the icy slope where she lay unconscious. It was *hopeless*... he was at the end of his rope...

333 And as his eyes adjusted to the dim yellow light from the weak flashlight, he wearily looked over at the bar. *Behind it a number of liquor bottles that'd survived the bullet and broken mirror behind them were all neatly lined up, ready for him to go get some---and drown his sorrows!* Lyle felt a fierce compulsion now to do just that: to "medicate" himself into a total, uncaring, unfeeling silliness... after all, wasn't that what they were there for? Weren't they there to let stressed-out, exhausted truckers get some relief on their journey? Didn't he deserve that relief just as much as some truck-driver? If Burt were here, wouldn't she happily---without a thought to the contrary---throw down a few shots?

334 "WELL, WHY NOT? WHY *SHOULDN'T* I DO IT TOO!?" Lyle shouted above the pounding of the storm. "I'VE NEVER USED ADDICTIVE DRUGS OR ALCOHOL BEFORE, LORD... BUT THERE'S ALWAYS A FIRST TIME! I DID EVERYTHING THE BEST I COULD AND NOW YOU'VE DONE ALL THIS TO ME! YOU'VE TAKEN AWAY EVERYTHING FROM ME! I'VE GOT NO SELF-RESPECT LEFT! I'M A TOTAL FAILURE! I CAN'T EVEN HELP MYSELF LET ALONE HELP ANYONE ELSE! AND BECAUSE OF ME POOR BURT IS OUT THERE DYING! I DISTRACTED HER WITH ALL MY STUPID 'CONVERSATION' SO SHE DIDN'T PAY ATTENTION TO HER BRAKING AND SHE COULDN'T CONTROL HER TRUCK! SHE CRASHED BECAUSE OF ME! IT WAS MY FAULT! SO WHAT DO YOU WANT FROM ME, LORD? DO YOU JUST WANT ME TO SIT HERE IN TERRIBLE PAIN STEWING IN MY OWN JUICES WHILE SHE DIES? IS THAT MY PUNISHMENT? I DON'T UNDERSTAND! I JUST DON'T UNDERSTAND! *WHY* ARE

YOU DOING THIS TO ME? I TOLD YOU TO GO AHEAD AND BURN ME UP! IF THAT'S WHAT YOU WANT, THEN JUST DO IT! LET THE LIGHTNING STRIKE THIS BUILDING AND BURN IT ALL DOWN WITH ME INSIDE! MAKE MY STUPIDITY AN OFFERING ON YOUR GRAND ALTAR! I'M READY TO BE YOUR BURNT OFFERING!" But... no answer... just silence---so *why not* take the ready-solution lined up there on the wall... so able and "willing" to take away his immediate pains? There it all was, just waiting for him---as much as he'd ever need! *Maybe that's why he'd ended up in a bar! Perhaps drugs weren't such a dead end after all! When nothing else is left to do, all sorts of powerful chemicals are easy to buy that can instantly get rid of any crippling pain!* And isn't that why people smoked? It's just another way to dull the pain of the moment, right? Maybe Burt and all the many others addicted to nicotine had the right idea after all? Cease the pleasure of the moment however it came---as a pill, a food, a vapor, or a drink! *"Come get me!"* seemed to shout-out the many bottles of gin, beer, whiskey, wine, vodka---and all the other concoctions of alcohol over there patiently waiting up on the wall, beckoning for him to come over and just *drink them up*!

335 But then... isn't that what the dark "Presence" would like him to do? As Lyle sat there slowly swaying back and forth from waves of sizzling pain in his leg and head he suddenly *felt the Thing was right there with him, that malignant Force! He now knew without doubt that the Presence had followed him from the crash of the truck. It was no longer at a distance, hovering above him. No, it was sitting right next to him in the booth, invisibly staring at him... silently demanding acknowledgement of its dark power, dominance, and ultimate physical authority...* and all Lyle had to do was to simply give-in to its inevitability... and all the disappointment, frustrations, confusion, and mind-numbing pain would just *fade away*...!

336 Unable to do anything more to try to help himself or Burt, Lyle abruptly *give up*... feeling a huge burden lift off his shoulders... finally able to relax his body... as---leaving the flashlight behind beaming its weak light upward---he levered himself up out of the booth... limping with the broom handle under his right armpit over to behind the bar... and reached up for the first, handy bottle; marveling at the seductively-smooth glass surface in his hand... bringing it down tenderly... and cradled it tenderly in both hands. In the gloom it seemed to glow with a light of its own... a soft, warm *gold*! He was just able to make out in the dim light the writing on its label: *"Buchanan's Deluxe Scotch Whisky Aged 12 Years"*... must be the good stuff... He held it up to his lips, kissed it gratefully, then fumbled at the red plastic seal on its top... managed to scrape off the protecting covering... but... no cork... another hard plastic cover there... what? *"How does this damn thing come off? I can't get it off! Really? I can't even open up some stupid bottle!? Auggggghhhhhh!*

I'LL OPEN YOU UP!" he screamed above the howl of the outside storm... as he savagely *SMASHED the bottle down into the countertop, spraying broken glass and liquid all over his chest and arms*! Then---laughing shrilly at the new cuts dripping even more blood from his hands and arms---he hopped on his left leg back to the booth, slumped down into it... put his head on his folded arms... and cried like a baby! *"It won't work..."* he sobbed. *"I'm in too deep... I know too much..."* he gasped, realizing the futility of trying to stop the now all-encompassing pain surrounding and smothering him with just alcohol... *"But... but..."* he whispered, now in his utter defeat realizing that the *only really effective way to end the pain was also there within his easy reach...* forcing himself to stand back up, jerk his body alongside the bar, grab the waiting *gun*, and stumble back to the booth... settling down now with the handle of the *heavy, solid, weapon* held firmly in his right hand...

337 Lyle wearily sighed, finally understanding the "Presence" that'd stalked him for so long... that horrible Evil that'd hovered over him for most of his journey... coloring everything in bloody hues: that *terrible black cloud* frightening his own spirit, plunging him into a bubbling caldron of misery and self-doubt, *magnifying every inevitable pain in living life...*

338 ---dogging his every step, making him lose heart, especially when he tried his hardest; knocking him backward whenever he felt he'd gained a little bit of forward momentum, crushing his initiative...

339 ---making nothing seem worthwhile, magnifying all the negatives, smearing all the positives, filling-in the last missing piece to the puzzle of the Meaning of Life: *negating even the cosmic, awesome Magnificence of God Himself*!

340 ---a smothering cosmic Evil manifesting not as some super-powered, hellish, spiritual cartoon sporting a pitchfork, horns, and forked tail... but the true *"Unholy Trinity"* of LADY LUCK, MOTHER NATURE, and HUMAN FRAILTY:

341 ---so vividly apparent in the terrible crash of Burt's decrepit pickup truck: slick roads from a passing shower on a steep downward decline (*Mother Nature*), the brakes going out right then (*Lady Luck*), and Burt not having gotten the brakes fixed or tires changed when she knew they were both going bad (*Human Frailty*)...

342 ---bringing down even the loftiest, smartest, most-worthy plans of little Man: teaching even the most arrogant of humans that his/her life is always uncertain and ephemeral...

343 ---proving that "meaningfulness" cannot be defined by important achievements when all such can be instantly derailed. Yes... there's a grim "finality" to *everything*! "SO I'M A NOTHING, AM I?" Lyle shouted angrily up at the ceiling, the awful pain in his leg and futility of all it coursing down his cheeks as a river of tears... "I'M JUST A USELESS BAG OF *SHIT*, IS THAT IT?" he screamed above the roar of the pounding rain. "IS THIS REALLY WHAT YOU WANT ME TO DO, LORD? DO YOU WANT ME TO PROVE BY MY *SUICIDE* THAT I'M NOTHING IN COMPARISON TO YOU? DESPITE EVERYTHING YOU'VE GIVEN TO ME IN THIS LIFE DO YOU WANT ME TO THROW IT ALL AWAY TO PROVE HOW STUPID AND WORTHLESS I AM? WELL, WHY NOT?! WHY THE BLOODY HELL NOT!?" he sobbed... then, speaking shakily and more quietly: "*It would be nice... though... to end it all---all the fear, the failure, the awful pain---even if it's to drift forever in the icy, black void...*" he choked in defeat as he deliberately and slowly hoisted the heavy handgun into the air, pointed it at the right side of his head, and placed the cold muzzle firmly against the bare skin of his temple... as, happily clustered around the table, HE SENSED THE SPIRITS OF HIS OWN PERSONAL TORMENTORS---the black-robed Fanatic, Critic, and Lawyer---cheering him on, urging him to end it all... chanting in ghostly unison: "DO IT! DO IT! DO IT!"---if not by their hands, then just as sweet for them would be him doing it to himself... now all three clapping their hands in unison while simultaneously swaying from side to side, singing as if at a Gospel revival meeting: "*DO IT! DO IT! DO IT!*"---as in an utter black depression of pain and defeat he slowly slid his finger into the gun's trigger guard to squeeze the trigger...

344 *Lyle closed his eyes, ready to have it all end... but... pausing for just a moment... perhaps... did he detect a glimmer of a bright lining at the edge of the dark cloud surrounding him? A pestering thought nagged at him, making him hesitate: could that malignant Presence* also *be the rainbow after the heaviest storm? What a strange idea! Maybe the Unholy Trinity didn't just empty life of its zest... but might it also punctuate and enhance noble efforts?*

345 ---so that even *when we have very good reason to give up and say "why bother trying anything else?"*...might we somehow still persist, "keeping on keeping on", refusing to accept defeat even when everything comes to nothing---because we are NOT walking down an ever-descending earthly road leading to inevitable, ignoble defeat... but rather are climbing UP an ever-ascendin*g*, Divine, Golden Path? But... when measured next to the reality of the moment... are those just empty words, comforting delusions? "*My words that I've spoken so arrogantly to others, so laughable...*" Lyle sobbed, his hand trembling as he maintained his tight grip on the handle of the gun thrust into his temple; eager to end

the soul-draining weariness... impatient with his own fevered meanderings: "*I see now... why so many preachers... become hypocrites...*"

346 Lyle's thoughts swirled in a confused maelstrom: his fevered, confused brain's "last gasp" before the bullet plowed through---scrambling and destroying those magnificent, intricate, delicate neuronal networks forever. *But what if the Unholy Trinity really did exist for a purpose...?* What if God allowed it to exist not just to torment mankind---but also to inform? What if that Malignant Presence was there to convince us to look beyond "success", since the Unholy Trinity causes everything to eventually crumble to dust? What if the ever-present Uncaring Evil was there to *constantly remind us to savor each precious moment*---doing what we can, where we can, when we can, however we can... fully living in the present while honoring the past extending our thoughts into the future: *proving that exercising the Gift of Godly Creativity is an infinitely sweet and precious elixir* more potent and addictive than even the finest whiskey! ...that is, if one were to embrace an Irrational Exuberance *continually struggling onward...* BUT NO! THE OTHER CHOICE IS MUCH FASTER, SIMPLE, AND FINAL! HOW NICE TO JUST GIVE-IN, BE CRUSHED BY REALITY, YANK THAT TEMPTING TRIGGER, AND TAKE THE EASY WAY OUT... when finding strength at the time of one's greatest weakness is, maybe, asking too much...

347 **Lawyer** (*leaning over the end of the table to whisper into Lyle's left ear*): "You've tried hard, Lyle. No one will fault you. The pain from your terrible injuries, society ignoring your writings... even those you count as your closest friends not interested in your strange religious ideas---it's an honorable ending! Everybody's got a breaking point! Stop the pain! Do it! Pull the trigger!"

348 **Lyle** (*his hand trembling as he held the gun firmly jammed into the right side of his head, wearily whispering back his reply*): "I have... tried... harder than anyone else would have... that's true... and I hurt... so very bad..."

349 **Critic** (*placing a comforting, red-gloved hand onto Lyle's left shoulder as the Lawyer's yellow mask moved back out of Lyle's immediate, blurred vision*): "Best to have a clean ending, Lyle. You'll be doing the world a favor! Think of your friends the Seeker and the Bystander. Now there won't be a chance at all that they'll be confused by your flawed thinking. By your suicide you'll wipe out any lingering doubt in others that your writings might have had any merit! After all, if your philosophy didn't save you, the Author... how could anyone else think that your pitiful ideas had any value for them? Whatever of your manuscripts that linger past your death will just be tossed into the trash, where they be-

long! You'll be doing the right thing for your friends.... So just pull the trigger! It's easy! Don't 'over-think' it! Just do it!"

350 **Lyle** (*nodding slightly in agreement, tears dripping from his squinted-up eyes*): "It is... better... this way... isn't it? I won't be... pestering... anyone... anymore..."

351 **Fanatic** (*laughing as he abruptly pushed the black-robed Critic to the side and grabbed Lyle's left forearm in a vice-like grip, leaning down so that the diamond-facets of his mask reflected dozens of little Lyle-heads*): "At last you've earned my respect, Lyle! Rather than slink away with a whimper---fading into obscurity---you're going out with a bang! Instead of being a 'nobody' that no one cares about... you'll be 'someone'! You'll be that 'failed author' that killed himself after breaking into a local bar! If nothing else, you'll get a write-up in the local newspaper or get mentioned on the nightly news! Hey, it might even cause a few curious people to go out and buy one of your existing books! Think about it! Suicide in a noble cause is certainly justified, don't you think? It's just too bad, though, that you're only taking with you a few broken bottles of booze... instead of killing a bunch of other people also! They deserve it, don't they? They turned their backs on your 'great' writings, didn't they? Even that stupid truck driver woman just talked with you for her own entertainment in her lonely drive back to town, didn't she? She didn't care anything at all about you, did she? She *deserves* to die on that slope! They *all* deserve to die! They're just a bunch of self-centered fools who turn their backs on you! And if you can't kill all those idiots, at least shake them up a bit with the violence of your ending! Show them all what jerks they are! And then they'll be sorry! They won't have Lyle to kick around anymore! THEY'LL SAY HE TOOK HIS FATE INTO HIS OWN HANDS! THEY'LL ADMIRE YOUR GUTS, LYLE! *MAKE* THEM TAKE NOTICE OF YOU, WHETHER THEY WANT TO OR NOT! PULL THE TRIGGER!!! *DO IT*! *DO IT NOW*! ISN'T THIS WHAT YOU REALLY WANT---TO GET PEOPLE'S ATTENTION? THIS WILL DO IT!"

352 **Lyle** (*addressing the dozens of reflected little Lyle-heads---identical tiny bloodied matted messes all leaning wearily against a comforting black muzzle*): "Yes... at least someone will... notice... if nothing more... that I died... for my convictions..."

353 **Lawyer, Critic, and Fanatic** (*standing straight at the end of the table, arms linked together, happily chanting all in unison as they swayed hypnotically back and forth*): "DO IT! DO IT! DO IT!"

354 Lyle pulled the trigger.

355 *"BANG! BANG! BANG!"* the loud explosions rang-out in the desolation of the bar... as Lyle fired the gun at the heart of each of his tormentors! As one, they lurched backward: clutching their black-robed chests, groaning and moaning as they fell to the floor out of Lyle's sight---as he lowered the smoking gun to the tabletop, dropped his head down to the smooth surface, and closed his eyes...

356 **Bystander** (*speaking hesitantly but with genuine concern*): "Mr. Lyle...? Are you ok?"

357 **Lyle** (*refusing to raise his head or open his eyes, groaning; wanting to be left alone in the prevailing gloom and continued-pounding of the outside storm*): "Go away..."

358 **Bystander** (*sliding into the booth opposite to Lyle, gingerly poking with a blue-gloved finger at Lyle's hand that still tightly gripped the gun*): "Were you... really going to... kill yourself?"

359 **Lyle** (*vaguely aware that the wounds on his face had opened up from the slashing movements he'd made when he fired the gun, managing to hit himself in the face with the hard metal... so that, yet again, hot blood was dripping down into his eyes*): "What the hell do you care, Bystander? You're just a stupid kid! All you want to do is play video games and giggle with your buddies. So go play games... grow up, get a job, fall 'in love', get married, live your little life... just leave me alone! You don't really care anything about me... "

360 **Bystander** (*pulling back his gloved hand, placing it under the chin of his sapphire-blue mask, his elbow placed solidly on the tabletop---rigidly staring behind black eyecups at Lyle, as Lyle in irritation lifted up his own head*): "But... I *see* you, Mr. Lyle... and... it would be interesting..."

361 **Lyle** (*with his trembling left hand wiping blood from his eyes... then unblinkingly staring back at the blue-masked, black-robed small figure stoically facing him across the booth*): "*What* would be 'interesting'?"

362 **Bystander** (*placing both of his blue-gloved hands now under his chin, leaning forward seemingly-eagerly*): "I've never seen anyone... *really* die..."

363 **Lyle** (*lifting up the gun still firmly cradled in his right hand and pointing it back at his own head*): "You'd like to see me blow my head off?"

₃₆₄ **Bystander** (*his blue masked head shimmering like a full moon on a dark night*): "Sure...!"

₃₆₅ "*BANG!*" the gun kicked in Lyle's hand... as he jerked it around, pulled the trigger, and fired a bullet though Bystander's looming mask--- Bystander squawking-out a startled "*Eep!*" as he slumped slowly to the side, blood squirting from a hole in his mask in the center of his forehead; dropping down out of sight, vanishing beneath the top of the table...

₃₆₆ **Seeker** (*gently pushing Lyle to the side as she slid into the booth right up next to him*): "That wasn't very nice of you, Dr. Lyle. Why did you shoot Bystander?"

₃₆₇ **Lyle** (*sighing in resignation as he shakily lowered the now-hot gun back again to the tabletop, fighting back the pain and fever raging in his body to answer her*): "Well, for one thing, he wasn't real... and neither are you!"

₃₆₈ **Seeker** (*tilting her emerald-green mask to the side as if puzzled*): "What do you mean?"

₃₆₉ **Lyle** (*feeling her warm, black-robed side pushed against him*): "It's just my... fever (cough)... or my exhaustion... maybe my lack of sleep... the pain... I don't know... I'm so tired... but I'm obviously hallucinating... however, come to think of it, you're the only one who ever really believed in me... the only one of them that gave me a fair hearing... I can't shoot you..."

₃₇₀ **Seeker** (*leaning her green-masked head over to rest tenderly upon his left shoulder*): "Why would you ever want to shoot me? I love you! You're wonderful!"

₃₇₁ **Lyle** (*laying his own head tenderly down upon Seeker's head, painfully lifting his hurt left arm up behind her to rest upon her thin shoulders*): "Do you... really... love me?"

₃₇₂ **Seeker** (*speaking softly with conviction*): "Of course, Dr. Lyle! I would do anything for you!"

₃₇₃ **Lyle** (*now feeling a twinge of hope, perhaps a rationale to abandon the weapon that he still held firmly in his right hand*): "Anything?"

₃₇₄ **Seeker** (*whispering seductively*): "Just ask!"

³⁷⁵ **Lyle** (*sighing, relaxing just a bit, and whispering out his most-cherished request*): "Would you... read my books?"

³⁷⁶ **Seeker** (*stiffening under his arm, drawing to the side, pulling away from him*): "Well... first we'd of course have to get married, have some children, raise them, think about all our obligations as to how best to spend our remaining time, energy, and money---and then, maybe...!"

³⁷⁷ **Lyle** (*lifting back his left arm off of her shoulders, speaking matter-of-factly*): "So you absolutely love me for what I can give to you..."

³⁷⁸ **Seeker** (*shrugging nonchalantly*): "Doesn't everybody?"

³⁷⁹ **Lyle**: "Yes... I suppose they do... and me as well. You've done me a big favor, Seeker..."

³⁸⁰ **Seeker**: "What's that, Darling?"

³⁸¹ **Lyle** (*wiping fevered sweat from his brow as he wavered back and forth in the booth's seat, whispering faintly*): "You've revealed my deepest hidden vice... my dear Seeker. I suspected it before... but now... I'm sure. Other people think of me as 'Mr. Perfect' but I'm not. Beneath the 'introverted' obsessions that I hide behind is a vile secret: the *real* thing that I *want more than anything else!*"

³⁸² **Seeker** (*attempting to put her arm around his shoulders as he angrily shrugs it off*): "You mean... deep down in your heart? You want *me*, don't you? How can that desire be 'vile'?"

³⁸³ **Lyle** (*now quietly sobbing, letting the tears dribble down his bloody cheeks*): "No, Seeker... it's *my* inexcusable *selfishness*..."

³⁸⁴ Lyle's heart went cold as he lifted the gun and shot her in the face. He didn't even hear the "bang" of the gun going off. His ears were still ringing from the previous discharges of the gun. But he did have a twinge of regret as her black-robed, slender body tumbled over out of the booth to join the others sprawled-out on the floor. She'd been a nice simulation of the real Seeker he'd met up on the peak. Too bad she wasn't more convincing. She might have given him a sweet excuse to not proceed with the inevitable...

³⁸⁵ **Lyle** (*addressing all the dead apparitions, shouting to be heard over the increasing roar of the outside raging storm*): "WELL, EVERYBODY, I SEE THAT THIS IS A TYPICAL HANDGUN WITH SIX BULLETS--- AND I'VE FIRED FIVE ROUNDS KILLING ALL OF YOU! THAT'S PERFECT! THAT MEANS THERE'S STILL *ONE* LEFT JUST FOR *ME*...!"

³⁸⁶ ---and as a new round of *THUNDER* shook the walls of the bar, with *brilliant lightning blazing* in the windows seemingly setting the bar on fire, Lyle jammed the muzzle of the handgun into his right temple and *pulled the trigger...*

. . . .

Back home

³⁸⁷ **Waitress** (*the next day casually unlocking the front door, stepping inside, startled in the early-morning light to see Lyle's bloody body sprinkled with broken glass and whiskey, sprawled-out in a booth---a gun on the tabletop to the side of his unmoving hand*): "HEY! WHAT THE HELL IS THIS? A DEAD BODY...?"

³⁸⁸ **Lyle** (*from far away hearing someone yelling at him... more than a call from beyond the pale... more than a waking dream... a pesky irritant pulling him back from the edge of death itself... causing him to wearily raise his head, blink himself awake, and gasp-out*): "Do you... have a cell phone?"

³⁸⁹ **Waitress** (*pausing a moment to realize from his calm words that the intruder was no threat; then reaching into her purse*): "Sure, doesn't everyone?"

³⁹⁰ **Lyle** (*smiling wryly as he managed to croak-out words past cracked, dry lips*): "The store's land-line phone is out.... there's been an awful accident up the road... can you please call for help?"

³⁹¹ In his delirium and confusion, Lyle had forgotten about the first bullet that got fired when he knocked the gun onto the floor while fumbling for a flashlight behind the bar. In total, six rounds had already been fired from the gun. So there wasn't another bullet left to fire into his head. All that happened was ineffectual "clicking" as he pulled the trigger multiple times. He was disappointed. But the experience sobered him greatly---cutting through his fevered confusion---making him realize that under the 'right' conditions anyone was capable of doing the unthinkable, even him! The Lawyer was right. Everyone does have a breaking point... It was very humbling. Despite all his many years of toil imagining and writing down incredibly-encouraging words... he'd fallen prey to the same crushing despondency that'd terminated many another would-be 'guru'! Instead of focusing on the positives of his life, he'd allowed the inevitable negatives to consume him... Surely, Lady Luck, Mother Nature, and Human Frailty were laughing at the irony. In the seemingly on-fire bar he'd been ready to end it all, but Lady Luck had saved him. Perhaps she wasn't such a bitch after all...

³⁹² It took a while, but Lyle made it safely home. And even though she'd been out on the cold slope for over a day, Burt was also alive. The emergency workers found her battered but conscious and at the head of a trail of blood...

393 ---having crawled half-way up the slope, dragging her limp legs along behind, refusing to stay helpless, fighting off unconsciousness to keep on keeping on...

394 ---persisting even when everything seemed hopeless, deliberately making the decision to continue her upward, defiant journey:

395 ---twisted with terrible pain yet still somehow managed to crawl many yards up the slope; with dignity and determination apparently refusing to surrender her Golden Path!

396 Lyle visited her in the hospital, where she was slowly healing. Feeling was returning to her legs, her back contused but not broken after all. Both her legs were in casts. She was lying in a hospital bed wearily watching a droning soap-opera on T.V. Looking away from the screen she seemed pleased to see Lyle limping in---a cane supporting his also-healing, white-cask-encased right leg---coming up to stand beside her bed, looking down at her with an apologetic expression on his face...

397 **Truck Driver** (*fingering the remote control with her thick fingers, turning off the T.V.*): "Well, look what the cat drugged in! It's that dirty bum again! So how you doin' thar, Dan? You're looking much better than last time ah saw you thar on that damn slope---cleaned up real good! You could maybe trim your shaggy beard and long hair a bit, but otherwise you're lookin' well-fed and chipper!"

398 **Lyle** (*carefully and slowly easing himself down onto a chair besides Burt's hospital bed*): "Yes, Ma'am! I'm doing better. All my aches, pains, bruises, and broken bones are coming along well. Also, it seems I really did have some bad virus scrambling my thinking... got over that also; though I was delirious for the first few days at the hospital! I kept seeing Lawyers... heh, no matter! The only thing that didn't get better was my pride... Anyway, they kept me there for a while, back in my hometown where they sent me. I finally just got out. So, the first thing I wanted to do was to fly back here and say 'howdy'! The Docs tell me you're doing well also---going to be up and at them soon enough. I just wanted to come and apologize in person for distracting you in the truck from your driving... and then taking so long to finally get help to you..."

399 **Truck Driver**: "Hah! The way you wuz beat up ah didn't even expect you to make it up to the road, least-wise all the way to the truck stand---and ah plumb forgot it was closed on the holiday, heh! Ain't that a kicker? Nothing for you to apologize fer at all! Ah'm still here, ain't I? And you can't keep an old bag like me down for long. Got me deliveries to make! As to the wreck, well, ah needed me a new truck anyways..."

400 **Lyle**: "I'd like to help you buy it. I've got a few debts to pay off first to that bar... lucky they didn't press charges for my break-in! They were nice about it all, though, since it was an emergency. But right after I pay off the damages from me shooting up their place, I'll help you pay for the wreck I caused you to suffer!"

401 **Truck Driver**: "Well, that's real considerate of you, Dan. From the news stories ah've heard seems you shore did have quite a time at that bar! And all that without even gettin' drunk! Hah! Yore one amazin' critter, Lyle! But twern't none of your affair that them there dad-blamed brakes of mine failed! You had nothing ta do with thet! In fact it was lucky of me to have you when it happened so you could go fer help! Ah sure wuz happy to see them ambulance workers comin' down the slope for me, I tell you the truth! It would have took me a week more of crawlin' to make it back up to the road on my own! Hah! But, seriously, Dan, I don't need money from you. I'm actually reasonably well off. Kept that old junker mostly for sentimental reasons, and... heh... also 'cause I'm a tightwad! The deliveries I do are, like you pried outta me before, mostly charity. Ah don't need the pay, bein' retired from my previous truck-drivin' career as I am. I do my present 'delivery-service' because it's something I'm capable of doin' that really helps others. Actually, what I *really* want from you is for you ta sell me one of the first copies of your new book!"

402 **Lyle**: "So you think I didn't just give up on my writing after all we went through---convinced at last that no one's interested in reading any of my junk?"

403 **TRUCK DRIVER**: "Dang it, Lyle! I just *told* you that *ah'm* interested!"

404 **Lyle** (*laughing gently*): "Well... seems *you're* an unusual specimen yourself, Burt. That's real nice of you to encourage me like that. And, yes, I'm not sure why, but I am indeed still writing on my 'next' book! I've actually gotten a fair amount done the last few weeks after our accident. It's a book about a grand spiritual Adventure! In fact, it's my spiritual autobiography up to this point in my life---and beyond! In fact, I'm typing the words right now as I sit at my kitchen table at home, working on my laptop computer. I'm almost to the end of the book...and *you* are one of the main characters! In a sense, you already have the book because you have become such an important part of it! Our God-given curiosity and imaginations are incredible---they have a life of their own! They fuel our Godly Creativity! So I'm here with you in this hospital room, as one might say, 'in the spirit'... and though I won't sell you a copy I'd be honored to *give* you one, if I could, that is..."

⁴⁰⁵ **Truck Driver** (*frowning in puzzlement before bursting out laughing*): "Hah! Got me again, Lyle! You're so serious I almost believed you! 'In the spirit' you say? I'm jist a character you invented in your book? I'm jist a figment of your 'lively' God-given imagination? I'm not real at all? Hey, that's great! Now jist write all my aches and pains gone away---and me hoppin' up out of this hospital bed completely healed! *Hah!*"

⁴⁰⁶ **Lyle** (*shaking his head in amused denial*): "Oh, you are real enough, Burt, that's for sure! In fact, you're an original! I absolutely believe that you are just as real as I! But you are more than just one person. You are a representation of many people. If I'm fortunate to actually finish and publish this book someday---which I'll call *'The Book of Lyle'*---then, hopefully many people may see their own selves reflected in you!"

⁴⁰⁷ **Truck Driver** (*laughing again before taking a swig at some bottled water sitting on a stand beside her hospital bed*): "You are a funny dude, Dan! You should be a stand-up comedian! If your writing skills are half as good as yore imagination---then that's gonna be one *heck* of a book! Too bad only two or three people in the world will ever want to read it, hah! Crank me up a bit, would you?"

⁴⁰⁸ **Lyle** (*reaching down to turn a crank at the side of the bed to raise up the top part of her hospital bed, putting Burt's pudgy grey-haired head at eye level to him as he sat in his chair*): "That better?"

⁴⁰⁹ **Truck Driver** (*nodding*): "Yup, shore is... thanks! Do you know, Dan, what wuz the first thing I asked for once they got me onto that stretcher, carried me up the slope, and slid me into that nice warm ambulance?"

⁴¹⁰ **Lyle** (*sighing in feigned resignation*): "A cigarette?"

⁴¹¹ **Truck Driver** (*her pudgy face hardened in resolution*): "A cell phone. I called my granddaughter, the one that started smoking sneaking out behind the barn when she wuz jist eight years old. Remember I mentioned her?"

⁴¹² **Lyle**: "I remember."

⁴¹³ **Truck Driver** (*tears welling up briefly in her eyes before hardening into a look of grim determination*): "I told her that her Granny didn't smoke... least wise, no more..."

⁴¹⁴ **Lyle** (*impressed*): "Really?"

⁴¹⁵ **Truck Driver** (*now grinning widely*): "Yup! Ah ain't had me a drag since thet last stogie ah had in the truck with you. Now mind you, ah've wanted me one *real bad*... 'cause I really enjoyed smokin' all that nicotine all those years! But something even *stronger* than the craving stopped me..."

⁴¹⁶ **Lyle** (*nodding knowingly*): "Your love for your granddaughter?"

⁴¹⁷ **Truck Driver**: "Damned straight. Of course she didn't stop smokin'. She said it was nice ah had stopped and wished me the best. But she said she liked smoking---just like me---and would keep doing it. Well, that's her decision ah guess. But I'm no longer her excuse for doing so. And... maybe... who knows... someday she may remember my example jist like you remembered your Dad's. And maybe she'll keep on rememberin' tell she gets a bit older, less stupid, and starts thinkin' with her brain rather than with her gut!"

⁴¹⁸ **Lyle** (*smiling in appreciation*): "Wow! I'm proud of you, Burt. I didn't think any less of you because you smoked. But now I'm ten-times as impressed with you for quitting. I know that must be incredibly hard for you to do."

⁴¹⁹ **Truck Driver**: "Yup. Shore 'nuff... Ah figured it'd be hell... and it was. But it's gettin' easier each day. I'm actually breathing better and even tastin' muh food! They say hospital food's bad, but now it seems great to me! Amazing how good things can taste when all that smoke-gunk is gone off one's taste buds! Also, I figure that maybe ah'm gonna have ten times the pull when it comes to influencin' young-uns. Ah even think ah might start going around to schools and volunteering myself to tell them about the negatives of smokin'. Maybe I'll catch some of them back when they're still eight years old and tempted to go out behind the barn to behave like a 'grown-up'! Ah kin tell them from experience about the tons of money ah've wasted on thet sweet poison. Ah kin tell them how ah've stunk so from it I was embarrassed to go out in public! Ah kin tell them how the stuff wrinkled me up and made me old-lookin' before mah time. Thet'll sure-nuf 'resonate' with them young cuties, fer shure! And them 'he-man' boys might get a bit less stupid when ah tells them how ah couldn't breathe good enough to play sports in school! And ah am goin' to tell the already-smokers how that---as the preachers like to say---'in God, all things are possible'. Thet, Dan, isn't jist preachifyin'... thet is smack straight from the Bible! It's jist like you told me back in the truck! Ah will tell them that they don't *have* to gum up their lungs and guts with stuff that's likely to give them emphysema and cancer! If they want to kick the habit, then by God---with God's help and the orneriness of a mule---they can do it! Think anyone'll listen to a fat old hag like me?"

⁴²⁰ **Lyle** (*taking Burt's large hand and giving it a friendly squeeze*): "Yes, I sure do. But I still say that you are without doubt a *beautiful* person... I'm proud of you...!"

⁴²¹ **Truck Driver** (*noting a peculiar strain in Lyle's voice; a forced enthusiasm lingering as he withdrew his hand*): "Ok, Dan. Spit it out! What's the problem?"

⁴²² **Lyle** (*not speaking for a moment, before answering in hushed tones that no one could hear outside the room in the corridor*): "Well... you said you heard what happened to me in the bar..."

⁴²³ **Truck Driver** (*lowering her voice also*): "Most of the news I heard on the T.V. said you were a hero... managed to stick it out, even with a broken leg, sick-to-death, and almost bled-out---while fighting off fever-created, imaginary demons!"

⁴²⁴ **Lyle** (*hanging his head*): "I guess that's what I told the responding officers... but it's not true, Burt... I... gave up. I really gave up. I was too ashamed to admit it to the investigators---but I came to the end my rope in that bar and I 'hung' myself... it's just blind luck I'm here today with my head intact instead of blown to pieces by my last shot from that gun I found... the chamber was empty when I pulled the trigger... my hangman's 'rope' broke! I'm no hero..."

⁴²⁵ **Truck Driver** (*nodding knowingly*): "Well... how about that... it... actually... makes me feel a bit better! You see, Dan, I managed to crawl up the slope a bit... and then, well, I gave up too... when they found me I was jist flat on the rocks waitin' to die! I wasn't goin' to move forwards one more inch... 'course I didn't tell all of that to the ambulance first-responders... heh... I got a reputation for toughness around these parts, don't you know..."

⁴²⁶ They both sat in silence for a while. Outside in the hospital corridor they heard people walking by, talking---a couple of respectful reporters down the hall were chatting, waiting for Lyle to emerge to get their 'follow-up' story---carts "clanking" past...

⁴²⁷ **Lyle** (*sighing*): "So we were just lucky, is that it? Some people get the 'hand up' and others get the boot? Today we're here but tomorrow we're gone?"

⁴²⁸ **Truck Driver**: "Sure, Dan. That's life!"

429 **Lyle**: "Then I guess I should just 'man-up' and tell those local reporters out there waiting for a story what really happened..."

430 **Truck Driver**: "Hell, *no!*"

431 **Lyle**: "But... Burt, it's like when I was a little kid and my parents took me to get a required vaccination!"

432 **Truck Driver** (*speaking suspiciously*): "Oh, yah?"

433 **Lyle** (*speaking firmly*): "Yes... they told me I had to have a shot in my arm! They were going to poke a big *needle* into my *arm*! I started crying and begging them not to do it! I was screaming-out: 'NO, DON'T SHOOT ME, DON'T SHOOT ME!' I was yelling and squirming and crying: "DON'T MAKE ME DO IT! DON'T STICK ME WITH THAT NEEDLE! I DON'T WANT TO HAVE A SHOT!"---making a big scene... everyone was looking at me---and..."

434 **Truck Driver** (*eagerly*): "Did you faint? Did they stop? Did they give you some gas to knock you out with first?"

435 **Lyle** (*quietly laughing*): "The nurse said 'It's done, Danny, it's all over!' ---AND I HADN'T EVEN FELT IT...!"

436 **Truck Driver** (*snorting*): "It twern't as bad as you'd thunk?"

437 **Lyle** (*shaking his head in sad denial*): "I was throwing a tantrum over something that was so trivial that I hadn't even felt it when they did it to me! I just hung my head and slunk out of that place trying to hide between my Dad and Mom! I was so *embarrassed*..."

438 **Truck Driver** (*laughing*): "Guess you never protested at having to get a shot again?"

439 **Lyle** (*looking up in exasperation at the ceiling*): "Never again... but everybody at that doctor's waiting room knew what a little idiot I was..."

440 **Truck Driver** (*sighing*): "Guess we're both not as grown up as we thought we were?"

441 **Lyle** (*slumping in his seat*): "Two little kids in wrinkled old bodies... still scared of what other people are going to think of us---it's so embarrassing to be so weak!"

442 Again they sat in an uncomfortable silence. It seemed they'd said everything needed saying, but yet not enough. Lyle felt like he should get up and walk away... but there was something more needed! What was it?

443 **Truck Driver** (*shrugging*): "Well... do whatever you think's best, Dan. Me, I'm keepin' quiet!"

444 **Lyle** (*looking at Burt with a curious frown*): "Why?"

445 **Truck Driver**: "Ain't no law you gotta tell people everything! You don't hang yore dirty undies out on the line to dry, do you? You wait tell they's washed and clean!"

446 **Lyle**: "But that's just logical, isn't it?"

447 **Truck Driver** (*taking in a big breath before replying*): "Shore, of course it's logical, Lyle! That's whut ah'm sayin'! You cain't jist sell 'gloom and doom', Dan... people need heroes!"

448 **Lyle:** "But... I'm not a hero... and from what you just told me, neither are you!?"

449 **Truck Driver**: "Nope! No heroes here... jist us grubby old, weak humans..."

450 **Lyle** (*speaking from sudden inspiration*): "---who, in God's eyes, are still *beautiful*! Yes! It's *not* logical, Burt... but somehow it's still our saving grace!"

451 **Truck Driver**: "Hah! So is that your 'big revelation' from all this we've been through? I thought you wuz tryin' to figure out what you really wanted outta life!?"

452 **Lyle** (*gritting his teeth together in intense concentration before replying*): "I've... got short-term goals. I've got a long-term AIM. Maybe that's enough... and our deepest motivations, perhaps we should leave that to the One that made us as we are...!"

453 **Truck Driver**: "Makes sense to me... but ah'm guessin' you don't find that a very satisfactory endin'?"

454 **Lyle** (*wryly laughing at Burt's keen insight*): "DAMN IT, BURT---I WANT TO *KNOW*...! But then... at the heart of all true religion, indeed, is *Un*knowable Mystery---and perhaps who we really are, deep down, is a part of that puzzle! It's a wonderful, beautiful, never-ending Adventure..."

455 **Truck Driver** (*snorting again as she settled back against her pillow, yawning widely*): "Well, me bein' 'beautiful' or not, Lyle---this 'figment' of yorn has gotta get her rest. Ah is still a wee bit shook up from *my* little 'adventure' with you! And talkin' makes me tired.... but ah'm healing up real good! Ah'm getting' better every day... and ah'm glad to still be here fer yet another day---whether it's from me bein' clever or me bein' lucky! And ah *am* lookin' forward to readin' yore book, which ah *am* gonna buy---your very first... or maybe your last... customer! Hah! Gotta get healed up, don't cha know! Ah've got lots of important things needin' fur me to get at! It's a *good day*, today... thanks fer stoppin' by, Dan. And thanks for stirrin' up my feeble little brain! Ah likes yore puzzlement..."

456 **Lyle** (*patting her weathered hand one more time before stiffly standing up*): "And I've got a lot of things to try to do also, Burt. And I thank *you* for *your* help. Your down-to-earth wisdom has encouraged me a lot---and I'm certain will continue doing the same for, hopefully, many others! There's no hiding the visible truth, but... you're right... we don't have to emphasize the inevitably-bad! *We can choose our outlook...*"

457 **Truck Driver** (*closing her eyes, drifting off to sleep, smiling*): "Yep! Who'd have thunk I'd wind up a Princess in a Crystal Castle...?"

458 **Lyle**: "Never doubted it for a moment."

- -

Lyle 32:1-40

BEYOND DEATH

¹ *And so Lyle continued to carefully explore, daring to express the Creativity of God, happy for any little successes but not discouraged by his many failures, choosing to Adventure as he went...*

² ---continuing on through life's challenging maze not allowing inevitable disappointments in himself or others to destroy a hopeful outlook; knowing that his own dreams were indeed limited by his own shortcomings, but accepting himself with all his many failings; choosing to give the many blessings in his life more weight than the unshakable curses; knowing his genetic programming to be a smart animal was beyond his control, but with God's help it might be transcended; whenever possible looking for a way to go over, under, or around the inevitable brick walls blocking his path; keeping on going forward step-by-step even when the destination seemed impossible; acutely conscious of his own weaknesses---and careful to avoid circumstances that would trigger them to be expressed;

³ Repeatedly stating his enabling Mantra of: "*What's next, Lord?*"---relentlessly focusing-down to details when the "big picture" seemed too difficult to pursue; choosing to find positives even when everything seemed to be going wrong; picking himself up when he fell, brushing off the dirt, and jumping right back into the exciting game of life;

⁴ Accepting bitter failure as the means to force important lessons to penetrate his thick skull; looking at hard problems as opportunities to use personal energy scrabbling to get himself into a better position; viewing slammed doors as welcomed redirection stopping him from wasting precious time, energy, and emotion on futile efforts; appreciating change forcing him to open up new, increasingly-interesting doors; accepting disappointing actions by others teaching him hard lessons on how other people think, feel, act, and prioritize *differently*---where irritating people engender fresh insights into the workings of his own brain; satisfied happily expressing his strengths rather than painfully fighting against his deficits;

⁵ Determined to whenever possible, where before there was nothing to put something that is *reasonable, useful, respectful, beautiful,* and *honorable*... universally implementing 'RURBAH';

⁶ *Making Truth more substantial---ever-eager to go deeper, wider, higher, more complex, and more substantial; seeking real enlightenment in transcendent Significance trying to make God happy in the best way possible...*

⁷ ---enjoying the many positive delights of this wonderful planet while trying to avoid hurting himself, others, nature, or God;

⁸ Responsibly experimenting actively forging Art of all possible sorts: not afraid to carefully attempt new things while conforming to all the enabling aspects of RURBAH;

⁹ Setting interacting Processes into motion as dynamic Systems: joining useful Vectors together marching bravely into the heart of stunningly-powerful Visions... defining Mission, Goals, and Objectives into one short, clearly-stated, motivating, and personal AIM: to *EXPRESS THE CREATIVITY OF GOD*!

¹⁰ Energized by the hard reality of his own fragile mortality; making each second precious in simultaneously honoring and defying the Unholy Trinity; attempting to achieve his top priorities not as vague generalities but as tangible specifics;

¹¹ Refusing 'worship' in service to lesser, baser objectives; upgrading the time required recognizing and respecting the weakness of others to include himself; harnessing personal criticism as the means for personal growth; questioning blind pursuit of happiness; rejecting enslavement to his own engrained survival instinct; not allowing tradition or small minds to define boundaries to God; resisting the temptation to put Divinity into his own preferred cage;

¹² Putting at a lesser priority ephemeral pleasure, emotional satiety, minor accumulation, a successful career, species perpetuation, societal approval, easy answers, empty rituals, meaningless tradition, forgettable lectures, empty spirituality, debatable doctrines... and even his own comfortable death; expanding his mind to appreciate even the cruelty of nature revealing weakness; accepting the capriciousness of luck giving you undeserved breaks; grateful for human weakness providing space for continual improvement; embracing the FIRE of life as a means not of destruction but of refinement, purification, and growth;

¹³ Using authoritative dictates as tentative starting frameworks within, around, and upon which to construct even better structures:

¹⁴ *Seeking, discovering, testing, and refining his own Golden Path expanding into a roomy Crystal Cathedral... continually improving all as-*

pects of his inclusive Temple to Godly Creativity by melding, molding, and joining his Portfolio wherever possible with like-minded travelers... becoming far more together than he could be all by his lonesome;

15 Delighting his approving & applauding heavenly Father edifying others while expanding his connection to all of Nature: finding ever more-meaningful ways to honor the eternal Divine;

16 *Until, at long last---beaten-down by the perpetual indignities foisted on him by Mother Nature, Lady Luck, and his own Human Frailty---Lyle finally died*:

17 Weakened but not beaten-down, crushed but not destroyed, stilled but not stopped, humiliated but never turned back...

18 Happy to cast aside hope for actual experience, delighted to find himself thinking beyond the death of his own brain:

19 **Lyle** (*speaking loudly his final message without voice; projecting powerfully without lungs; resonating broadly without atmosphere*): "AND SO I, DANIEL BASIL LYLE---HAVING MOVED BEYOND TIGHT LIMITATIONS, HAVING SURPASSED SPACE-ENERGY-MATTER-TIME---FIND MYSELF IN A SUPREME PLACE, WHERE ALL OF HUMAN ENDEAVOR IS BUT ONE NOTE IN A NEVER-ENDING CELESTIAL SYMPHONY;

20 FREED FROM BREATHING, EATING, DRINKING, AND EXCRETING I DISCOVER MYSELF RELIEVED OF AN ENORMOUS BURDEN:

21 FIRST AMONGST ALL THE IMPRINTED SURVIVAL-INSTINCT'S CONSTANT DREAD OF DEATH, EXPLODED LIKE A ROCKET FIRED OUT OF MY SOUL... A FESTERING, PUTRID, PAINFUL SORE EXPUNGED;

22 ME ESCAPING UP OUT OF EARTH'S CONSTRICTING THIN FILM OF AIR... FEAR FROZEN AND LEFT FAR BEHIND, DROPPED INTO AN ICY VOID OF BOTTOMLESS BLACK VACUUM, ITS ETERNAL DARK GRAVE RECEDING;

23 WHILE I AM INSTANTLY EXPANDED-ENLARGED-INFUSED-BEAUTIFIED AND AMAZED TO FIND MYSELF ZIPPING-OUT INTO A VAST EXPANSE THAT IS PARADOXICALLY ALIVE & ABLAZE WITH COUNTLESS OVERLAPPING AVENUES:

24 INFINITE POSSIBILITIES POPPING UP BEFORE ME, BECKONING ME WITH MANIFOLD POTENTIAL, PATIENTLY AWAITING MY EXPLORATION;

25 AS I, AT LAST, BEGIN TO GRASP THE FULL & TRUE REALITY OF 'GOD' NO LONGER LIMITED BY QUAINT HUMAN CONCEPTS & EMOTIONS;

26 AND I AM AT ONCE STUNNED, EMBARRASSED, AND GRATEFULLY HUMBLED AS I AM CAUGHT-UP IN THE LORD'S WARM EMBRACE AND WELCOMING GREETING;

27 MAKING ME FEEL LIKE NOTHING I EVER BEFORE CONCEIVED OR IMAGINED, FREEING MY THOUGHTS FROM WORLDLY-ANIMAL CONSTRAINTS---AS I AM SWALLOWED UP BY A WONDERFUL AND HEADY EXHILARATION;

28 LOOKING BACK ON MY FADING PAST-EXISTENCE WITH AMUSEMENT... AS A CURIOUS PHASE, A FRIENDLY JAIL, AND AN INVOLUNTARY ISOLATION:

29 WHERE MY POTENTIAL AND POWER WAS CAGED, CONTAINED, AND SHAPED BY HARD BOUNDARIES DISTORTING THE INFINITE CONTENT OF MY CHARACTER;

30 NECESSITATING NOW A RADICAL, MIND-BENDING TRANSFORMATION... A CONVERSION FROM WHAT I WAS BEFORE INTO WHAT I AM NOW... AND WHAT I WILL BECOME:

31 CRACKING-THROUGH THE UTTER BLACKNESS OF HEARTLESS, COLD, OUTER-SPACE... I SIMULTANEOUSLY SLICE–INTO WHITE LIGHT CONTAINING THE GLORIOUS MULTIVERSE;

32 AND I LOOK BACK WITH FONDNESS ON WHAT NOW IS NAKEDLY REVEALED AS A GLITTERING, SWIRLING CLOUD OF SUSPENDED, VIBRATING MARBLES... GLOWING AS THEY CONTINUALLY MERGE, CONVERGE, AND DIVERGE...

33 AND I 'WILL' MYSELF A 'HAND' TO HOLD IT ALL GENTLY IN MY 'PALM'... SENSING THE WARMTH OF BILLIONS OF BILLIONS OF BILLIONS OF STARS;

34 KNOWING THAT IN ONE STRONG *CLENCH* I COULD *CRUSH* IT ALL, LEAVING ONLY DRIFTING DEAD STELLAR DUST, OR MEGA-BLACK-HOLE VACUUMING IT ALL AWAY...

35 RATHER, IN ANOTHER WILLED 'HAND' I ALSO 'WILL' AN EXACT DUPLICATE, SHINING BRAND-NEW AND PREPPED TO EVOLVE... AND REALIZE THAT THE AWESOME POWER NOW IN ME IS BUT A HINT OF GOD'S LOVE BEAMING DOWN AND DRAWING ME AWAY...

36 AS I AM TORN FROM WHAT IS REALIZED, DONE WITH, AND FINISHED... TO WHAT YET BECKONS... AND WITH MORE EXCITEMENT AND JOY THAN I EVER DREAMED POSSIBLE I SAY 'GOODBY' TO ALL YOU WHO---FOR BUT A SHORT WHILE---REMAIN BEHIND:

37 THAT YOU BE NOT DISCOURAGED DISMAYED, NOR NEEDLESSLY AFRAID... BUT REVEL IN YOUR OWN BRIEF EXISTENCE, *EN*COURAGED;

38 NOT STOPPED BY THE CONFOUNDING COMPLAINTS OF THOSE SURROUNDING AND CONSTRAINING YOUR DREAMS; NEITHER ALLOWING YOUR OWN WEAKNESS AND FAULTS TO STOP YOUR UPWARD STRUGGLE; REFUSING THE TEMPTATION TO RETREAT BACK INTO THE COMFORTABLE CAVE; FINDING THE COURAGE TO BRAVE THE FIRES OF LIFE; USING THE FIERCE PAIN AND TRIALS OF *UN*COMFORTABLE STRUGGLE TO FUEL YOUR PURSUIT OF THE UNKNOWABLE MYSTERY; ACCEPTING THAT YOU'LL NEVER KNOW ALL THE ANSWERS NOR EVEN ALL THE QUESTIONS AS YOU ENJOY TACKLING THE GRAND PUZZLE; RELISHING THE EFFORT MORE THAN THE RESULT; *REVILING* IN THE INCREDIBLY-GRAND ADVENTURE OF LIFE...

39 WORKING TO REALIZE ALL YOUR EARTHLY POTENTIAL WITH DILIGENCE; DELIGHTING YOURSELVES PRACTICING IN A LIMITED BUT SIGNIFICANT WAY A *HOLY CREATIVITY* THAT'S A MERE TASTE OF THE FEAST TO COME:

40 WHERE GLADLY TAKING YOUR PLACE AT THE TABLE TO PARTICIPATE, YOU DISCOVER YOURSELF AS HONORED GUEST AND FEATURED SPEAKER."

DBL, 4-22-2006

* *

About the Author:

Daniel B. Lyle, Ph.D. holds a Ph.D. in Biology, earned from the University of California, Riverside. He has directed laboratory research programs in identifying environmental hazards, how to assay the function & health of blood vessels, what can over-stimulate the immune system, how cancer develops, and new aspects of treating diabetes. This research has been conducted in academic, hospital, and government regulatory settings. In addition, he has taught academic courses at all levels up to graduate school, been a life-long practitioner of religious-application, has constant interaction with Mother Nature, and is a Quality Management executive.

As a "Student of Life" (biologist) Dr. Lyle has a deep interest in both what hurts us (causing diseases like diabetes, heart attacks, and cancer) and what makes us healthy; and *why* we choose one or the other---in all aspects of life: whether physically, mentally, or spiritually.

To help others in understanding what helps versus hurts us---and how to implement Quality methods and techniques to better our lives---Dr. Lyle established and maintains ***LylePublishing.com*** and ***Creative-Theology.org***---places where people from all over the world, from all walks of life, can come to share online their experiences in living life: in a mutual search for what it really means to make a difference and have our lives be "Significant".

Dr. Lyle's books deal with figuring out the real nature of Life: in which knowledge becomes achievable steps that CHANGE our lives for the better. The established doctrine is rarely enough. Rather than be satisfied with the "status quo" Dr. Lyle insists on going back to Principles and their underlying Assumptions. As such, he is a radical thinker anchored in what is practical. He joins with many other "life-long learners" in cherishing and celebrating the many incredibly-interesting challenges and Adventures of life!

OTHER BOOKS BY DR. LYLE:

Creative-Theology®: Definitions and implementation.

In Search of Quality: Principles & Mechanisms.

The God Debate: Intelligent arguments about the idea of God.

The Real Jesus: A Creative-Theologist worthy of being followed.

The Jesus Lectures 1: How to find the Kingdom of God.

The Jesus Lectures 2: How to understand one's own heart.

The Jesus Lectures 3: How to deal with difficult people.

The Jesus Lectures 4: How to best express Godly Love.

The Jesus Lectures 5: How to master true Compassion.

The Jesus Lectures 6: How to capitalize on Connectivity.

The Jesus Lectures 7: How to best understand God.

The Jesus Lectures 8: How to make your life Significant.

The Jesus Lectures 9: How to enjoyably avoid Damnation.

The Jesus Lectures 10: How to learn to cherish true Salvation.

* *

www.ingramcontent.com/pod-product-compliance
Lightning Source LLC
LaVergne TN
LVHW051824080426
835512LV00018B/2709